STAR FOODS
FOR HEALTHY EATING

Star Foods for Healthy Eating

Kirsten Hartvig

Thorsons
An imprint of HarperCollins*Publishers*
77–85 Fulham Palace Road
Hammersmith, London, England W6 8JB

Published in the United States by Thorsons in 2002

Conceived, created and designed by Duncan Baird Publishers
Duncan Baird Publishers Ltd
Sixth Floor
Castle House
75–76 Wells Street
London W1T 3QH

Managing Editor: Judy Barratt
Editor: Richard Emerson
Editorial Assistant: Jessica Hughes
Managing Designer: Manisha Patel
Designer: Suzanne Tuhrim
Commissioned Photography: William Lingwood
Stylists: David Morgan, Helen Trent, Sunil Vijayakar

Library of Congress Cataloging-in-Publication Data is available

10 9 8 7 6 5 4 3 2 1

ISBN: 0-00-764486-8

Typeset in Helvetica Neue
Colour reproduction by Scanhouse, Malaysia
Printed and bound in Singapore by Imago

PUBLISHER'S NOTE: *Star Foods for Healthy Eating* is not intended as a replacement for professional medical treatment and advice. The publishers and authors cannot accept responsibility for any damage incurred as a result of any of the therapeutic methods contained in this work. If you are suffering from a medical condition and are unsure of the suitability of any of the therapeutic methods in this book, or if you are pregnant, it is advisable to consult a medical practitioner. Essential oils must be diluted in a base oil before use. They should not be taken internally and are for adult use only. The detox program should be avoided by children, elderly people, and women who are pregnant or breast-feeding.

The abbreviation BCE is used in this book:
BCE Before the Common Era (the equivalent of BC

STAR FOODS
FOR HEALTHY EATING

THE ILLUSTRATED GUIDE TO STRENGTHENING THE BODY'S DEFENSE SYSTEMS

KIRSTEN HARTVIG

Thorsons
Directions for Life

contents

KEY TO SYMBOLS USED IN
STAR FOODS

★ IMPORTANT NUTRIENTS AND
OTHER ACTIVE INGREDIENTS

✓ IMMUNE-BOOSTING ACTION
AND OTHER BENEFICIAL
PROPERTIES

! WARNING

💡 INTERESTING FACTS AND
HANDY HINTS

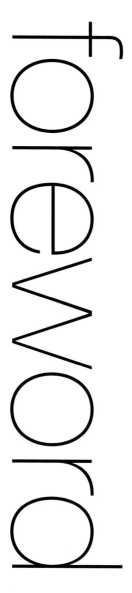

Readers who digest and act on the advice in this book are likely to improve their enjoyment of life into middle and old age. I hope that, as you read this foreword, you think of yourself not just as an individual, but as a member of a family and community, whose choices and actions affect others. In general, people live longer, and also suffer from disease for more of their lives, than ever before in history. In rich countries, such as those in North America and Western Europe, people on average suffer some serious disability for around a quarter of their lives, and often die from diseases likely to cause intense suffering in the last years of their lives. But disease is not an inevitable function of ageing. I am writing this foreword during a visit to the headquarters of the World Health Organization (W.H.O.) in Geneva. Colleagues here envision a world in which it is normal to live a long, healthy, and active life and to die of old age in good health.

feed the mind, body, and spirit

If you want to change the world, begin with yourself, within your community. *Star Foods for Healthy Eating* is full of useful information and good advice. Its most important message can be expressed in a few words: Food and nutrition is crucial to health. And as health is not only physical but also mental, emotional, and spiritual, it is better to say that the nature and quality of what we eat and drink are the most important determinants of our state of being. This is an old truth to which writers such as my colleague and friend Kirsten Hartvig are bearing new witness.

The incidence of tooth decay, constipation, gut diseases, obesity, high blood pressure, diabetes, osteoporosis, stroke, heart disease, and most cancers, in all populations and communities, is mostly determined by food and nutrition, together with tobacco habits and level of physical activity. The W.H.O. is currently launching an initiative designed to prevent chronic diseases throughout the world, with that message. Secure, adequate and, varied food supplies are essential to prevent deficiency diseases; and nutritional deficiency not only remains a massive public health issue in Africa and Asia, but is also quite common among impoverished people who live in rich countries like the U.S.A. A vital message for parents, is that a diet exclusively of breast milk until 6 months old, followed by weaning on to nutrient-dense plant-based foods, gives babies and children the best protection against infectious diseases at the time, and also throughout life.

natural and fresh is best

But that is not all! As *Star Foods for Healthy Eating* shows, a diet that is based on fresh or minimally processed foods (above all wholegrain starchy foods combined with pulses such as beans, and a variety of vegetables and fruits, rich in vitamins, minerals, phytochemicals, essential fats, and fiber), and that is correspondingly low in highly processed foods, total fat, saturated fat, sugar, salt, and alcohol, protects the health of all systems of the body. And yes, this includes the nervous system— of which the brain is one part, the source of our thoughts, feelings, and beliefs. Some people still suppose that the best diets for humans, and especially children, are those that promote growth, and that tall and heavy people are superior to those who are small and slim. In fact, *homo sapiens* evolved to grow and mature slowly, and diets high in protein and fat and often sugar, have created populations in the richest countries who resemble human rhinos, in more ways than one.

Those of us who are lucky enough to have homes and jobs, and who enjoy international travel, electronic technology, and shops full of fresh foods, do not want to revert to any kind of primeval existence. What we can achieve now, is the best of all worlds. Kirsten has assembled, summarized, and displayed a vast amount of knowledge, designed to convince you that excellent food and nutrition is the rational way to avoid disease, and also that natural foods and drinks contain prudent remedies for most illnesses. Don't be daunted by the detail. The fundamental message is simple—the basic nourishment for your body, mind, and spirit, and those of your family and community, is in your local supermarket now.

Geoffrey Cannon

Author, *The Politics of Food*; Chief editor, *Food, Nutrition, and the Prevention of Cancer: a Global Perspective*; Advisor on nutrition policy, Ministry of Health, Brazil.

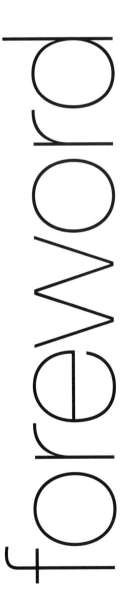

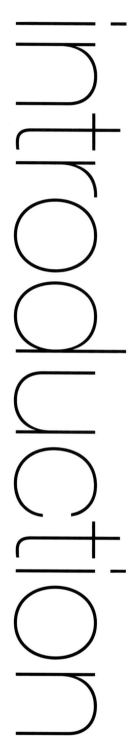

ABOUT STAR FOODS...

Star Foods for Healthy Eating gives you a strategy to maximize your self-healing potential and develop a better understanding of health and disease. It is divided into four parts:

● Part One, A Guide to the Immune System, explains the components of the immune system and how they work together to maintain health and combat disease.

● Part Two, Superfoods for the Immune System, looks in detail at 150 foods that support the immune system.

● Part Three, Coping with Common Ailments, highlights some common ailments, and explains how you can use the foods described in Part Two to prevent illness and promote health.

● Part Four, Immune Foods in Practice, shows you how to incorporate immune-enhancing foods into your daily diet with 180 recipes and a range of diet plans.

You don't need to read *Star Foods for Healthy Eating* from cover to cover before using it. Keep it in the kitchen and use it as a reference source of good food and better health.

When making the recipes in Part Four, choose organic ingredients whenever possible, since chemical farming involves the use of many different substances that are harmful to immunity. Eating organic is also the best way of avoiding genetically engineered foods, the long-term health effects of which are unknown.

food for life

Over the last 30 years, systematic scientific studies have confirmed that poor nutrition impairs the immune response, and that a diet based primarily on minimally processed and chemically unadulterated plant foods is the most effective way of enhancing immunity.

A recent global survey carried out by the World Cancer Research Fund together with the American Institute for Cancer Research concluded that plant-based diets protect against cancer. Hundreds of reliable studies show that fresh vegetables, fruits, nuts, grains, and pulses are packed with immune-boosting phytochemicals.

Since the early 1960's, research has repeatedly confirmed that a diet high in natural fiber from vegetables, fruits, and unrefined grains protects from a wide range of serious diseases.

Nutrition experts and scientists worldwide agree that high intakes of saturated fats from meat, dairy products, and convenience foods are linked with coronary heart disease, and that the activity of the immune system is improved by decreased total fat intake.

Large numbers of fish caught for human consumption have been shown to contain toxic heavy metals, hydrocarbons, and radioactive contaminants, and those reared in fish farms are commonly dosed with antibiotics and treated with dyes. Oily fish contain unsaturated fatty acids that may protect against coronary thrombosis, but increasing fish oil intake without also reducing saturated fat intake is unlikely to have any significant effect on the development of coronary heart disease.

Taking fish oils in a concentrated form may cause excessive production of free radicals, which can interfere with immunity. Unlike fish oils, plant sources of polyunsaturated fatty acids are high in natural antioxidants, which combat the effects of free radicals.

Despite its reputation as a natural staple food, cow's milk may compromise immunity. Some people (particularly children) are allergic to milk protein and may develop eczema, hay fever, or asthma as a result of consuming it, and people with mucus problems and allergy often experience substantial relief when they exclude milk products from their diet. Milk is also high in cholesterol and thus associated with an increased risk of heart problems.

Milk sugar (lactose) is digested in the stomach by an enzyme (lactase) that most humans stop producing at around the age of five, making it difficult to digest milk products efficiently. Contamination of milk products with hormones, antibiotics, and other agricultural chemical residues may also produce unpredictable and unexpected adverse reactions.

Based on this overwhelming evidence, *Star Foods for Healthy Eating* follows a plant-based approach to improving immunity that is relevant to every style of eating—carnivore, piscatarian, vegetarian, and vegan. It is designed to help you tailor your personal food choices to the benefit of your immune system, increasing your intake of health-enhancing foods and cutting down on those that increase immune system workload.

dos and don'ts

Star Foods for Healthy Eating can be used by nearly everyone, although people suffering from serious acute illness and young people under the age of eighteen are advised to follow the diet recommendations under the guidance of a suitably qualified medical practitioner. During pregnancy and while breast feeding, stringent diet regimes are not recommended, but eating a varied diet rich in fresh fruits, nuts, seeds, grains, and vegetables is beneficial for both mother and baby.

The health suggestions in this book are intended to complement and enhance other treatments, not to replace them. Increasing your intake of some foods can change your body's reaction to medication (for example, cholesterol-lowering drugs), so if you are currently under medical treatment consult your practitioner before making any major dietary changes. If you are being treated for diabetes, you should follow your normal dietary guidelines and discuss the implications of change with your medical adviser.

side effects

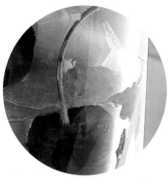

The diet plans in *Star Foods for Healthy Eating* are extremely unlikely to produce any unpleasant adverse reactions, but you may notice that withdrawing from caffeinic tea and coffee, and abstaining from alcohol and smoking makes you feel more edgy, headachey, lethargic, and short-tempered for a few days. An increase in fruit and vegetable intake may also make your bowels more loose, and the extra fiber may cause excess gas. Such symptoms soon pass, and are not a cause for concern.

As always, if you have any particular concerns or worries, or if you have any doubt about the suitability of the advice contained in this book in relation to your current situation, you should seek advice from your doctor (or, if he or she should feel unable to offer advice, from a registered naturopath or other suitably qualified medical practitioner).

Happy—and healthy—eating!

Kirsten Hartvig

a guide to the immune system

A fully functioning immune system is one of the most vital aspects of a healthy body, helping to prevent and combat disease. However, for many people, the immune system does not function as effectively as it should. In some cases, the immune response fails to offer protection from disease, such as infection or cancer. In other cases, the immune system actively turns against its host, triggering a range of autoimmune and other disorders, such as rheumatoid arthritis, or allergies, that are increasingly prevalent in the modern world. Part One explains how the immune system works, why it sometimes breaks down, and what you can do to strengthen it and keep it in tip-top condition.

NATURAL DEFENSE

When it comes to maintaining good health, the immune system is the body's most precious asset. By helping the body to resist infection and avoid cancer, it offers protection against many of the world's most widespread and deadliest diseases. Yet, despite modern scientific understanding and major advances in medical treatments, infection is still the commonest cause of illness and death worldwide. And cancer of the lung, stomach, breast, cervix, bowel, and prostate continue to be scourges of the world—responsible for over two and a half million deaths worldwide per year.

What is going wrong? Why hasn't our detailed knowledge of the immune system enabled us to enhance our body's defense mechanisms in a sustainable way? In the process of developing ever more powerful means of attacking and destroying micro-organisms and cancer cells, have we lost sight of the need to strengthen our innate protective systems and nurture our inner environment?

In the early 1950s, with antibiotic therapy, general vaccination programs, radical cancer surgery, radiotherapy, and chemotherapy moving into the medical front line, it seemed clear to most people that scientific know-how was going to provide more effective solutions to disease than old-fashioned naturopathic methods designed to encourage the self-healing processes. Now, 50 years on, we are faced with the specter of malaria and tuberculosis on the rise once again, new strains of drug-resistant superbugs outwitting our most powerful technologies, vaccinations that may harm as well as protect, a rising incidence of cancer, and the engulfing tide of collapsed immunity that is A.I.D.S.

History suggests that, when things go wrong, human beings have a tendency to continue doing what doesn't work—only doing it harder. Despite valuable short-term tactical advances in the management of infectious disease and cancer, we are signally failing in our strategic goal of improving world health in a sustainable manner. This is because we have attempted to usurp the power of the natural world, attacking it with crude weapons, and losing ourselves in a maze of technical detail, instead of working with nature and doing everything we can to enhance our natural powers of healing and self-defense.

Just as the pioneers of microbiology—Didier Béchamp, Claude Bernard, and Louis Pasteur—explained that micro-organisms should be thought of as agents of disease and not as causes, we need to understand that our detailed, valuable, and hard-won knowledge of the process of immunity is not the same as an understanding of its purpose. We have superimposed a dualistic, male-oriented, warlike model on to the remarkable scientific observations we have made, and are assuming that life is a battle between ourselves and the micro-organisms and cancer cells; that we inhabit a dog-eat-dog, kill-or-be-killed biological universe.

The effect has been to focus our attention on external factors, while neglecting an inward-looking, broader approach to healing that attempts to observe the interaction between the physical, mental, emotional, and spiritual aspects of self, and to understand how these affect health and our susceptibility to disease. As a result, we have developed a range of medical weapons that are becoming increasingly hazardous to use.

As a society, we seem to find it easier to spend our money on weapons and drugs rather than on good food, basic sanitation and clean water for those most at risk of disease. Therefore, we do not even keep faith with the knowledge that we do possess—that immunity is profoundly compromised by malnutrition; that poverty creates the perfect environment for the spread of infectious disease; that the typical Western diet and lifestyle lead to cardiovascular problems and cancer; that fear and stress create an internal bodily environment that is prone to disease and degeneration.

This section is written in the knowledge that good health involves paying attention to body, mind, and spirit, that the immune response is the fundamental physical process of healing, and that health and healing are encouraged and enhanced by good food. On the following pages, we take a look at the history, mechanisms, language, and science of immunity, and explain how it operates both in health and disease, and how it can be influenced by diet and lifestyle. You are welcome to use it as a reference as you explore other parts of the book, and as an aid to a better understanding of how the body heals and protects itself.

WHAT IS IMMUNITY?

At the beginning of the 18th century, Mary Pierrepont, an English noblewoman living in Constantinople, became interested in the local method for preventing smallpox, which involved taking scrapings from smallpox crusts and scratching them into the skin. This was an early form of vaccination. Although successful in some cases, the risk of actually developing smallpox from this procedure was very high, and her attempts to introduce inoculation into Britain were largely unsuccessful. However, with smallpox ravaging the 18th-century world (approximately 50 million people died from the disease in Europe between 1700 and 1800), the search for an effective preventive strategy continued.

Some years later, Edward Jenner, an English country doctor from the county of Gloucestershire, noticed that dairymaids who caught cowpox (a relatively minor condition causing spots on the hands) had a strong capacity to resist smallpox. In 1796, he inoculated a young boy with material taken from cowpox spots and then, in an experiment that caused much controversy at the time, inoculated the same boy several times with actual smallpox, without causing any ill effects! Not surprisingly, this dramatic demonstration led to large numbers of people visiting Jenner's country home seeking vaccination, and the success of his smallpox-prevention treatment paved the way for the development of the worldwide vaccination programs we see today.

However, at the time, Jenner's work did little to stimulate new thinking on the nature and causes of infectious disease. Since Roman times, doctors had been trying to discover the reason for the epidemics that decimated the population periodically, but the "germ" theory central to our current understanding of infection did not gain wide acceptance until the mid-19th century. It was then that an Italian, Agostino Bassi, proved that a disease of silkworms was caused by micro-organisms. Although not directly related to human health, his research formed the basis for later discoveries by the "giants" of microbiology—Pasteur, Robert Koch, Joseph Lister, and Paul Ehrlich—that revolutionized biomedicine.

Modern-day research into infectious disease follows two parallel tracks—the first investigating the form, nature, and lifestyle of pathogenic (or disease-causing) micro-organisms, and the chemicals that can be used to destroy them; the second looking into the nature of the body's inherent capacity to resist infection, and how this in-born immunity can be stimulated.

While this research has produced much valuable information and given us important new treatments, the commonly-held belief that germs are malign micro-foes, constantly out to get us—and that the best way of dealing with them is to zap them with increasing doses of powerful antibiotics—is, in fact, a misunderstanding of what the pioneers of microbiology and immunology were saying.

Pasteur, together with the other early holistic medical thinkers—Béchamp, Bernard, and Max von Pettenkofer—emphasized that microbes are only a part of the story, best thought of as agents of disease rather than the causes, their effects largely dependent on the nature of the bodily "terrain" they encounter. In other words, he understood that the state of the body's natural defense systems was paramount to the maintenance of good health.

what the immune system does

The immune system is the body's first line of defense against invasion by micro-organisms and "foreign" materials, and the basis for vaccination and the differences between blood groups. It also protects against the development of cancer by destroying mutant (abnormal) cells. However, immune reactions are not always helpful. If the immune system overreacts to the presence of harmless substances, it produces allergic conditions such as hay fever and asthma. When it is weakened and fails to protect us from infection, the body suffers from immunodeficiency states such as A.I.D.S. When it starts to attack its own body cells as if they were "foreign," the immune system causes autoimmune diseases such as rheumatoid arthritis and systemic lupus erythematosus (S.L.E.).

Thus, the immune system can help or harm the body, depending on the nature and strength of its reactions. There is no fundamental difference between the mechanisms underlying "protective" immunity and those that cause disorders such as allergy and autoimmunity. The part that the immune system plays in health and disease can be divided into two helpful effects—active and passive immunity—and two harmful effects—overactivity and underactivity:

● Active immunity involves the body's own defensive cells and chemicals, which act against bacteria, viruses, fungi, parasites, tumors, and foreign blood groups. Some forms of vaccination stimulate active immunity in the body.
● Passive immunity includes the antibodies acquired by a fetus from its mother, and also refers to vaccination with pre-formed antibodies taken from people or animals.
● Overactivity includes allergy and hypersensitivity to external substances, autoimmunity, and adverse blood transfusion reactions (rhesus incompatibility).
● Underactivity includes inherited immunodeficiency, and acquired immunodeficiency (for example, associated with H.I.V. infection, drugs, radiation, or environmental toxins).

components of the immune system

The immune system is an elaborate, interactive system of cells, chemicals, and tissues distributed throughout the body. When any of these components come into contact with any cells or substance to which they are programed to respond (such as bacteria, viruses, and pollen grains), a series of reactions is triggered that results in the "foreign invader" being destroyed or rendered harmless.

Any cell or chemical substance that triggers a reaction by the immune system is known as an antigen. The reaction may be innate or adaptive (see page 18) and a property of adaptive immunity is that it is specific to the antigen that stimulated it. The cells and antibodies involved in an adaptive immune reaction to a particular antigen won't respond to any other antigen unless it is very similar indeed to the original.

Among the most important components of the immune system are the lymphocytes, or white blood cells, chemicals such as cytokines, antibodies, and the complement system, and tissues such as the lymph nodes. These form the "sharp end" of the immune system. They are the tools that the body uses to dismantle, destroy, and eliminate harmful antigens such as bacteria, viruses, and tumor cells. The way in which these various components interact determines how efficiently the immune system will function.

cells

The principal cells of the immune system are T cells, B cells, antigen-presenting cells (A.P.C.s), neutrophils and mast cells. All have clearly defined roles in the immune system.

● T cells are a type of white cell, or lymphocyte, found in the blood, bone marrow, and lymph nodes. They stimulate B cells (see below) to produce antibodies and can also act directly to destroy antigens (such as viruses) that invade the body's own cells, by secreting chemicals called cytokines. T cells are divided into three groups, according to function— T helper cells, cytotoxic T cells, and T suppressor cells.

● B cells are another group of white cells, also found in the blood, bone marrow, and lymphoid tissues. When stimulated by T cells and cytokines, they turn into plasma cells and secrete antibodies, which enhance the body's response to a disease. Antibodies produced by any group of plasma cells react against only one specific antigen. After infection, some B cells remain in the circulation as "memory" cells, capable of recognizing the disease should it strike again. This function is described in more detail on page 21.

● Antigen-presenting cells are a group of cells found in the skin and throughout the lymphoid tissues. These process antigens in a way that ensures the T cells recognize the presence of foreign cells and other substances as efficiently as possible, and do not confuse them with naturally occurring cellular material. Macrophages—a type of A.P.C. whose name means "big eaters"—are the waste-disposal units of the immune system, eating up all types of foreign matter and the debris that results from immune activity.

● Neutrophils are the commonest form of white blood cells. Like macrophages, they are capable of engulfing bacteria and foreign matter.

● Mast cells are found throughout the body. When activated by antibodies during an immune reaction, they release chemicals (such as histamine) that trigger inflammation.

chemicals

Antibodies are also known as immunoglobulins (Ig). They are proteins secreted by plasma cells that activate enzymes and stimulate various blood and tissue cells to destroy bacteria

and other pathogens. There are five types of antibody:

● IgG is the most abundant immunoglobulin, found in the blood and throughout the body tissues. It activates the complement system (see opposite), and stimulates neutrophils and macrophages to destroy antigens.

● IgM is also found in the bloodstream. It, too, activates the complement system and is particularly important in the fight against bacteria.

● IgA is found in tears, saliva, and the secretions from mucous membranes (such as the lining of the intestines and the respiratory and reproductive tracts) and so is one of the first lines of defense against invading micro-organisms. It helps resist gastro-intestinal infections, and maintains a healthy gut flora. Like IgG and IgM, it also activates complement enzymes (see below).

● IgE is found in the body tissues and can trigger allergic reactions, such as hay fever, by stimulating mast cells to release histamine.

● IgD is present in the body in very low concentrations. Its role in the immune response is unclear.

Surface membrane molecules (also known as CD molecules) are antibody-like molecules found on the outer surface of T cells. They enhance the ability of T cells to trigger immune responses, and help them to recognize the difference between antigens and our own body cells. The number of T cells in the blood carrying CD surface molecules is important in the diagnosis of some diseases. A low level of CD4-carrying T cells is characteristic of A.I.D.S.

Cytokines are a group of chemicals secreted by T cells and other white cells (including macrophages, mast cells, and neutrophils). They stimulate the immune response and improve its efficiency. Four are particularly important:

● Interleukin 1 is secreted by blood cells in response to injury and tissue damage.

● Interleukin 2 is secreted by T cells in response to the presence of antigens. It increases the rate of production of B cells and other T cells.

● Tumor necrosis factor alpha (T.N.F.) is secreted by lymphocytes, macrophages, and neutrophils. As the term "tumor necrosis" (tumor death) suggests, T.N.F. attacks and destroys tumor cells. It also plays a role in activating the immune response to disease, and is responsible for a number of symptoms of illness (including fever, weight loss, and feeling generally unwell).

● Interferon gamma is produced by activated T cells (and other white blood cells) after they have been exposed to an antigen. It encourages macrophage activity and has a strong anti-viral action. It also works with T.N.F. to destroy tumor cells and, like T.N.F., is responsible for some of the general symptoms of acute illness.

Complement is a group of enzyme proteins, made in the liver and found in the blood. When an immune reaction is triggered, antibodies start attaching themselves to antigens and this triggers a chain reaction by the complement enzymes that amplifies the immune response and produces the classic symptoms of inflammation—swelling, redness, and pain.

● Human leucocyte antigen (H.L.A.) markers were discovered in the latter half of the 20th century by scientists researching the phenomenon of transplant rejection. The scientists found a cluster of genes on chromosome six of human D.N.A. that they called the major histocompatibility complex. As well as containing the instructions for making some of the complement proteins, these "histocompatibility genes" are responsible for the presence of so-called H.L.A. "markers" on the surface of body cells. These markers identify cells as belonging uniquely to that body. They provide the means by which the immune system can distinguish between its "own" body cells and "foreign" cells (such as bacteria).

A T cell will respond to the presence of an antigen only when it comes across that antigen stuck to an H.L.A. marker on the surface of an antigen-presenting cell. The fact that H.L.A. markers are genetically determined explains some of the variation in immune response shown by different individuals.

tissues

While many immune reactions happen in the bloodstream, there are other "lymphoid" tissues equally important to immunity— namely lymph nodes ("glands"), mucosa-associated lymphoid tissue (M.A.L.T.), the spleen, the bone marrow and the thymus.

● Lymph nodes are collections of lymphoid cells found throughout the body, including the neck, the armpits, and the groin. They are joined by a network of lymph-carrying vessels (the lymphatics), and are the main sites of storage, activation, and production of the lymphocytes. They are also places where macrophages swallow up and process foreign antigenic particles. Lymph is a pale

straw-colored fluid, similar to blood plasma, from which it is produced, but more watery and containing only lymphocytes plus some protein, fat, and salts. It circulates throughout the body via the lymphatics, and acts as a transport and communications medium for immune cells.

● M.A.L.T. is a diffuse collection of patches of lymphoid tissue found in many parts of the body, including the lining of the gastro-intestinal tract, the appendix, the tonsils, the breasts, and the lungs. It contains clusters of B cells, T cells, and mast cells.

● The spleen, like other lymphoid tissues, contains B cells, T cells and macrophages. In the developing fetus, the spleen also produces red blood cells.

● The bone marrow is the main production site for red and white blood cells and is a constantly renewing reservoir of small, "primitive" immune system cells. Immature B cells leave the bone marrow to take up residence in the other lymphoid tissues. Immature T cells leave the bone marrow at an even earlier stage of development, and migrate to the thymus (hence the name "T" cell) where they are taught to recognize the difference between "self" (the body's own cells) and "other" (foreign cells and other material) before moving on to other lymphoid tissues. The thymus was named by the second-century physician Galen, who thought it looked like a bunch of thyme flowers. It is situated in the upper part of the chest and is crucial to the proper development of T cells and thus to the function of the immune system as a whole.

how the immune system works

We all have an innate, genetically determined ability to produce an immediate, non-specific immune response to disease-causing antigens that enter the body. Cells in the lymphoid tissues (including macrophages and primitive lymphocytes) are genetically pre-programed to secrete cytokines when foreign antigens enter the body. These cytokines stimulate B cells to change into plasma cells and secrete antibodies against the invader, and also stimulate T cells to turn into "killer" cytotoxic T cells that are capable of destroying pathogens directly. However, there is such a wide variety of potentially pathogenic organisms in the world that we have also evolved a powerful system of adaptive immunity that enables us to mount a massive, specific defense against individual pathogens, and also protects us against future exposure to those same pathogens. This adaptive immune response is triggered by an interaction between antigen-presenting cells and T helper cells, which leads to the production of antibodies, cytokines, and cytotoxic T cells specifically directed against the particular strain of invading pathogen that is posing a threat.

The first time the immune system is exposed to a new antigen, the adaptive response takes about 10 days to reach full intensity, during which time the balance between resisting and succumbing to the disease can be very fine. Assuming we recover, the next time the immune system meets the same pathogen, the defensive response is powerful and immediate, giving us resistance to the disease.

recognition and defense

Innate or adaptive, our immune response is always a two-stage process. First, we have to recognize that a foreign, potentially harmful antigen has entered (or is trying to enter) the body. Second, we have to do something to defend ourselves from the invasion. In the process of recognition, we have to be sure as far as possible that we are not mistaking the surface characteristics of our own cells (or other harmless substances) for those of pathogens.

In the defense process, we have to be able to adapt and respond efficiently to a huge variety of potentially harmful antigens, yet without letting the intensity of the immune response cause damage to the body. And we have to do it fast enough to ensure that the invaders don't get the upper hand. Then we have to be able to remember past battles, in order to respond more quickly and effectively if faced with the same challenge in the future.

In summary, for antigen recognition we have primitive T cells, T helper cells, antigen-presenting cells, "virgin" killer T cells, and B cells. For defense, we have T helper cells, cytotoxic "killer" T cells, macrophages, antibody-producing plasma cells, mast cells, neutrophils, macrophages, and the complement system, all kicked into action by cytokines. As well as these specific responses, the body also has a number of non-specific protective mechanisms that amplify the effects of immunity, and which are triggered by immune activity. These non-specific responses can be grouped together under the general term "inflammation."

inflammation

This is one of the oldest recognized features of disease, first described by the Roman medical writer Celsus. It is the body's initial response to tissue or cell damage (internal or external), and the symptoms of heat, redness, swelling, and pain it causes are well known. Much orthodox medical treatment of illness is directed toward the suppression of inflammation, and in many cases (especially in chronic inflammatory conditions such as arthritis) this is both rational and humane.

However, the bad press that inflammation usually receives is misleading because, for most people, it is the process of inflammation that actually allows the immune system to do its work quickly and efficiently. To the naturopathic physician, inflammation is not an unwelcome event but the primary sign that the body is starting to heal itself. Naturopathic treatment seeks to keep the patient comfortable while allowing natural healing mechanisms to do their work unsuppressed.

The inflammatory process follows a set course. First, a cell or tissue is injured, or attacked by pathogens. As a result, chemicals are released from damaged cells or immune cells that cause blood vessels in the damaged area to widen, bringing more blood to the damaged area and slowing down the rate of blood flow. In addition, the blood vessels around the area become "leaky," allowing the free flow of immune cells and fluid into the tissues.

White cells in the blood line up along the blood vessel walls and pass into the damaged area. These cells come into contact with micro-organisms and foreign particles, triggering an immune reaction. Swelling caused by the fluid immobilizes and localizes the damage, and the other components of the immune system—including antibodies, cytotoxic T cells, and complement—then come into play and neutralize the antigens. The debris is swallowed up by macrophages and neutrophils.

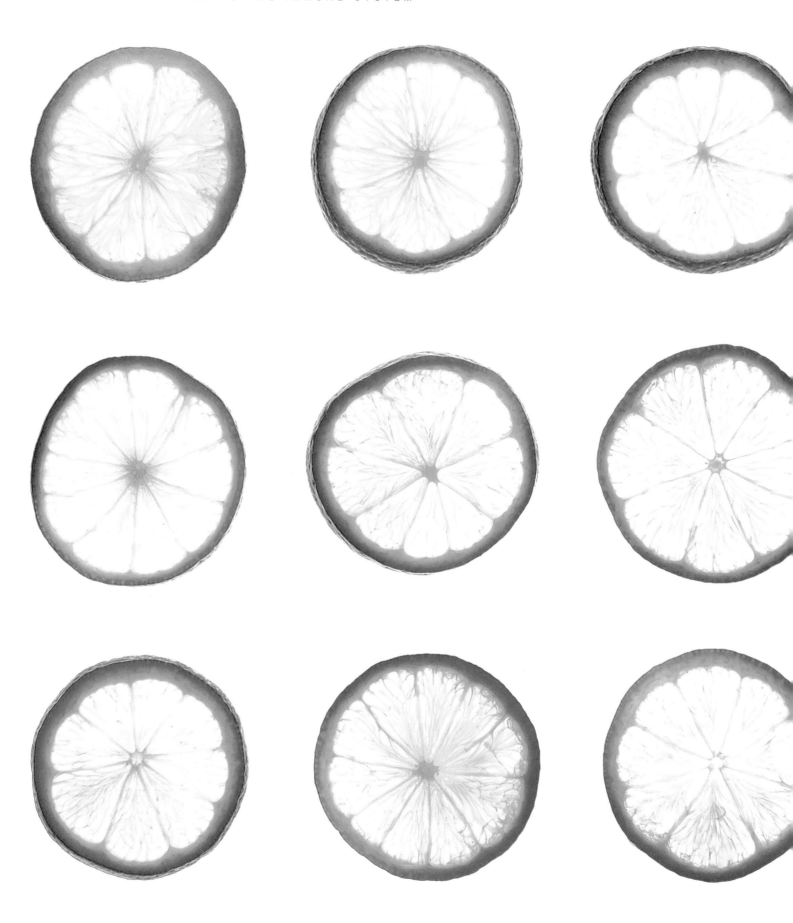

control of immune reactions

With all this cellular and chemical firepower at its disposal, the immune system needs to include certain safeguards to ensure that its reactions do not get out of hand and start attacking healthy body cells. One simple control mechanism built into the system is that, because the intensity of the immune response depends on the amount of antigen present, as soon as immunity starts destroying antigen, the strength of the response fades naturally. This means that the immune response is inherently self-limiting.

As a further safeguard, some of the cytokines damp down the immune response, and there is also a sub-group of T cells, called T suppressor cells, that act to keep immune system activity in check. (In cases of deficient T-cell function, such as immunodeficiency states and malnutrition, this suppression function is lost, leading to an increase in allergic and autoimmune reactions; see pages 24 and 25.)

immune memory, tolerance, and vaccination

The capacity for immunological memory is one of the most important features of the immune system. When B cells are activated by the presence of antigens, many of them turn into plasma cells that produce antibodies, but a proportion remain as B cells and form a "memory population" capable of multiplying rapidly and mounting a swift immune response if the body is exposed to the same antigen at a later date.

This response to the antigen may be so effective that the symptoms of disease are much milder than on the first occasion—or there may be no symptoms at all (in which case, the person is said to be immune to that disease). However, each antigen is recognized by its unique chemical characteristics, and immunological memory relates only to those antigens that have been encountered before. An individual who is immune to one kind of pathogen does not have immunity to other pathogenic organisms. The capacity for immunological memory underlies the concept of vaccination in its two forms—"active" and "passive." In active vaccination, immunity is induced artificially by exposing the body to small amounts of dead or inactivated micro-organisms, usually by injection. The protective response generated in the body by this form of vaccination can last for many years. However, for some diseases, it is not possible to produce a safe, active vaccine, but some measure of short-term protection can be given by passive vaccination—which involves injecting "ready-made" antibodies against the disease, usually derived from animals.

The debate over the safety and effectiveness of vaccination continues to smolder, with protagonists pointing to successes in the control of epidemic diseases such as smallpox, diphtheria, polio, and tuberculosis, and opponents claiming that it can cause brain damage and autism, and pointing to the increased incidence of allergy and autoimmune disease that has coincided with the widespread use of vaccination.

Whatever view you hold over the risks and benefits of vaccination, it is important to remember that vaccines necessarily contain antigens that have been altered from their original state, and that our understanding of the body's reactions to such antigens is far from complete.

Another extremely important property of the immune system is that, in general, it can distinguish between cells from its "own" body and "foreign" cells and antigens. As already explained, this is owing to the presence of "markers" on our body cells that signal "self" to the immune system.

In the developing fetus, these surface markers are "learned" by the immune system because the only cells passing through the unborn baby's lymphoid tissues are its own. In fact, if a newborn baby (whose immune system has not yet fully matured) is exposed to antigenic material there is a good chance that it will develop tolerance to the antigen rather than mount an immune response against it. (The same is true in some elderly people whose immune systems become progressively less efficient.) This means that it is ineffective to vaccinate very young babies, because their capacity to develop tolerance to antigens at this stage in life might leave them unprotected, despite the vaccination.

IMMUNITY AND DISEASE

For many years, it was thought that the symptoms and signs of infectious disease were caused by pathogens, and that the immune system was purely a protective shield, destroying microbes and eliminating dangerous toxins from the body. While the second part of this idea is still held to be true, it is now known that many of the unpleasant, painful, and damaging effects of infection are a direct result of the immune response itself, and that the protection we enjoy from the immune system carries a cost.

When it comes to infectious disease, most of us are happy to pay the price of short-term discomfort as long as we receive the longer-term benefit of recovering from the illness. If, on the other hand, the immune system begins to react to substances in the environment that would ordinarily pose no threat to health—or worse, starts attacking our own body tissues for no apparent reason—we get justifiably concerned. Before looking in detail at allergy and autoimmunity, it is helpful to look at the ways in which the immune system causes illness, and at what it is that makes us susceptible to immune-based diseases.

The following are important conditions caused by immune system activity:

● Heart—carditis in rheumatic fever, cardiomyopathy, and post-heart attack syndromes
● Lungs—alveolitis and asthma
● Gastro-intestinal and liver—celiac disease, ulcerative colitis, and some forms of hepatitis
● Skin—contact dermatitis, pemphigus, pemphigoid, and dermatitis herpetiformis
● Endocrine—Addison's disease, thyroiditis, and type I, insulin-dependent (early onset) diabetes mellitus
● Ear, nose, and throat—hay fever, otitis media ("glue ear")
● Eyes—uveitis, allergic conjunctivitis, and keratoconjunctivitis sicca
● Children—atopic eczema, milk allergy, food allergies, juvenile chronic arthritis, and Henoch-Schönlein purpura
● Blood—pernicious anemia, autoimmune hemolytic anemia, thrombocytopenia and blood transfusion reactions
● Reproductive—rhesus disease of newborn, and infertility
● Kidneys—glomerulonephritis
● Joints—rheumatoid arthritis, S.L.E., and dermatomyositis
● Nerves—multiple sclerosis, myasthenia gravis, polyneuritis, polymyositis, post-vaccination/post-infection encephalitis
● Infections—immune activity is responsible for a variety of syndromes associated with tuberculosis, malaria, Chagas' disease, and leprosy
● General—anaphylaxis, graft rejection, serum sickness.

immune-based disease

Anaphylactic (reaginic) immune reactions are caused by the release of histamine and other chemicals from mast cells, resulting in inflammation, edema, and contraction of smooth muscle. Anaphylaxis evolved to protect us against parasites, and to provide an immediate response to foreign antigens, but it is also responsible for allergic asthma, hay fever, atopic eczema, and food allergies. In its most severe form, acute anaphylaxis, reaction to an antigen causes a rapid onset of nausea, wheezing, itching, low blood pressure, abdominal pain, urticaria (hives), and loss of consciousness. Untreated, acute anaphylaxis can be fatal.

Cell reactive immune reactions involve antibodies sticking to the surface of body cells and triggering various inflammatory responses. Originally designed to destroy invading micro-organisms, these reactions are also responsible for blood transfusion incompatibility, rhesus disease of the newborn, acute graft rejection, and a variety of autoimmune conditions including hemolytic anemia, thyrotoxicosis, pemphigoid, and myasthenia gravis.

Immune complex reactions are caused by antibodies binding with soluble antigens (such as bacterial toxins) in the blood or body fluids. The resulting "immune complexes" are then deposited in the tissues, clogging small blood vessels, and triggering inflammation. Intended as a way of ridding the body of toxins, these reactions are a common cause of immune-related disorders including rashes, vasculitis, alveolitis, serum sickness, glomerulonephritis, rheumatoid arthritis, and systemic lupus erythematosus.

Cell-mediated reactions (or delayed hypersensitivity reactions) involve T cells and macrophages and offer protection against parasitic infection. They are also responsible for the clinical features of tuberculosis, leprosy, pernicious anemia, "contact" dermatitis, type I, insulin-dependent (early onset) diabetes mellitus, graft rejection and to "sensitization" to common substances (such as household chemicals and latex).

susceptibility to immune disease

One of the big unanswered questions in modern immunology is: "Why are some people more prone to immune-based diseases than others?" Research into this subject is ongoing but scientists have uncovered important clues that might point to possible answers. The first involves an immune phenomenon called "atopy." At least 5 per cent of the population have an inherited tendency to produce high levels of IgE, which reacts with common substances, such as pollen and food additives, to cause atopic allergic reactions—such as itching and sneezing. A popular but unproven theory suggests that children develop atopy because they are raised in oversanitized environments and eat "non-natural" diets (such as formula infant milks and convenience foods). The theory is that, because modern children are exposed to few disease microbes but are repeatedly in contact with artificial substances, such as industrial chemicals, the immune system directs too much of its attention toward harmless environmental antigens and hence lacks an adequate response to disease organisms. The allergic child, constantly suffering upper respiratory-tract infections, is an example of this mechanism at work.

There is some evidence that an inherited lack of some of the components of the complement system is responsible for the tendency to develop some immune disorders. Research has also shown that an individual's inherited H.L.A. type has a bearing on the development of a wide range of immunologically based diseases, including ankylosing spondylitis, celiac disease, Graves' disease, S.L.E., rheumatoid arthritis, and pernicious anemia.

Research in West Africa has shown an association between H.L.A. type and the capacity to resist malaria. Although useful in the diagnosis of some conditions, the reason for these associations is not yet clear.

allergy, autoimmunity, and immunodeficiency

Allergy (an unpleasant reaction to non-microbial, "harmless" environmental antigens) and autoimmunity (an immune response against one's own body tissues) are now major causes of illness, particularly in the Western world. Between them they are responsible for much of the daily workload of family doctors, and also generate a huge market for pharmaceutical products that control or suppress the immune response.

allergy

As we saw on page 22, allergic reactions fall into two categories: anaphylactic (or reaginic), rapid allergic responses caused by histamine released from mast cells; and cell-mediated, a slower response to environmental antigens involving T cells and macrophages. A significant proportion of the population have an inherited atopic tendency to anaphylactic allergic reactions of the skin, lungs, eyes, nose, and digestive tract causing conditions such as eczema, hay fever, conjunctivitis, asthma, and food allergy.

Celiac disease (an allergy to wheat gluten, which causes malabsorption), dermatitis herpetiformis (a blistering skin disease also caused by gluten), and allergic alveolitis (for example, farmer's lung, a potentially serious allergic lung inflammation usually caused by occupational exposure to molds) are other important conditions caused by allergy to environmental antigens. Allergic asthma is most often caused by tiny particles of antigenic material. Allergic rhinitis or hay fever is triggered by larger particles. The most common environmental antigens are: plant pollens, house dust mites, insect stings, pet dander (fur and feathers), fungal molds, food proteins, vaccines, drugs, household/industrial chemicals, latex, and heavy metals (especially chromium, cobalt, and nickel).

However, not all adverse reactions to environmental substances are caused by allergies. The term "allergy" is sometimes wrongly attached to any unpleasant reaction to a food or drug. Favism is a hemolytic anemia caused by an inherited lack of the enzyme glucose-6-phosphatase dehydrogenase, which is vital for the health of red blood cells. When a sufferer eats fava beans, inhales fava bean pollen, or takes certain drugs, including sulfonamide antibiotics and certain anti-malarial drugs, red blood cells are rapidly destroyed causing fever, abdominal pain and, in severe cases, coma and even death. The sensitivity of some asthma sufferers to drugs such as aspirin is more often a chemical, rather than an immunological, problem.

Orthodox treatment of allergy is a two-stage process. First, it involves reducing exposure to the allergen responsible (where possible) and, second, the use of drugs. Common drugs used for allergies include:
● Nasal sprays and inhalers (such as antihistamines and sodium cromoglycate), to inhibit the release of histamine from mast cells.
● Bronchodilators, to reduce muscle spasm in the lungs and open the airways.
● Corticosteroid drugs ("steroids"), which counteract inflammation.

autoimmunity

In normal circumstances, the immune system is able to distinguish clearly between "self" and "non-self." During their "education" in the thymus, developing T cells that may react to the body's own tissues are destroyed, and any self-reacting cells that do survive are suppressed by other cells in the immune system. However, for reasons not yet clearly understood, these safety mechanisms sometimes break down, resulting in an autoimmune disease.

Autoimmune diseases are usually chronic, and cause slow, progressive damage to organs and tissues. These conditions cover a spectrum ranging from "organ specific" disorders, in which only one "target" organ is damaged, to "multi-system" diseases involving a variety of body systems, and producing complex patterns of symptoms and signs.

Organ-specific autoimmune diseases include:
● Thyroid—Hashimoto's thyroiditis, and Graves' disease
● Adrenal gland—Addison's disease
● Pancreas—Type I (early onset) diabetes mellitus
● Nerves and muscles—multiple sclerosis, and myasthenia gravis
● Skin—pemphigus, pemphigoid, and vitiligo
● Kidney—Goodpasture's syndrome
● Liver—primary biliary cirrhosis
● Stomach—pernicious anemia

● Hair—alopecia
● Ovaries—premature ovarian failure
● Reproductive organs—endometriosis.

Autoimmune disease is growing increasingly common, so the search for a cause is generating an enormous research effort. This research has uncovered important clues suggesting possible trigger mechanisms for autoimmune reactions. It seems, for example, that certain infections (particularly viruses), vaccinations, and environmental factors can cause subtle changes in lymphocyte function that lead to a breakdown in self-recognition by the immune system.

Some microbes even stimulate B cells to produce "auto-antibodies" directly, by mimicking the actions of T helper cells, and it is possible that other micro-organisms contain proteins that closely resemble those of human tissues. If the immune system makes antibodies to such micro-organisms, it will unwittingly produce antibodies that damage the body's own cells as well.

Many of those suffering from autoimmune diseases have an inherited immunological instability that affects their ability to control immune responses. In particular they may lack T suppressor cells, which normally keep stray "auto-reactive" T helper cells under control.

immunodeficiency

In order to cope with the huge diversity of potentially harmful micro-organisms (and other antigens) that we are exposed to in life, the immune system has evolved into a highly complex system of many inter-related components. Although this gives a wide repertoire of immune responses, it also means that damage or deficiency in any part of the system makes us susceptible to illness.

Immunodeficiency is now an increasingly common cause of disease worldwide. The basic feature of immunodeficiency is the tendency to suffer more frequent and more serious infection than normal, often from micro-organisms not usually considered dangerous.

Immunodeficiency can be divided into two categories: primary—a genetic defect involving the lack of a vital immune system component; and secondary—the direct result of another disease process, or the consequence of exposure to drugs, chemicals, or ionizing radiation. Primary immunodeficiency is usually diagnosed early in life (most often in a child suffering frequent ear, nose, throat, and chest infections), and in some cases (such as in severe combined immunodeficiency—S.C.I.D.) it may lead to early death. When primary immunodeficiency is owing to a lack of B cells (such as X-linked hypogammaglobulinemia—Bruton's disease), lifelong injections of immunoglobulin are necessary to maintain health. Deficiency of complement enzymes can also be managed with drugs and enzyme injections.

Secondary immunodeficiency is more common than the primary type, and has a wide variety of possible causes. The commonest are leukemia, Hodgkin's lymphoma, myeloma, burns, severe kidney disease, Down's syndrome, chronic inflammation, chronic infection (such as malaria and leprosy), congenital rubella (German measles), surgery/radiation of lymphoid tissues, drug therapy (especially corticosteroids and anti-cancer drugs), and poverty.

Of these, poverty is probably the most common cause of immunodeficiency worldwide. Protein-energy malnutrition causes decreased cellular immunity, atrophy of lymph nodes, a reduction of T cells, and an overall decrease in the capacity of the immune system to deal with infection.

H.I.V. and A.I.D.S.

Of all the possible causes of immunodeficiency, in the last 20 years the most important has undoubtedly been acquired immune deficiency syndrome (A.I.D.S.). This is a slow, progressive deterioration of immune function and to date has been responsible for more than 15 million deaths worldwide, with the brunt of the disease borne by the populations of sub-Saharan Africa, south and south-eastern Asia, and South America. A.I.D.S. is now probably responsible for more deaths per year than malaria, and is a major factor in the re-emergence of tuberculosis as a world health problem.

As in other immunodeficiency states, the central problem faced by the A.I.D.S. sufferer is susceptibility to severe infections by viruses, bacteria, fungi, and parasites. The other important feature of full-blown A.I.D.S. is the development of tumors such as lymphoma (cancer of

lymphoid tissue) and Kaposi's sarcoma (a type of skin tumor). When H.I.V. is active, the number of CD4 T cells in the blood (see page 16) falls progressively.

The commonest A.I.D.S.-related infections are Herpes simplex, Herpes zoster, cytomegalovirus (C.M.V.), tuberculosis, salmonella, toxoplasma, cryptosporidium, giardia, pneumocystis, cryptococcus, histoplasma, candida, and strongyloides.

There has been extensive worldwide debate over the cause of A.I.D.S., but the current consensus is that infection with either the H.I.V.1 or H.I.V.2 virus is at the root of the problem. H.I.V. viruses belong to a family of retroviruses thought to have originated in primates. H.I.V.2 infection is most common in West Africa.

How H.I.V. causes immunodeficiency is not well understood, but it is known that the H.I.V. virus has the ability to stick on to CD4 molecules on the surface of T helper cells, which seriously interferes with T-cell function. H.I.V. infection also damages the thymus (where T cells develop), and affects antigen-presenting cells such as macrophages, altering their pattern of cytokine release.

The fact that the H.I.V. virus is able to fuse with T cells and commandeer their internal workings—and that it is capable of assuming a wide range of antigenic forms during the course of the disease—enables it to evade the body's protective immune response, and makes the development of effective treatments very difficult.

Combination anti-viral drug therapy with reverse transcriptase inhibitors helps raise the CD4 lymphocyte count, and antibacterial and antifungal drugs are also used to treat infections. Health education programs about the need for safer sex, safe blood transfusion procedures, and reducing shared-needle use by intravenous drug users are the mainstays of prevention, and much research is being devoted to the development of a safe and effective vaccine.

Given the close link between nutrition and immunity, it is not surprising that diet and the treatment of H.I.V. infection are also intimately related. It has been shown that good nutrition greatly improves the outcome of drug therapy and chances of long-term survival. Maximizing the quality of the diet can also play a major role in improving the quality of life of A.I.D.S. sufferers (see page 92–3).

IMMUNITY AND FOOD

Like the lungs, the gastro-intestinal tract is a major "meeting place" in which the body comes into contact with the outside world. All food and drink has to pass through it before being absorbed and used for nutrition, and its lining is rich in lymphoid tissue called Peyer's patches.

The challenge for the immune system is that it has to be tolerant of the wide variety of "foreign" food proteins that we consume habitually, while at the same time being able to recognize and destroy potentially harmful micro-organisms that might contaminate our food and water.

It manages this by suppressing the production of any IgG and IgM antibodies that might react against food protein molecules, and by increasing the amount of IgA antibody in gut secretions. IgA has the ability to bind directly to pathogenic micro-organisms, and to neutralize them without activating the complement system or causing inflammation.

However, when the immune system is combating an infection elsewhere in the body, gastro-intestinal lymphoid tissue can get caught up in the action and start attacking harmless food antigens. This, in turn, causes inflammation and damage to the lining of the gastro-intestinal tract. Severe malnutrition can also damage the lining of the intestines and disturb the pattern of immune responses.

allergy or intolerance?

Sometimes—and especially in those with a family tendency to atopic conditions such as eczema, asthma, and hay fever —the immune system reacts against certain foods. In addition to triggering general allergic symptoms, this causes inflammation of the intestinal lining and increased contraction of intestinal muscle, leading to abdominal discomfort, diarrhea, wind, and poor absorption of nutrients. Deficiencies of vitamins, minerals, and other nutrients can, in turn, affect the immune system. For example:
● Essential fatty acid deficiency causes atrophy of lymphoid tissues and decreased ability to produce antibodies.
● Vitamin A and E deficiency affects the immune defenses of skin and mucous membranes, decreases T-cell activity and antibody production, and so increases infection risk.
● Vitamin B6, folate and pantothenate deficiency decreases T and B cell activity.
● Iron deficiency (or excess iron) increases infection risk.
● Zinc deficiency causes atrophy of lymphoid tissue, decreases B and T cell responses and inhibits development of the immune system in the fetus.

There is a tendency these days to label all unpleasant reactions to food as "food allergy," but for accurate diagnosis and effective treatment, it is necessary to classify such reactions under their correct headings: food intolerance; food allergy; and psychological intolerance.

Food intolerance is a general term covering all negative reactions to foodstuffs, including those caused by inherited enzyme deficiencies, interactions with drugs and medicines, and chemical irritations (for example, by chilli pepper).

Food allergy means that a particular food is triggering a specific immune response. True food allergy is more common in children, and can express itself in a variety of ways including eczema, asthma, urticaria (hives), mood disturbance, severe anaphylactic reactions, epilepsy, poor growth, diarrhea, vomiting, and gastro-intestinal bleeding. (The association between childhood hyperactivity and food allergy is not clearly established.)

Food allergy in adults tends to cause urticaria, asthma, migraine, or "irritable bowel syndrome"-type symptoms such as nausea, bloating, abdominal pain, and alternating constipation and diarrhea. There is also some evidence implicating food allergy in arthritis and depression. Accurate diagnosis of food allergy is time-consuming and usually involves elimination diets followed by "challenges" with the suspect food(s). Patch and scratch tests, cytotoxic blood testing, hair analysis, applied kinesiology, vega testing, and iridology are also used, with varying degrees of success.

Psychological intolerance means reacting to a food which, although causing unpleasant symptoms when eaten in a recognizable form, causes no reaction when it is disguised or made unrecognizable by mixing with other foods. Generally speaking, orthodox medical practitioners tend to over-diagnose psychological intolerance, whereas complementary therapists tend to under-diagnose it.

cow's milk allergy

Despite its status as a staple food in the West, cow's milk is a common cause of food allergy in children and is responsible for a variety of symptoms—including eczema, asthma, diarrhea, vomiting, and malabsorption of nutrients causing slow growth.

The allergen responsible is beta-lactoglobulin, a protein that forms part of milk whey, and most children (and many adults) have antibodies to milk protein in their blood . Babies can become sensitized to milk protein via the breast milk if the mother's diet contains cow's milk and milk products. Although the majority of children have developed "tolerance" to cow's milk by about one year old, the lining of the intestine continues to show abnormalities. Excluding cow's milk from the diet resolves the problem.

Allergy to cow's milk is not the same as lactose intolerance, another common cause of gastro-intestinal upset in children. Babies and young children produce the enzyme lactase, which can digest lactose, a sugar found in breast milk. Production of this enzyme drops sharply after weaning and in most races (except Western Caucasians) is practically non-existent in adults. If an individual with lactase "deficiency" drinks cow's milk, the lactose will not be digested and so will pass into the colon, causing diarrhea, wind, and abdominal discomfort. Lactose intolerance is a common cause of "unexplained" abdominal pain in children and is also common after bouts of gastroenteritis.

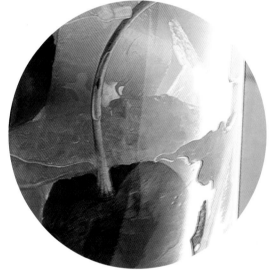

celiac disease

Celiac disease is another immune-related gastro-intestinal condition, in which eating wheat gluten causes inflammation and damage to the lining of the small intestine. This leads to severe malabsorption of important nutrients resulting in multiple health problems including diarrhea, weight loss, flatulence, edema, anemia, muscle wasting, bone problems, and disturbance of heart rhythm. The exact nature of the immune reaction that causes celiac disease is unclear, but it is known that people with the condition have an inherited genetic susceptibility, and that the components of gluten that cause the problem are called gliandins. Although potentially serious, celiac disease can be managed by eating a gluten-free diet. This means avoiding wheat, barley, rye, and, usually, oats—for life. However, rice, maize, and soy products are safe, and not everyone with the disorder is sensitive to oats.

IMPROVING IMMUNITY

Immunity that harms and immunity that heals are both caused by the same basic mechanisms, so knowing which nutritional and lifestyle factors influence immunity gives us a powerful way of enhancing personal health, and of coping with many common ailments that have immune disturbance at their root. A healthy immune system is the basis of well-being, so making it more efficient, and avoiding anything that might compromise or weaken it, are the fundamental steps to life-long health.

Later sections of this book look in detail at how you can select the right foods to optimize immune function, but clinical experience and modern research also show that other factors have powerful effects on immunity, particularly stress, environmental pollution, alcohol, cigarettes and recreational drugs, medical interventions, obesity, lack of exercise, and age factors.

managing stress

Chronic stress causes the adrenal glands to secrete higher levels of corticosteroids, which depress immune function. In acute stress reactions, high epinephrine levels also decrease T helper cell activity, increase T suppressor cell activity and lead to degeneration of lymphoid tissues. Changes in mood alter the amount of IgA present in secretions from mucous membranes, and depression interferes with T and B cell function. Therefore, chronic stress is a major risk factor for illness, particularly cancer and heart disease, and making the lifestyle changes necessary to reduce its impact on our lives is a vitally important preventive health strategy. Stress-management techniques such as yoga, deep breathing, meditation and autosuggestion can also have a significant effect on immune function and reduce our susceptibility to disease.

avoiding pollution

Environmental pollutants are broadly divided into three categories:
● Radiation—from microwave appliances, mobile phones, television and radio transmitters, television and computer screens, high-tension overhead electricity cables, and nuclear installations and reprocessing plants.
● Chemicals—including garden and agricultural pesticides and herbicides, aerosols, industrial emissions, engine exhaust fumes,

smoke, paints, fungicides, and household products such as air fresheners, detergents, and furniture polish.

● Biological—such as house dust and dust mites, pet dander, and molds.

All of these can compromize immunity and should be avoided where possible. Minimizing the use of household chemicals, buying organic produce, using dust-covers on mattresses, exchanging carpets for wood or tiled flooring, avoiding smoking and smokers, ensuring good ventilation in the house, limiting the amount of time spent in front of television screens and computer monitors, and regular household maintenance to avoid damp and mold formation are all achievable ways of improving immune-system health.

avoiding alcohol, cigarettes, and drugs

In many parts of the world, alcohol is one of the most important controllable risk factors for serious illness. It depresses the immune response and is clearly associated with heart disease, hypertension, stroke, gastritis, pancreatitis, peptic ulcers, serious liver damage, and deterioration of mental function. As with hard-drug use, it is a major cause of poor nutrition, which further damages immune competence. Tobacco smoke contains high concentrations of dangerous chemicals including benzene, carbon monoxide, and cadmium (a powerful immuno-suppressant also found in fungicides, fertilizers, and rubber tires). Cannabis inhibits both T cell and macrophage activity. Put simply, drinking, smoking, and recreational drug use are not compatible with a healthy immune system.

taking treatment —with caution!

Medicinal remedies used to control the symptoms of allergic reactions—antihistamines, bronchodilators, decongestants, sodium cromoglycate, corticosteroids—are designed to dampen immune system activity, but many other drugs—including anti-inflammatories, blood thinners, oral contraceptives, hormone replacement therapy (H.R.T.), antibiotics, and anti-cancer drugs—can cause unintentional suppression of normal immune responses. Diagnostic and therapeutic X-rays and other ionizing radiations also carry a risk of immune-system damage. Informed and appropriate use of medical drugs, plus avoidance of unnecessary high-energy imaging procedures, should form part of any strategy for immune health.

controlling weight

Obesity is a global epidemic, which is clearly related to the high incidence of coronary heart disease worldwide, and strongly implicated as a risk factor for cancer, especially of the breast, uterus, cervix, and ovary in women, the prostate in men, and the colon and rectum in both sexes. As immunity plays a major role in protecting against cancer, and as it is proven that obese people are more likely to die earlier than the non-obese, maintaining a healthy body weight is a common-sense way of encouraging long-term immune health, as well as improving general well-being.

taking exercise

Research confirms that regular moderate exercise enhances immune function and protects against cancer, heart disease, and osteoporosis, as well as being an effective way to relieve stress. Three or more 30-minute exercise sessions a week, such as brisk walking, jogging, cycling, or swimming, are ideal for optimizing immunity, but beware overexertion—it suppresses T cell function and other immune responses.

for young and old

At both extremes of age, the immune system is less efficient, so paying special attention to the above factors is particularly important for children and the elderly. As far as children are concerned, breastfeeding, avoiding cow's milk, allowing minor illnesses to take their course without suppressing the symptoms with drugs, and eliminating unnecessary exposure to environmental antigens, are the basics of healthy immune-system development.

superfoods
for the immune system

The medicinal value of food for warding off illness has been acknowledged for thousands of years. More recently, scientific research has discovered hundreds of beneficial nutrients in the foods we eat. By applying our knowledge of these nutrients and of how they work to our diet, we can eat foods that boost our immune system and so help protect ourselves against a host of ailments.

   Part Two presents profiles of 150 foods packed with disease-fighting nutrients, including nine "star foods," such as beet and shiitake mushrooms, that are particularly effective in boosting the body's natural defenses. All recipes serve four people unless otherwise stated.

fruits and vegetables
ROOTS AND BULBS

CARROT

★ VITAMINS A, K, FOLATE; CALCIUM, MANGANESE, PHOSPHORUS; CHROMIUM, IRON, ZINC; CAROTENOIDS; FIBER

✓ ANTI-CANCER, ANTIOXIDANT, GOOD FOR SKIN AND EYES

! HIGH CARROT INTAKE CAUSES ORANGE/YELLOW SKIN COLORING; THIS EFFECT IS HARMLESS AND GOES ONCE INTAKE IS REDUCED

Carrots (*Daucus carota*) support the immune system, aid wound healing and promote healthy skin. They can also be useful in treating chronic viral infections, such as herpes simplex. Carrots help prevent the formation of cancer cells and can protect against heart disease and arthritis. They play a role in regulating blood-sugar levels and thus may help protect against diabetes.

RECIPES carrot 'n' beet salad (page 119), carrot and lemon with garlic (page 124), healing soup (page 104)

ONION

★ VITAMINS B1, B6; SULFUR COMPOUNDS

✓ ANTI-ASTHMATIC, ANTIBACTERIAL, ANTI-CANCER, ANTISEPTIC, DIURETIC, LOWERS BLOOD PRESSURE, LOWERS CHOLESTEROL

! MAY CAUSE INDIGESTION IN THOSE WITH GASTRO-INTESTINAL DISORDERS

Onion (*Allium cepa*) is a natural antibiotic that also helps the body's metabolism by lowering blood cholesterol, blood fat and blood sugar. Onions decrease the formation of blood clots, too. They inhibit the activity of *Helicobacter pylori* (the bacterium thought to be responsible for gastritis and stomach ulcers), and may protect against stomach cancer by decreasing the conversion of nitrates to nitrites in the stomach. Onion syrup (prepared like garlic oxymel—page 129) is a useful remedy for colds and coughs.

RECIPES french onion tart (page 115), samosa parcels (page 108), tofumasalata (page 108)

POTATO

★ VITAMINS C, B1, FOLATE; POTASSIUM; IRON; SOLANIDINE ALKALOIDS; FIBER, COMPLEX CARBOHYDRATES, PROTEIN

✓ ANTIOXIDANT, ENERGY-BOOSTING, NUTRITIONAL VALUE

! GREEN AND DAMAGED POTATOES HAVE AN INCREASED ALKALOID CONTENT THAT MAKES THEM TASTE BITTER, AND WHICH CAN BE TOXIC IN LARGE AMOUNTS

Potatoes (*Solanum tuberosum*) boost energy and strengthen immunity. They lower blood-fat levels, improve tissue oxygenation, promote a healthy nervous system, and improve wound healing. They help the body absorb and use other nutrients and alleviate digestive and malabsorption disorders. For most benefit, eat in their skins. Hot potato water and raw potato juice are traditional remedies for arthritis and gout.

RECIPES shepherdess' pie (page 116), hasselbach potatoes (page 118), welsh leek and potato soup (page 106)

SWEET POTATO

★ VITAMINS A, B1, B3, FOLATE; CAROTENOIDS (IN YELLOW VARIETY); COMPLEX CARBOHYDRATES, FIBER, SUGARS

✓ ANTIOXIDANT, ANTIVIRAL (YELLOW VARIETY), ENERGY-BOOSTING

There are two varieties of sweet potato (*Ipomoea batatas*)—yellow and white. The yellow variety contains high levels of vitamin A and carotenoids, which enhance the immune response and help the body deal with viral infections and cancer. Therefore sweet potato is useful in the treatment of ailments such as cancer and A.I.D.S., in which the immune response is compromised. Both kinds boost resistance to infection and help maintain optimum energy levels. They nourish the nervous system, help maintain healthy muscles, and keep skin and mucous membranes in good condition.

RECIPES nettle and sweet potato mash (page 45), sweet potato curry (page 116), vegetable kebabs (page 107)

YAM

★ VITAMINS A, B1; CAROTENOIDS (IN YELLOW YAM); COMPLEX CARBOHYDRATES, FIBER, PROTEIN

✓ ANTIOXIDANT, ANTIVIRAL (YELLOW YAM), ENERGY-BOOSTING

There is a yellow and a white variety of yam (*Dioscorea spp.*). The yellow kind aids immunity and inhibits cancer growth. Both kinds help maintain healthy heart, nerves, muscles, and metabolism.

RECIPES use as sweet potato (above)

VEGETABLE FRUITS

BUTTERNUT SQUASH

★ VITAMINS A, E; MAGNESIUM; CAROTENOIDS

✓ ANTI-CANCER, ANTIOXIDANT

Butternut squash (*Cucurbita sp.*) helps protect against cancer, heart disease, and mental dysfunction. It aids normal blood cell function and encourages healthy skin, muscles, and nerves.

RECIPES butternut squash with bell pepper and tomato (page 113)

OKRA (GUMBO, LADIES' FINGERS)

★ FOLATE; CALCIUM, MAGNESIUM, PHOSPHORUS, POTASSIUM; IRON; FIBER

✓ ANTIDEPRESSANT, IMMUNO-STIMULANT

Okra (*Abelmoschus esculentus*) helps protect against colon cancer and other disorders related to low fiber intake, such as diverticulitis. It strengthens the immune system by supporting lymphatic tissue and white blood cells, aids the development and maintenance of a healthy nervous system, and reduces the risk of heart disease.

RECIPES okra in sweet and sour tamarind sauce (page 116)

PUMPKIN

★ VITAMIN A; CAROTENOIDS

✓ ANTIOXIDANT, ANTI-CANCER

Like butternut squash, pumpkin (*Cucurbita maxima*) helps prevent the formation of cancer cells and promotes healthy skin.

RECIPES pumpkin soup (page 105)

RED BELL PEPPER

★ VITAMINS A, C, B6; CAROTENOIDS; FIBER

✓ ANTI-ALLERGIC, ANTIOXIDANT, ANTI-CANCER, SUPPORTS NERVES

! ONE OF SOLINACEAE FAMILY OF VEGETABLE FRUITS AND MAY CAUSE ADVERSE REACTIONS IN THOSE WITH FOOD ALLERGIES OR ARTHRITIS

Red bell pepper (*Capsicum sp.*) boosts immunity and helps protect against cancer. It also helps maintain normal blood-fat levels, and aids production of hemoglobin by the red blood cells. It encourages a healthy nervous system, and may protect against asthma, migraine, and depression.

RECIPES broiled bell peppers (page 107), catalan salad (page 120), vegetable kebabs (page 107), paella (page 112)

TOMATO

★ VITAMINS A, C, B3; LYCOPENE; FIBER

✓ ANTI-CANCER, ANTIOXIDANT, ANTIVIRAL

! ONE OF SOLINACEAE FAMILY OF VEGETABLE FRUITS—MAY CAUSE ADVERSE REACTIONS IN THOSE WITH FOOD ALLERGIES OR ARTHRITIS

Tomatoes (*Lycopersicon sp.*) are packed with antioxidants, including vitamins A and C, and lycopene. They improve the immune response while also helping to maintain energy levels. This combination makes tomatoes a useful addition to the diet of those suffering from energy-compromising conditions such as cancer and A.I.D.S. They boost resistance to infectious disease, encouraging wound healing and keeping the skin and mucous membranes in good condition.

RECIPES baked tomatoes on toast (page 102), beans and tomatoes on toast (page 102), cool tomato soup (page 104), tomato and cucumber canapés (page 110), tomato cocktail (page 127), tomato salsa (page 118), tomato ketchup (page 111)

beet

BEET HAS BEEN USED AS A FOOD AND A MEDICINE SINCE EARLY TIMES. ITS UNIQUE MIXTURE OF MINERALS AND PHYTOCHEMICALS RESISTS INFECTION, BOOSTS CELLULAR INTAKE OF OXYGEN, AND TREATS DISORDERS OF THE BLOOD, LIVER, AND IMMUNE SYSTEM.

The origin of beet

A native of southern Europe, beet (*Beta vulgaris rubra*) is now cultivated worldwide. It is derived from the sea beet, which grows wild around the Mediterranean. Beet has an unmistakable sweet flavor that is strongest when the food is eaten raw. Its leaves taste like spinach and, as with spinach, can be cooked, or eaten raw in salads. Modern Western medicine makes little use of the healing power of beet, but the vegetable is held in high regard by practitioners of natural medicine all over the world.

Beet was prized in ancient Greece, where people would offer it up to the god Apollo. Legend has it that Aphrodite ate beet to retain her beauty. In the old English medical tradition, beet was regarded as an important remedy for blood ailments. Herbalists and naturopaths of today still use beet as an effective treatment for disorders of the blood and the immune system, and often refer to it as "the vitality plant."

Immune-boosting properties

Beet stimulates the immune system by improving cell respiration and tissue oxygenation. It does this by encouraging the production of new red blood cells (a process called *erythropoiesis*). The enhanced cell respiration helps keep the heart, muscles, and nerves in good condition. There is evidence that eating beet causes cancer cells to either revert to normal or die, by altering their rate of cell respiration. This may not cure the disease, but may help to boost the length and quality of life of sufferers. Beet also helps stabilize the body's pH (acid–alkaline balance). This is important for

immunity because bacteria thrive when the body's pH is disturbed. Beet can be used to treat chronic infections, cancers (particularly leukemia), skin problems, inflammatory bowel disease, liver disease, and in the prevention and treatment of heart disease and rheumatoid arthritis. It also aids fat metabolism and liver function.

Using beet

Beet has no harmful side effects and is well tolerated by most people. It needs to be eaten over a relatively long period of time to improve general health and vitality in all cases of chronic illness. The average dose is two medium-size beets per day. Beet is just as effective cooked as it is eaten raw or juiced. Try this recipe for a blood-purifying drink: juice equal amounts of beet, carrot, celery, tomato, and a lemon. Drink 1 to 2 wineglassfuls per day for three weeks.

IMMUNE-BOOSTING PROFILE

★ FOLATE; CALCIUM, MANGANESE, POTASSIUM; IRON; BETANIN, MALONIC ACID, PHYTOSTEROL, SAPONIN; FIBER, PROTEIN, SUGARS

✓ ANTI-CANCER, ANTI-INFLAMMATORY, ANTIOXIDANT, DETOXIFYING, IMMUNO-STIMULANT, BOOSTS CELL OXYGENATION, REJUVENATING

! BETANIN, THE PIGMENT IN BEET, MAY COLOR FECES AND URINE RED; THIS IS HARMLESS AND THE EFFECT DISAPPEARS ONCE YOU STOP EATING THE VEGETABLE

! THE LEAVES CONTAIN OXALIC ACID AND SHOULD BE AVOIDED BY PEOPLE SUFFERING FROM KIDNEY STONES OR ARTHRITIS

baked beet salad *(above)*

2 beets, washed but
  not peeled
1 scallion, finely
  chopped
1 bunch of watercress, finely
  chopped
1 tbsp balsamic vinegar
2 tbsp safflower oil

Dry the beets gently and rub in a little oil. Bake in a medium hot oven (350°F) for about an hour. Cool under running water, peel and chop into sticks. Place in a salad bowl and mix with the rest of the ingredients.

beet and horseradish salad

3 medium beets, grated
1 cup plain soy yogurt
1–2 tbsp fresh horseradish,
  grated
4 tbsp fresh mint, finely chopped
Salt to taste

Mix the yogurt, horseradish, and salt. Gently fold the beet into the dressing and garnish with mint.

scandinavian beet burgers

3 cups white rice, well cooked
4 oz firm tofu, grated
2 medium beets, grated
2 tbsp breadcrumbs
1 tbsp balsamic vinegar
1 tbsp olive oil
1 tbsp marjoram
Salt and pepper
  to taste
Flour for dipping
Oil for frying

Mix the rice, tofu, beet, breadcrumbs, vinegar, oil, and marjoram in a bowl. Season and shape into flat cakes. Dip in flour and fry at high temperature for 2 minutes on each side. Turn down the heat and continue frying for about 5 minutes on each side. Serve in burger buns, with salad, slices of tomato, cucumber, raw onion, and mustard and tomato ketchup (*see page 111*).

LEAVES AND FLOWERS

AMARANTH LEAVES (LOVE LIES BLEEDING)

★ VITAMINS A, C, B2, FOLATE; CALCIUM, MAGNESIUM, MANGANESE, PHOSPHORUS, POTASSIUM; IRON; FIBER, PROTEIN

✓ ANTI-ALLERGIC, ANTI-CANCER, ANTIOXIDANT, ENERGY-BOOSTING

! AMARANTH HAS A HIGH PROTEIN CONTENT, WHICH MAY MAKE IT HARDER FOR CHILDREN TO DIGEST LARGE AMOUNTS

The leaves of amaranth (*Amaranthus candatus*) are high in protein and other important nutrients. This makes amaranth a useful support to the immune system and a good source of energy. Amaranth leaves aid liver function and wound healing, help regulate blood-fat levels, and are good for the digestion. They may also help protect against heart disease, cancer, and rheumatoid arthritis. The leaves can be used like other greens in salads, or steamed or creamed like spinach. Amaranth tisane is taken to treat bronchitis and irritable bowel syndrome.

RECIPES *amaranth and tofu puffs (page 112)*

ASPARAGUS

★ VITAMINS B3, FOLATE; POTASSIUM; ZINC; RUTIN, SAPSONIN, TANNIN; FIBER, PROTEIN

✓ ANTISPASMODIC, DIURETIC, GENTLY LAXATIVE, SOOTHING TO THE URINARY TRACT, WOUND HEALING

Asparagus (*Asparagus officinalis*) is a gentle diuretic that is used to stimulate urine flow and hence alleviate water retention. It also helps combat urinary-tract infections, and ease the pain of cystitis. As a general tonic, it helps keep the skin and mucous membranes in good condition, and to maintain the health of blood-vessel walls. It may have a role in regulating blood cholesterol levels and inhibiting the growth of cancer cells.

RECIPES *asparagus with ravigote (page 106), asparagus asian-style (page 113), catalan salad (page 120), pasta salad (page 120), scrambled tofu (page 102)*

BELGIAN ENDIVE

★ VITAMINS A, B1, FOLATE; PHOSPHORUS; BITTER PRINCIPLE; FIBER

✓ ANTI-ALLERGIC, ANTI-CANCER, ANTIOXIDANT, ANTI-STRESS

Belgian endive (*Cichorium intybus*) has a delicate, slightly bitter taste that is popular in France. It stimulates the liver and digestion, supports the immune system and helps to regulate and maintain energy levels. Endive is also good for the health of the skin and mucous membranes.

RECIPES *broiled endive and brazil nut salad (page 57), grapefruit salad (page 49)*

BROCCOLI (GREEN- AND PURPLE-SPROUTING)

★ VITAMINS A, C, E, B3, B5, FOLATE; CALCIUM, PHOSPHORUS, POTASSIUM; IRON, ZINC; GLUCOSINOLATES

✓ ANTI-CANCER, ANTIOXIDANT, ANTI-STRESS, ENERGY-BOOSTING

💡 SEE GLOSSARY FOR INFORMATION ON GLUCOSINOLATES

Broccoli (*Brassica oleracea var.*) is a useful aid to detox and boosts energy and strength. It protects the health of the heart, skin, nerves, and muscle tissue, and helps prevent heart disease, cancer, and immune disorders.

RECIPES *sweet potato curry (page 116)*

BRUSSELS SPROUT

★ VITAMINS C, B2, B5, B6, FOLATE; POTASSIUM; GLUCOSINOLATES; FIBER, PROTEIN, SUGARS

✓ ANTI-ALLERGIC, ANTIOXIDANT, ANTI-STRESS

♀ SEE GLOSSARY FOR INFORMATION ON GLUCOSINOLATES

Brussels sprouts (*Brassica oleracea gemmifera*) strengthen the immune system and help maintain the health of the skin, nerves, and mucous membranes. They also help maintain normal energy and blood-fat levels, and may protect against asthma, migraine, depression, and cancer.

RECIPES serve steamed or boiled as side dish.

BUTTERHEAD LETTUCE

★ VITAMINS A, C, B3, FOLATE; CALCIUM, POTASSIUM; ZINC

✓ ANTI-CANCER, ANTIOXIDANT

Butterhead lettuce (*Lactuca sativa sp.*) improves oxygen transport in the blood and aids liver function and wound healing. It also helps to regulate blood-fat levels and maintain the strength of the heart, nerves, and muscles.

RECIPES provençal mesclun salad (page 119)

CAULIFLOWER

★ VITAMINS C, B3, B5, B6; PHOSPHORUS, POTASSIUM; ZINC;
  GLUCOSINOLATES; FIBER, PROTEIN

✓ ANTI-ALLERGIC, ANTI-CANCER, ANTIOXIDANT, ANTI-STRESS

♀ SEE GLOSSARY FOR INFORMATION ON GLUCOSINOLATES

Cauliflower (*Brassica oleracea botrytis*) encourages antibody and hemoglobin production and protects against allergy, asthma, migraine, and depression. It improves the health of the skin and mucous membranes, helps maintain energy levels, and regulates blood-fat concentration.

RECIPES creamy cauliflower soup (page 105), green lentil salad (page 120)

FLORENCE FENNEL

★ VITAMIN B3, FOLATE; POTASSIUM; ZINC; VOLATILE OILS, BITTER
  PRINCIPLES; FIBER

✓ ANTI-INFLAMMATORY, CARMINATIVE, DIURETIC, CIRCULATORY
  STIMULANT

Fennel (*Foeniculum vulgare dulce*) is an important remedy for digestive upsets. It also helps regulate blood-fat levels and maintains the health of the heart, muscles, skin, mucous membranes, and nerves.

RECIPES florence fennel salad (page 120), green party (page 124), black-eye pea and wild marjoram soup (page 105)

GLOBE ARTICHOKE

★ VITAMINS B3, B5, BIOTIN, FOLATE; ZINC; BITTER PRINCIPLE; PROTEIN

✓ ANTI-ALLERGIC, ANTI-STRESS

Globe artichoke (*Cynara scolymus*) stimulates the appetite and enhances liver function. It is a good source of energy, which improves the health of the skin, hair, bone marrow, mucous membranes, and nervous system, and helps regulate blood-fat levels.

RECIPES artichoke hearts, fava beans and shiitake (page 112), paella (page 112), artichoke salad (page 119)

MUSTARD CRESS

★ VITAMINS A, C, B3, FOLATE; CALCIUM; IRON, ZINC;
  GLUCOSINOLATES, SULFUR, VOLATILE OIL; FIBER

✓ ANTI-ALLERGIC, ANTIBACTERIAL, ANTI-CANCER, ANTIOXIDANT,
  STIMULANT

! LARGE QUANTITIES OF MUSTARD CRESS CAN CAUSE DIGESTIVE
  UPSET BECAUSE OF THE SULFUR AND MUSTARD OIL CONTENT

♀ SEE GLOSSARY FOR INFORMATION ON GLUCOSINOLATES

Mustard cress (*Brassica hirta*) improves iron absorption, oxygen transport, and wound healing, and helps balance blood-fat levels. It is also good for the heart, liver, nerves, skin, and muscles.

RECIPES provençal mesclun salad (page 119)

NASTURTIUM

★ VITAMIN C; GLUCOSINOLATES, VOLATILE OIL

✓ ANTIBACTERIAL, ANTIMICROBIAL, ANTIOXIDANT, ANTIVIRAL

♀ SEE GLOSSARY FOR INFORMATION ON GLUCOSINOLATES

Nasturtium (*Tropaeolum majus*) leaves and flowers are powerful natural antibiotics, and are particularly useful in relieving respiratory-tract infections such as bronchitis, influenza, and colds.

RECIPES toasted tempeh with herb salad (page 108), tropical sunshine salad (page 121), green leafy salad (page 41)

RADICCHIO

★ VITAMINS B2, B3; POTASSIUM; ANTHOCYANIN, BITTER PRINCIPLES;
  FIBER

✓ ANTI-CANCER, ANTIOXIDANT

Eating radicchio (*Cichorium var.*) helps the body maximize energy release from food, prevents cholesterol buildup and the formation of blood clots.

RECIPES orange mango salad (page 120)

curly kale

CURLY KALE IS A MEMBER OF THE BRASSICA FAMILY, WHICH INCLUDES CABBAGE, BROCCOLI, AND BRUSSELS SPROUTS. IT IS PACKED WITH VITAMINS, MINERALS, AND PHYTOCHEMICALS THAT GUARD AGAINST BACTERIAL AND VIRAL INFECTION, HEART DISEASE, AND CANCER.

The origin of curly kale

Curly kale (*Brassica oleracea acephala*) is also known as "Borecole," from the Dutch word "Boerenkool" meaning "peasants' cabbage." It is derived from the wild cabbage (*Brassica oleracea*), which is a native of southwestern Europe and the Mediterranean region and grows on seaside cliffs. Opinions differ over when the wild cabbage was first cultivated (estimates range from a few hundred to thousands of years ago!) but it has been developed into a number of edible varieties.

Other members of the cabbage family form "heads" but curly kale retains its ancestral shape—leaves set loosely on a stem. The leaves are blue-green and, as the name implies, curly and crimped. Although kale and the other edible brassicas originated in temperate zones, they are now cultivated all over the world.

A characteristic of the brassicas is that they hold a lot of water in their leaves, making them fleshy and succulent foods. Like other members of the family, curly kale is a biennial—it grows for two years, storing a large amount of nutrients in its leaves. We can benefit from this nourishment only if the leaves are harvested during its first year. In its second (final) year, the plant will use the stored nutrients to produce flowers and seed.

Immune-boosting properties

Curly kale is a valuable winter vegetable, highly nutritious, and rich in vitamins, minerals, and protective phytochemicals. It is one of the tastiest of the cabbage family and easily overwinters to provide important nutrients when little else is growing in temperate regions. Its phytochemicals facilitate oxygen transport to the tissues,

support the immune system, aid liver function, and play a part in controlling blood-fat levels, and helping the body to release and utilize the energy contained in food. Curly kale thus promotes the health of the heart, nerves, and muscles and protects against high blood pressure, vascular disease, and rheumatoid arthritis.

Curly kale is good for the skin, encourages wound healing and the maintenance of healthy cell membranes, and may protect against estrogen-linked cancers such as those of the breast and ovaries. It helps regulate protein and fat metabolism and, because of its vitamin K content, encourages normal blood clotting. It also improves iron absorption from food and facilitates the production of hemoglobin and red blood cells. It may offer protection against asthma, migraine, and depression, and aid the nervous system.

Packed with protection

Curly kale contains three important groups of protective phytochemicals: glucosinolates, bioflavonoids, and sterols (phenylpropanoids). Glucosinolates include indoles, dithiolthiones, sulphoraphane, and isothiocyanates. Indoles, in particular, protect against various carcinogens. They also help reduce the activity of estrogen in the body and therefore have a dual role in protecting against estrogen-related cancers.

Bioflavonoids stimulate the immune system. They chelate (combine with) metals and make blood platelets less sticky, thus protecting against abnormal blood clotting and preventing heart disease.

Sterols influence the absorption of cholesterol from food and its metabolism in the body. They also affect the production of steroid hormones.

IMMUNE-BOOSTING PROFILE

★ VITAMINS A, C, E, K, B2, B3, B6, FOLATE; CALCIUM, MAGNESIUM, PHOSPHORUS, POTASSIUM, MANGANESE; IRON, ZINC; BIOFLAVONOIDS, GLUCOSINOLATES, KAEMPFEROL, STEROLS; FIBER, PROTEIN

✓ ANTI-ALLERGIC, ANTI-CANCER, ANTIOXIDANT, DETOXIFYING, IMMUNO-STIMULANT

💡 SEE GLOSSARY FOR INFORMATION ON GLUCOSINOLATES

curly kale parcels (above)

1 lb fresh curly kale, chopped
2 tbsp olive oil
8½ oz tempeh, cut into small cubes
1 tbsp soy sauce
2 garlic cloves, finely chopped
1 onion, finely chopped
1 tsp turmeric
1 tsp cumin
Pinch of cayenne
Salt and pepper to taste
1 packet phyllo pastry

Stir-fry the curly kale in the oil for 2 minutes. Add the other ingredients one by one, stirring in between. Add a little water and simmer gently for 5 minutes (until the kale goes soft). Open out sheets of phyllo pastry (as many as you have filling for), brush with oil and place a generous portion of the filling in the middle of each one. Fold each sheet into a parcel. Brush each parcel with oil and bake at 425°F until golden.

curly kale, tomato, and fava beans

3 tbsp olive oil
1 red onion, chopped
2 lb fresh fava beans, shelled
1 lb curly kale, chopped
1 lb tomatoes, in wedges
4 garlic cloves, finely chopped
Salt and pepper to taste
2 tbsp lemon juice
2 scallions, chopped

Heat the oil gently in a deep saucepan. Sauté the onion for 2 minutes, add the beans and cook for 5 minutes. Add the curly kale and the tomatoes and stir-fry for 2 minutes, then add the garlic, salt and pepper. Add enough water to cover, bring to the boil and simmer for 30 minutes (or until all the liquid is reduced). Add lemon juice, check seasoning, garnish with scallions and serve with couscous.

green leafy salad

1 handful of fresh curly kale, finely chopped
1 handful of iceberg lettuce, shredded
1 handful of lamb's lettuce
1 small handful of parsley sprigs, finely chopped
1 small handful of fresh mint, finely chopped
1 small handful of nasturtium flowers and calendula (pot marigold) petals (optional)
Lemon tahini dressing (see page 111)

Mix the green leaves in a bowl. Decorate with the flowers. Pour the dressing over and mix gently. Serve with bread or cooked bulgur.

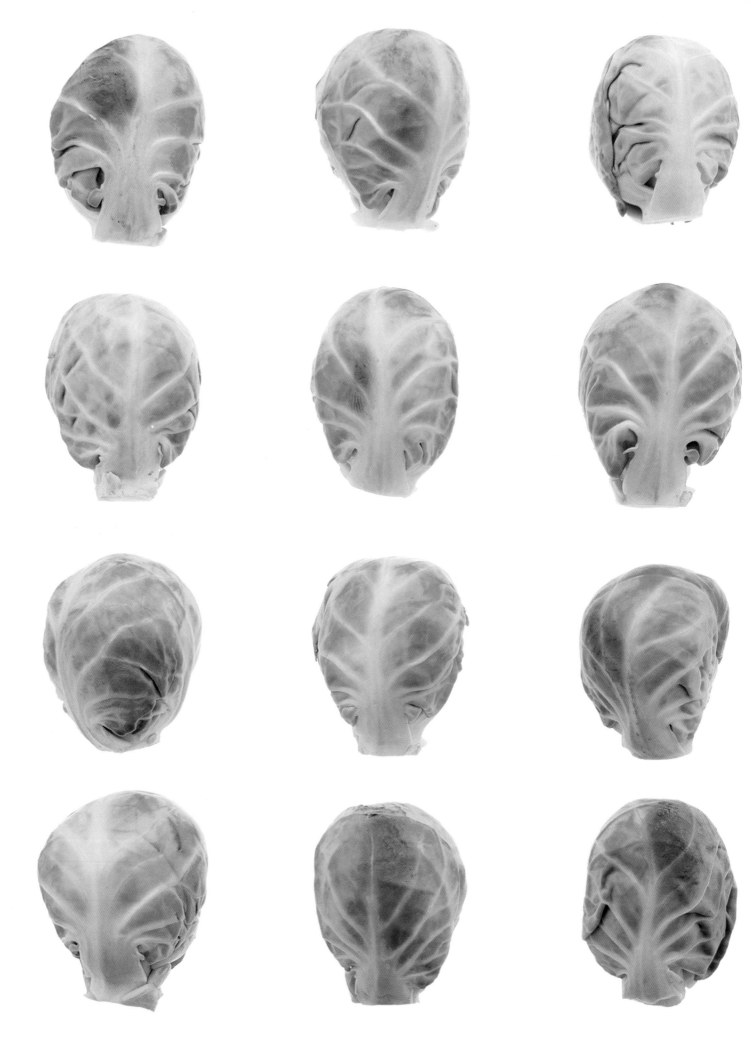

ARUGULA

★ VITAMINS A, C; BITTER PRINCIPLE, VOLATILE OIL; FIBER

✓ ANTI-CANCER, ANTISCORBUTIC, ANTIOXIDANT

Arugula (*Eruca sativa*) keeps the skin in good condition, and improves immunity and wound healing as well as helping the body to maintain healthy blood-fat levels.

RECIPES arugula salad (page 119), corn and sun-dried tomato salad (page 120), green party (page 124), vegetable cocktail (page 127), shiitake salad (page 75)

SAVOY CABBAGE

★ VITAMINS A, C, B3, FOLATE; CALCIUM, POTASSIUM; IRON; GLUCOSINOLATES; FIBER, PROTEIN

✓ ANTI-CANCER, ANTIOXIDANT, ENERGY-BOOSTING

♡ SEE GLOSSARY FOR INFORMATION ON GLUCOSINOLATES

Savoy cabbage (*Brassica oleracea capitata*) aids the liver's detoxifying capabilities and improves oxygen transport in the blood and tissues. It is a good source of vitamin B3, which boosts energy and strength, and helps keep the heart, muscles, skin, mucous membranes, and nerves healthy.

RECIPES garlic and savoy cabbage (page 69)

SPINACH

★ VITAMINS A, E, B2, B3, FOLATE; CALCIUM, MAGNESIUM, MANGANESE, POTASSIUM; ZINC; CAROTENOIDS, OXALIC ACID; FIBER, PROTEIN

✓ ANTI-CANCER, ANTIOXIDANT, ANTIVIRAL, IMMUNO-STIMULANT

❗ FOODS CONTAINING OXALIC ACID ARE BEST AVOIDED IF YOU SUFFER FROM KIDNEY OR BLADDER STONES, OR RHEUMATOID ARTHRITIS

Spinach (*Spinacia oleracea*) originated in Iran and spread east via China, Korea, and Japan. It reached Spain with the Arabs in the 11th century and was being used throughout Europe by the 18th century. It stimulates the immune response and helps protect against heart disease and some cancers, particularly of the lung, breast, and cervix, as well as keeping the skin, mucous membranes, blood, muscles, and nerves in good condition. It is a good source of energy, aids normal liver function, and regulates blood-fat levels.

RECIPES spinach bouillabaisse (page 115), sweet potato curry (page 116), tomato cocktail (page 127)

SPRING GREENS

★ VITAMINS A, C, B2, B3, B5, FOLATE; CALCIUM, PHOSPHORUS, POTASSIUM; IRON, ZINC; GLUCOSINOLATES; PROTEIN, FIBER

✓ ANTI-ALLERGIC, ANTI-CANCER, ANTIOXIDANT, ANTI-STRESS, DETOXIFYING, ENERGY-BOOSTING, WOUND HEALING

♡ SEE GLOSSARY FOR INFORMATION ON GLUCOSINOLATES

Spring greens (*Brassica oleracea var.*) evolved from wild cabbage, which is a native of southwestern Europe and the Mediterranean region. They support the liver's detoxifying action, and enhance the action of the immune system as a whole. Spring greens help protect against cancer and help maintain the health of the heart, skin, mucous membranes, and nerves, and maintain energy levels.

RECIPES spring greens and macadamia nuts (page 118)

SWISS CHARD

★ VITAMINS A, C, FOLATE; POTASSIUM; IRON

✓ ANTI-CANCER, ANTIOXIDANT

Also known as "seakale-beet," Swiss chard (*Beta vulgaris cycla*) is closely related to beet and spinach beet. It increases natural resistance by supporting oxygen transport via the blood to nerves, muscles, and liver, and helps in the regulation of blood-fat levels.

RECIPES swiss chard and juniper berries (page 119)

WATERCRESS

★ VITAMINS A, C, E, B3, B6; CALCIUM, MANGANESE; IRON; GLUCOSINOLATES, VOLATILE OIL; PROTEIN, FIBER

✓ ANTI-CANCER, ANTIOXIDANT, ANTISCORBUTIC, EXPECTORANT, PURGATIVE

❗ EXCESSIVE INTAKE OF WATERCRESS MAY CAUSE KIDNEY PROBLEMS, AND SHOULD BE AVOIDED IN THOSE WITH KIDNEY DISEASE

♡ SEE GLOSSARY FOR INFORMATION ON GLUCOSINOLATES

Traditionally used in spring cures to stimulate metabolism and aid detoxification, watercress (*Nasturtium officinale*) was once considered a specific cure for tuberculosis. Nowadays, the principal medicinal use of watercress is in the relief of arthritic conditions and congestion problems affecting the upper respiratory tract. Watercress stimulates the immune and lymphatic systems.

RECIPES avocado, watercress, and cumin salad (page 53), grapefruit salad (page 49), baked beet salad (page 37), green lentil salad (page 120), chinese salad (page 120)

nettle

THE NETTLE MAY JUST BE A HUMBLE WEED, BUT IT IS PACKED WITH NUTRIENTS THAT STRENGTHEN THE IMMUNE SYSTEM AND FORTIFY THE BODY AGAINST DISEASE. THIS VERSATILE PLANT CAN ALSO ENRICH AND PURIFY THE BLOOD TO HELP ALLEVIATE CIRCULATORY DISORDERS.

The origin of the nettle

The nettle (*Urtica dioica*) is one of the world's commonest weeds. It quickly colonizes any piece of reasonably fertile and well-watered land, and is found in fields, gardens, woodland, and wasteground throughout the world's temperate zones. Being a "greedy" plant, the nettle stores up large quantities of vital nutrients that promote health and restock depleted tissues and body systems. This makes nettle a fortifying remedy that strengthens the whole body.

Immune-boosting properties

In immunodeficiency states, chronic degenerative diseases, and cancer, nettle has a unique ability to revitalize and replenish, helping the body to cope better in difficult circumstances, and providing many of the building blocks necessary for health and healing. As a gentle but efficient diuretic, nettle can be very effective in the management of disorders of the heart and circulation, helping to rid the body of excess fluid while toning up blood-vessel walls. It has a beneficial effect on the kidneys, enhancing their ability to excrete uric acid and so relieving gout (which is caused by excess uric acid in the tissues and joints). The nettle's ability to cleanse the body of accumulated waste also promotes the healing of chronic skin problems such as eczema. Being rich in iron, nettle is a useful treatment for anemia.

Using nettle

Nettle tea has been used for centuries as a blood purifier and "spring tonic," and is an excellent aid during convalescence from illness. As both a circulatory stimulant and a diuretic, it is a powerful aid to detox and thus helpful in the management of arthritis, urinary-tract disorders, and skin problems such as psoriasis. Cold nettle tea is a useful external remedy for the relief of burns and minor wounds. The green tips of the plant can be used fresh or dried. For drying, it is best to pick the young shoots on a fine morning, after the sun has dried the dew. The young tips can be harvested almost all year round to provide a nutritious, healing, and tasty addition to any diet. Pick and wash the nettle tops. Boil them in a little water for about 10 minutes, then remove them with a slotted spoon (preserve the liquid for use as a bouillon or a medicine). Chop finely and use with other vegetables in soups, stews, and pasta sauces. As a side dish, precooked nettles are delicious stir-fried with leeks, garlic, salt, and pepper. They can also be used as a substitute for spinach (although they need a little more cooking water). Cooked nettles have a surprisingly full-bodied flavor. Try nettle lasagne, which uses cooked nettles and lentils for the filling instead of meat.

IMMUNE-BOOSTING PROFILE

★ VITAMINS A, C, K, B1, B2, B3, B5; CALCIUM, MAGNESIUM, PHOSPHATE, PHOSPHORUS, POTASSIUM; BORON, BROMINE, COPPER, IRON, SELENIUM, SILICA, ZINC; ACETYLCHOLINE, CHLOROPHYLL, FORMIC ACID, LYCOPENE, GLUCOQUINONE, HISTAMINE, SEROTONIN, TANNIN; FIBER, OMEGA-3, -6, AND OLEIC FATTY ACIDS

✓ ANTI-CANCER, ANTI-INFLAMMATORY, ANTIOXIDANT, ASTRINGENT, CIRCULATORY STIMULANT, DETOXIFYING, DIURETIC, LOWERS BLOOD SUGAR, TONIC

! USE GLOVES WHEN HANDLING THE FRESH PLANT; NETTLE SHOULD NOT BE EATEN UNCOOKED

nettle and sweet potato mash (above)

1 lb sweet potatoes, peeled and chopped
8½ oz fresh nettle tips
3 tbsp olive oil
1 red onion, sliced
6 oz green peas
Salt and pepper to taste

Pick and wash the nettles (wearing gloves). Boil the sweet potatoes in lightly salted water until soft. Mash and set aside. Boil the nettles in a little water until soft. Remove from water and chop. Heat the oil in a pan or wok and stir-fry the onion until soft. Add the peas, then the nettles and the sweet potato. Mix well, season, and serve hot.

spiced nettle soup

8 oz fresh nettle tips
2 tbsp olive oil
½ tsp cayenne
1 tsp turmeric
1 bay leaf
1 garlic clove, chopped
1 leek, chopped
2 potatoes, chopped into cubes
1 carrot, chopped
1 parsley root or parsnip, chopped
2 tbsp flour
7½ cups basic vegetable bouillon (see page 104)
Salt and pepper to taste

Pick and wash the nettles (wearing gloves). Steam in a little water until soft, then chop finely. Heat the oil gently in a big saucepan. Add the spices, stir for ½ minute, then add the vegetables. Stir-fry for a few minutes, but don't let them brown. Sprinkle with the flour at low heat, mix well and add the bouillon. Bring to the boil and simmer for 10–15 minutes, then add the nettles (together with their cooking water). Heat through and simmer for another 5 minutes. Season and serve.

nettle and lime tisane

2 fresh nettle tips or 1 tsp dried nettle
1 thick slice of lime
1 cup boiling water

Wearing gloves, place the nettle in a tea filter in a large cup or mug. Add the boiling water and the lime. Leave to infuse, covered with a lid, for 5 minutes.

SWEET FRUITS

APPLE

★ VITAMIN C; POTASSIUM; MALIC ACID, TANNIN, VOLATILE OIL; FIBER, PECTIN, SUGARS

✓ DETOXIFYING, LOWERS CHOLESTEROL

Apples (*Malus domestica*) stimulate the secretion of digestive juices and aid protein digestion. They contain pectin, which binds with cholesterol and bile acids, enhancing their excretion from the body. The pectin makes apples a remedy for simple diarrhea. Apples protect the body against the effects of some environmental toxins.

RECIPES yogurt with fruit (page 103), baked apples (page 122), beet and apple (page 124), guava and apple (page 126)

APRICOT (FRESH AND DRIED)

★ VITAMINS A, B2, B3, B5; CALCIUM, MAGNESIUM, POTASSIUM; COPPER, IRON, ZINC; FIBER, SUGARS

✓ ANTIOXIDANT, DETOXIFYING, IMMUNO-STIMULANT

! BRIGHT-ORANGE DRIED APRICOTS HAVE BEEN TREATED WITH SULFUR AND SHOULD BE AVOIDED

Apricots (*Prunus armeniaca*) promote detoxification and waste elimination. They also contribute to efficient antibody production. Apricots help stabilize blood-sugar levels, keep muscles, nerves, enzymes, and hormones working properly, facilitate the release of energy from food and tissue stores, and enhance the transport of oxygen in the blood.

RECIPES fruity pancakes (page 103), muesli (page 103), apricot and ginger (page 124), nirvana (page 127), soft tutti fruity (page 127)

BANANA

★ VITAMINS C, B3, B5, B6, BIOTIN; MAGNESIUM, MANGANESE, POTASSIUM; FIBER, SUGARS

✓ ANTI-STRESS, ENERGY-BOOSTING, DIGESTIVE STIMULANT

Bananas (*Musa cavendishii*) help prevent high blood pressure, heart disease, cancer, and rheumatoid arthritis. They enhance the metabolism of protein, carbohydrate, and fats, stabilize blood-sugar levels, and promote healthy skin, hair, nerves, and bone marrow. Easy to digest, they are useful in the management of gastro-intestinal disorders.

RECIPES baked apples (page 122), blackberry cream (page 124), caribbean smoothie (page 124), creamy mango (page 124)

CANTALOUPE MELON

★ VITAMINS A, C, B3; CAROTENOIDS; SUGARS

✓ ANTIOXIDANT

With its high level of carotenoids, cantaloupe melon (*Cucumis melo cantalupensis*) may inhibit the growth of cancer cells, and also help maintain vitality. It aids wound healing, and helps maintain the health of all body tissues, including the skin. It also enhances release of energy from other foods.

RECIPES: ruby red melon salad (page 102), mint and melon soup (page 105), melon and orange (page 126)

GRAPE

★ VITAMINS B3, B6, BIOTIN; MAGNESIUM, PHOSPHORUS; COPPER, IRON, SELENIUM, ZINC; ANTHOCYANIN, TARTARIC ACID; SUGARS

✓ ANTI-INFLAMMATORY, ANTIOXIDANT, DETOXIFYING

Fresh grapes (*Vitis vinifera*), and dried grapes (sultanas, raisins, and currants), are "biological response modifiers"—inhibiting the action of allergens, viruses, and carcinogens. They also act as free-radical scavengers, making them ideal detoxifiers, particularly of the skin, liver, kidneys, and bowels. (See traditional grape fast—page 133.)

RECIPES fresh fruit salad (page 102), grape and raisin smoothie (page 127), oatmeal with dried fruit and quinoa (page 102)

GUAVA

★ VITAMINS A, C, B3; FIBER, SUGARS

✓ ANTIOXIDANT, DETOXIFYING, IMMUNO-STIMULANT

Guava (*Psidium guajava*) is an excellent natural antioxidant, combining vitamins A and C, which mop up free radicals before they can do the body harm. It has a major role to play in serious immunodeficiency disorders, heart disease, and cancer, as well as reducing the severity of autoimmune diseases.

RECIPES fruity pancakes (page 103), guava and apple (page 126)

KIWI (CHINESE GOOSEBERRY)

★ VITAMINS A, C, B3; FIBER, SUGARS

✓ ANTIOXIDANT

An advantage of kiwi fruit (*Actinidia chinensis*) is that it keeps well for a long time after harvesting with little loss of its nutritional value—even after 6 months' storage, 90 per cent of the vitamin C is still intact. Kiwi fruits encourage the health and repair of all body tissues, and promote the release of the energy from other foods.

RECIPES fresh fruit salad (page 102), tropical fruit salad (page 123)

MANGO

★ VITAMINS A, C, E, B3; CITRIC ACID, PAPAIN; FIBER, SUGARS

✓ ANTI-ALLERGIC, ANTIBIOTIC, ANTI-CANCER, ANTIOXIDANT, DETOXIFYING, ENERGY-BOOSTING, IMMUNO-STIMULANT

! IN RARE CASES, MAY CAUSE DERMATITIS

Mango (*Mangifera indica*) stimulates the immune system and helps protect mucous membranes from pathogens. Mango contains papain, a protein-digesting enzyme that may help anyone suffering gluten intolerance or wheat allergy.

RECIPES creamy mango (page 124), mango and lime (page 126)

PAPAYA (PAW-PAW)

★ VITAMINS A, C; CAROTENOIDS, PAPAIN; FIBER, SUGARS

✓ ANTI-ALLERGIC, ANTIBACTERIAL, ANTIOXIDANT, DETOXIFYING

Papaya (*Carica papaya*) can help prevent skin disorders, gastro-intestinal ulcers, pancreatic disorders, cancer, and other conditions related to dysfunctional immunity. The papain in papaya promotes the breakdown of protein and can play an important role in alleviating digestive disorders and detoxifying the body.

RECIPES fresh fruit salad (page 102), papaya power (page 127)

PASSION-FRUIT

★ VITAMINS A, C, B2, B3; MAGNESIUM, PHOSPHORUS; IRON, ZINC; CITRIC ACID; FIBER, SUGARS

✓ ANTI-ALLERGY, ANTI-CANCER, ANTIOXIDANT

Passion-fruit (*Passiflora edulis*) helps ensure healthy nerves, skin, and mucous membranes, boosts energy levels, relieves muscle cramps, and alleviates insomnia and depression.

RECIPES passion-fruit sorbet (page 122), height of passion (page 126), passion and lime (page 127)

PINEAPPLE

★ CALCIUM, MAGNESIUM, MANGANESE, PHOSPHORUS, POTASSIUM; COPPER, IRON, ZINC; BROMELAIN, CITRIC ACID; FIBER, SUGARS

✓ ANTI-CANCER, ANTI-INFLAMMATORY

Pineapple (*Ananas comosus*) modifies the body's inflammatory response, speeds up tissue repair and alleviates fluid retention. It aids digestion, helps prevent blood clots and atherosclerosis, relieves angina, and lowers blood pressure.

RECIPES piña colada (page 127), pink pineapple (page 127)

grapefruit

GRAPEFRUIT IS A POWERFUL DETOXIFIER, HELPING TO RID THE BODY OF HARMFUL MICROBES AND STRENGTHENING THE IMMUNE SYSTEM AGAINST FURTHER ATTACK. IT MAY ALSO AID TISSUE REPAIR AND HELP RESIST THE GROWTH OF TUMORS.

The origin of grapefruit

Grapefruit (*Citrus paradisi*) is thought to have originated in Jamaica, possibly as a mutation of the pomelo (*Citrus maxima*), or as a hybrid between the pomelo and the sweet orange (*Citrus sinensis*). By 1750 it had become popular throughout the West Indies, and its fame then spread rapidly to the American mainland and the rest of the world. Depending on the variety, grapefruits are lemon-yellow or orange-yellow when ripe, with a juicy, fragrant, light yellow, pink, or ruby-red pulp, and a distinct sweet-sharp acid flavor. When buying grapefruits, choose ones that feel heavy for their size, with firm, shiny skin. Avoid very soft or dull-colored fruits. The nutritional content varies with type and color. Fruits with ruby-red and pink pulp contain more vitamin A than the yellow variety.

Immune-boosting properties

Grapefruit is a natural detoxifier, acting on the digestive system and liver. Its detoxifying action, combined with a strong growth-inhibiting effect on bacteria, fungi, parasites, and viruses, means that grapefruit can be beneficial in immunodeficiency states, as well as for colds and flu. Grapefruit contains a wealth of protective phytochemicals that enhance immunity and wound healing, and may inhibit tumor growth. Although citrus fruits in general are best avoided by those suffering from autoimmune disorders, there is evidence that grapefruit improves some inflammatory conditions.

Grapefruit is an effective pick-me-up when stress takes its toll on energy levels. It also aids healing by strengthening bones, blood vessels, and other tissues. The soluble fiber in grapefruit helps lower blood cholesterol (and other blood fats) by binding with excess cholesterol and bile acids and promoting their excretion from the body. This makes it useful in the prevention and treatment of heart and artery disease and gallstones. By aiding digestion and waste elimination, grapefruit relieves constipation. The fruit also inhibits the formation of calcium oxalate kidney stones, by reducing the amount of calcium salts in the urine.

Grapefruit boosts fat metabolism, which explains its popularity as a "fat burning" aid in weight-loss diets. An average serving of grapefruit is less than 100 calories and yet its high fiber content helps satisfy hunger. Its bitter principles aid the digestion of other foods, thus enabling dieters to gain maximum nutritional value from their meals while keeping their appetite under control.

Citricidal—grapefruit seed extract—is a natural, broad-spectrum antimicrobial agent active against streptococci, staphylococci, salmonella, mycobacteria, and other pathogens. Grapefruit oil is a powerful astringent and antiseptic that can be used to cleanse oily skin and as a gentle treatment for acne and other minor skin conditions.

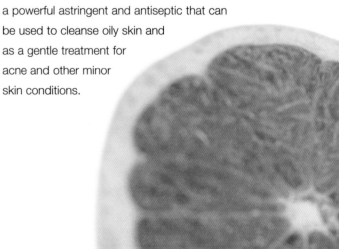

IMMUNE-BOOSTING PROFILE

★ VITAMINS A, C, FOLATE; POTASSIUM; BITTER PRINCIPLE,
BIOFLAVONOIDS, CITRIC AND PHENOLIC ACIDS, LYCOPENE;
FIBER, PECTIN, SUGARS

✓ ANTI-ALLERGIC, ANTI-CANCER, ANTIMICROBIAL, ANTIOXIDANT,
LOWERS BLOOD PRESSURE, LOWERS CHOLESTEROL LEVELS,
DETOXIFYING, DIGESTIVE STIMULANT, IMMUNO-STIMULANT

❗ GRAPEFRUIT JUICE MAY INTERACT WITH SOME PRESCRIBED
DRUGS SO CHECK WITH YOUR MEDICAL PRACTITIONER IF YOU
ARE TAKING ANY MEDICINES

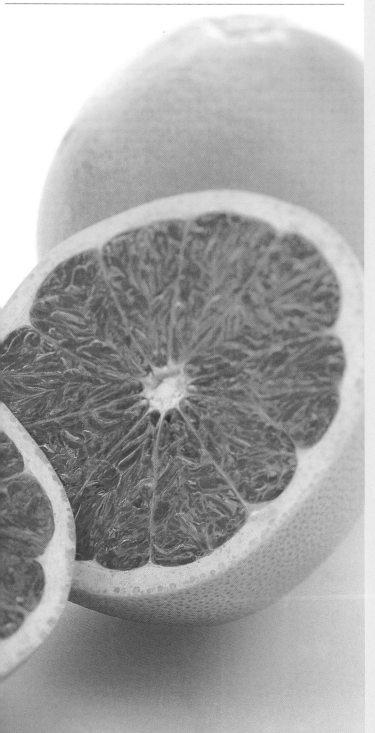

stuffed grapefruit *(above)*

2 grapefruits, halved, flesh removed, and chopped	1 pear, core removed, in cubes
1 avocado, pitted and peeled, in cubes	1 small green bell pepper, deseeded, finely chopped
1-in cube fresh ginger root, finely chopped	2 black olives, pitted
	2 tbsp fresh lemon balm, finely chopped

Mix the grapefruit flesh with the avocado, ginger, pear, and green bell
pepper. Divide the filling between the two half shells. Garnish with
olives and lemon balm.

grapefruit and peppermint fizz

1 bunch of fresh peppermint	2 ruby-red grapefruits
2½ cups boiling water	1 lime
2 tbsp maple syrup	Ice cubes

Put the mint in a teapot or bowl, pour the boiling water over and then
leave to infuse for 5 minutes. Add the maple syrup and leave to cool.
Squeeze the grapefruit and the lime and divide the juice between four
tall glasses. Add the peppermint infusion when cool. Serve with ice.

grapefruit salad

1 grapefruit, peeled and cut into segments	2 stalks of celery, thinly sliced
1 avocado, peeled, pitted and sliced	3½ oz bean sprouts
1 endive, thinly sliced	1 bunch of watercress
	Lime dressing (*see page 111*)

Combine all the ingredients in a salad bowl. Add some dressing,
garnish with watercress and serve immediately.

CITRUS FRUITS

LEMON

★ VITAMIN C, FOLATE; CALCIUM, POTASSIUM; CITRIC ACID; FIBER

✓ ANTI-ALLERGIC, ANTIBACTERIAL; ANTIOXIDANT

Lemons (*Citrus limon*) contain high levels of vitamin C, which boosts the body's resistance to infection, as well as enhancing iron absorption, aiding efficient wound healing, and strengthening cell membranes. Lemons also lower blood-fat levels, and help maintain the health of the heart, nerves, and muscle tissue.

RECIPES *guacamole (page 110), lemon tahini dressing (page 111), carrot and lemon with garlic (page 124), cold buster (page 128)*

LIME

★ VITAMIN C, FOLATE; CALCIUM, POTASSIUM; CITRIC ACID, FIBER

✓ ANTI-ALLERGIC, ANTIBACTERIAL, ANTIOXIDANT

Like lemon, lime (*Citrus aurantifolia*) improves the health of all body tissues and enhances iron absorption. It may speed up wound healing and increase the efficiency of the immune system. It therefore has a role in the prevention and treatment of cancer.

RECIPES *lime dressing (page 111), mango and lime (page 126), passion and lime (page 127), piña colada (page 127), tempeh kebabs (page 63), nettle and lime tisane (page 45)*

ORANGE

★ VITAMINS C, B3, B5, FOLATE; POTASSIUM; BETA-SITOSTEROL; FIBER, SUGARS

✓ ANTIOXIDANT, ANTI-STRESS, LOWERS CHOLESTEROL

! ORANGES CAN TRIGGER MIGRAINE ATTACKS IN SOME CASES

! IT MAY BE BEST TO AVOID ORANGES IN YOUR DIET IF YOU SUFFER FROM RHEUMATOID ARTHRITIS

The high vitamin C content in oranges (*Citrus sinensis*) helps to maintain healthy blood cells, and increases resistance to infections. Oranges also lower blood cholesterol, and may protect against cancer, improve iron absorption and wound healing. Eating oranges helps to maintain optimum energy levels, keeps skin and mucous membranes in good condition, aids antibody production, and protects against high blood pressure and allergy.

RECIPES *orange mango salad (page 120), melon and orange (page 126), pink pineapple (page 127), sunrise (page 127), oriental salad with tempeh (page 63)*

BERRIES

BILBERRY (BLAEBERRY, WHORTLEBERRY, WINBERRY)

★ VITAMIN C; ANTHOCYANIN; FIBER, SUGARS

✓ ANTIBACTERIAL, ANTI-INFLAMMATORY, ANTIOXIDANT, ANTISEPTIC, TONIC

Bilberries (*Vaccinium myrtillus*) are helpful in the treatment of rheumatoid arthritis. They inhibit free radicals, strengthen blood capillaries, tone up the cardiovascular system, and help prevent abnormal blood clots. Bilberries can be used for gastro-intestinal disorders and throat infections, and are effective as a tisane (1 tablespoon per cup).

RECIPES *use in place of blackberries, raspberries, or cranberries*

BLACKBERRY

★ VITAMINS C, E, B3, FOLATE; MANGANESE; IRON; CITRIC ACID; FIBER

✓ ANTIOXIDANT, TONIC

Blackberries (*Rubus ulmifolius or R. alleghanensis*) improve iron absorption, increase energy release from food and enhance oxygen transport to the tissues. They aid liver function, speed up protein and fat metabolism, help regulate blood-fat levels, and encourage wound healing. They may also offer a degree of protection against heart disease and some cancers.

RECIPES *blackberry crumble (page 123), blackberry cream (page 124), yogurt with fruit (page 103)*

SWEET CHERRY

★ POTASSIUM; ANTHOCYANIN, MALIC ACID; FIBER, SUGARS

✓ ANTI-INFLAMMATORY, ANTIOXIDANT, DETOXIFYING, REJUVENATING

♡ TISANES MADE FROM CHERRY STALKS ARE A TRADITIONAL REMEDY FOR CYSTITIS

Cherries (*Prunus avium*) boost energy and are beneficial to the heart, muscles and nerves. Eating cherries can lower uric acid levels in the blood and so is a traditional way of avoiding gout. They reduce platelet "stickiness" and help prevent blood clots, and can help relieve the symptoms of rheumatoid and osteoarthritis.

RECIPES *ruby red melon salad (page 102)*

CRANBERRY

★ VITAMIN C; IRON; ANTHOCYANIN, BENZOIC, CITRIC AND QUINIC ACIDS; FIBER

✓ **ANTI-CANCER, ANTIOXIDANT**

The juice of cranberries (*Vaccinium vitis-idaea*) prevents harmful bacteria from sticking to the bladder wall, and so has long been used to relieve urinary-tract infections. Cranberry juice has powerful antioxidant effects that improve cardiovascular health and help prevent cancer. It may also reduce kidney stones.

RECIPES cranberry spritzer (page 124)

ELDERBERRY

★ **VITAMINS A, C, B2, B3, B6, BIOTIN; IRON; ANTHOCYANIN, TANNIN; SUGARS**

✓ **ANTI-ALLERGIC, ANTI-CANCER, ANTIOXIDANT, ASTRINGENT, DIURETIC, ENCOURAGES SWEATING, LAXATIVE**

Elderberries (*Sambucus nigra*) are an effective remedy for disorders of the upper respiratory tract, such as excess mucus, colds, and influenza, and can be used to relieve all types of inflammation, including rheumatic complaints. They improve iron absorption from food and aid hemoglobin production, benefit blood-fat levels, and fat metabolism, aid liver function, and boost energy.

RECIPES elderberry cordial (page 128)

HAWTHORN

★ **VITAMIN C; ANTHOCYANIN, GLYCOSIDES, SAPONINS, TANNIN**

✓ **ANTI-INFLAMMATORY, ANTIOXIDANT, LOWERS BLOOD PRESSURE, TONIC**

Hawthorn berries (*Crataegus monogyna*) benefit the whole cardiovascular system. They are gentle in action and can help support the heart in heart failure, as well as being used to treat hypertension, arteriosclerosis, and angina. They reduce the "stickiness" of blood platelets and may help prevent thrombosis (abnormal blood-clot formation). They may also inhibit the growth of some cancers, especially of the lung, skin, and esophagus.

RECIPES circulation booster (page 128)

MULBERRY

★ **VITAMINS C, B3, BIOTIN, FOLATE; MANGANESE, POTASSIUM; IRON; ANTHOCYANIN, CITRIC ACID; FIBER, SUGARS**

✓ **ANTIOXIDANT**

! **UNRIPE MULBERRIES CAN BE TOXIC AND SHOULD NOT BE EATEN**

Mulberries (*Morus nigra*) boost energy and strength, support nerve, heart, liver, muscle, and bone marrow function, and help to keep cell membranes healthy. They enhance iron absorption, reduce

blood-fat levels, improve oxygen transport to the tissues, and aid protein and fat metabolism. They may also protect against heart disease, cancer, and rheumatoid arthritis.

RECIPES use in place of blackberries in recipes

RASPBERRY

★ **VITAMINS C, B3, BIOTIN, FOLATE; MANGANESE; IRON; CITRIC ACID; FIBER, SUGARS**

✓ **ANTIOXIDANT, DETOXIFYING, LAXATIVE, TONIC**

💡 **RASPBERRY LEAVES ARE ALSO USED MEDICINALLY TO HELP ENSURE HEALTHY PREGNANCY AND BIRTH**

Raspberries (*Rubus idaeus*) activate the body's natural self-cleansing ability, and improve the health of the skin, hair, sweat glands, nerves, liver, bone marrow, and mucous membranes. They enhance wound healing and their powerful antioxidant properties mean they also help protect against heart disease, cancer, and rheumatoid arthritis. Raspberries boost the body's energy levels, and also encourage efficient protein and fat metabolism.

RECIPES raspberry gateau (page 122), raspberry sorbet (page 123), fruity pancakes (page 103)

ROSEHIP

★ **VITAMIN C; CAROTENOIDS, TANNIN; PECTIN**

✓ **ANTI-ALLERGIC, ANTIOXIDANT, HEALING, MILD LAXATIVE**

Rosehips (*Rosa canina*) are extremely rich in vitamin C and therefore improve immunity to infections, especially the common cold. They boost energy levels, help maintain healthy mucous membranes, enhance wound healing, and help prevent heart disease and the formation of cancer cells.

RECIPES pick-me-up (page 130), rosehip syrup (page 130), tea for ear infections (page 131)

STRAWBERRY

★ **VITAMINS C, B3, B5; CITRIC ACID; FIBER, SUGARS**

✓ **ANTIOXIDANT, ASTRINGENT, DIURETIC, LAXATIVE**

Strawberries (*Fragaria x ananassa*) can be used to treat fever and to relieve the symptoms of rheumatoid arthritis. Good for the health of the skin and mucous membranes, strawberries improve wound healing, encourage iron absorption, and reduce blood-fat levels. They may reduce the tendency to develop high blood pressure and allergic reactions. They can also help the body cope with stress.

RECIPES fruity pancakes (page 103)

avocado

AVOCADO IS PACKED WITH ENERGY AND IMMUNE-BOOSTING PHYTOCHEMICALS THAT CAN HELP GUARD AGAINST CERTAIN CANCERS AND PREVENT FUNGAL DISEASES. THIS TASTY FRUIT ALSO STABILIZES BLOOD FATS AND HELPS MAINTAIN HEALTHY BLOOD PRESSURE.

The origin of avocado

The avocado pear is thought to have originated in Central America, where it was an important component of the diet of the native Aztec people. It was discovered by the Spanish conquistadors in the 16th century, but was little-known to the rest of the world until the early 20th century. Avocados are now popular all over the world and are grown commercially in many tropical and subtropical regions, mainly in Australia, Brazil, USA, Israel, Mediterranean Europe, South Africa, and southeast Asia.

Avocados are usually thought of as a savory food, even though, botanically speaking, they are fruits. The avocado grows on an evergreen tree (*Persea americana*) with small green-yellow flowers. The tree starts producing fruit when it is three years old. A mature tree can display one million flowers on its branches, of which only 100 to 400 will set fruit. Healthy avocado trees can continue to produce fruit for hundreds of years.

Avocados are normally picked before they are fully ripened. On average, an avocado takes about a week to ripen at room temperature. The process can be accelerated by placing the unripe avocado in a paper bag along with an apple. The flesh of the fruit is yellow/green and discolors easily when exposed to the air. You can prevent this by rubbing lemon juice on to the exposed surface of the flesh.

Immune-boosting properties

The avocado is a highly nutritious food that houses several important nutrients and phytochemicals. It contains glutathione, a powerful antioxidant phytochemical that mops up free radicals—the destructive molecules known to trigger the development of cancer and heart disease. In particular, glutathione has been shown to reduce the risk of cancer of the mouth and throat. Recent research has discovered a new group of phytochemicals in the avocado that have strong antifungal properties. They work by inhibiting the germination of fungal spores, and so make avocado useful in the treatment of internal and external yeast infections.

The particular combination of nutrients and micro-nutrients found in the avocado offers other beneficial effects. It stimulates the immune system, enhances antibody production and acts as a mild vasodilator, relaxing the muscles surrounding blood vessels and thus reducing blood pressure. The avocado can help protect the skin by slowing down the effects of ageing, and maintaining hair, mucous membranes, sweat glands, nerves, muscles, and bone marrow in good condition. New research suggests that avocados can enhance male fertility by improving sperm health.

Energy-rich

Avocados differ markedly from other vegetable fruits in being extremely high in calories—about 90 per cent is fat. Some 80 per cent of this fat is oleic acid. There are many health benefits associated with eating a diet high in monounsaturated fat such as this. In particular, such fats reduce levels of L.D.L. cholesterol in the blood, and have a beneficial effect on the composition of blood fats in general. Monounsaturated fat also helps to stabilize blood-sugar levels. Most of the rest of the fat found in avocados is polyunsaturated. As the fruit ripens, the small amount of saturated fat it contains steadily turns into polyunsaturated fat. Avocados also contain phytochemicals called beta-sitosterols, which reduce the absorption of cholesterol from food (these chemicals are widely used in the manufacture of blood-cholesterol-lowering drugs).

IMMUNE-BOOSTING PROFILE

★ VITAMINS E, K, B1, B2, B3, B5, BIOTIN, FOLATE; POTASSIUM; ZINC;

BETA-SITOSTEROLS, CAROTENOIDS, GLUTATHIONE; FIBER,

UNSATURATED FATTY ACIDS (INCLUDING OLEIC)

✓ ANTI-CANCER, ANTIFUNGAL, ANTIOXIDANT

! PEOPLE WHO ARE ALLERGIC TO NATURAL RUBBER (LATEX) HAVE

A ONE IN TWO CHANCE OF BEING ALLERGIC TO AVOCADO

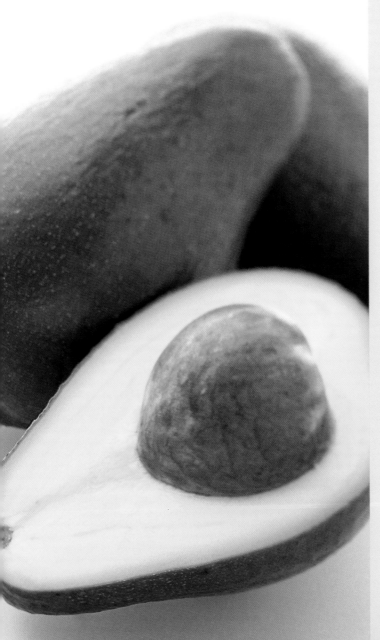

filled avocados *(above)*

2 avocados, halved, stone removed	1 tbsp tarragon vinegar (or wine vinegar)
2 ripe tomatoes, finely chopped	4 tbsp sunflower oil
½ cucumber, finely chopped	1 garlic clove, crushed
1 bunch of chives, finely chopped	½ tsp soy sauce
	½ tsp tabasco

Place the avocado halves on separate plates. Gently mix the tomato, cucumber, and chives, and divide on top of the avocado halves. Beat the dressing ingredients together and drizzle over the avocados. Serve with French bread.

avocado smoothie

Per serving:	1 tsp fresh ginger root, finely chopped
1 avocado, peeled and chopped	
1 pear, peeled, deseeded, and chopped	½ cup soy milk
½ grapefruit, squeezed	4 tbsp plain soy yogurt

Blend all the ingredients. Serve immediately in a glass.

avocado, watercress, and cumin salad

2 tsp cumin seeds	thinly sliced
1 bunch of watercress, chopped	Lemon tahini dressing
3 large ripe avocados,	*(see page 111)*

Roast the cumin seeds in a dry skillet. Remove and crush. Place the watercress on a large plate. Arrange the avocado on top. Sprinkle with dressing and garnish with the roasted cumin.

nuts and seeds

ALMOND

★ VITAMINS E, B2, B5, BIOTIN, FOLATE; CALCIUM, MAGNESIUM, MANGANESE, PHOSPHORUS, POTASSIUM; BORON, COPPER, IRON, SELENIUM, ZINC; STEROLS; FIBER, PROTEIN, UNSATURATED FAT

✓ ANTIOXIDANT, LOWERS CHOLESTEROL, NUTRIENT-RICH

! BEWARE BITTER-TASTING ALMONDS—THEY CAN BE TOXIC

Almonds (*Prunus dulcis*) help maintain healthy blood-fat levels, strengthen the cardiovascular system, and reduce the risk of coronary heart disease. They also enhance antibody production, strengthen cell membranes, and help protect against cancer.

RECIPES *muesli (page 103), toasted nuts and seeds (page 108)*

CASHEW

★ VITAMINS B1, B2, B3, B5, B6, BIOTIN, FOLATE; MAGNESIUM, MANGANESE, PHOSPHORUS, POTASSIUM; BORON, COPPER, IODINE, IRON, SELENIUM, ZINC; FIBER, PROTEIN, UNSATURATED FAT

✓ ANTIOXIDANT, LOWERS CHOLESTEROL

Cashews (*Anacardium occidentale*) help to maintain healthy blood-fat levels, aid hemoglobin production and fat metabolism, enhance the body's ability to cope with stress, and help keep skin, hair, glands, nerves, mucous membranes, blood cells, and bone marrow in good condition.

RECIPES *toasted nuts and seeds (page 108), paella (page 112)*

FLAXSEED (LINSEED)

★ GLYCOSIDES; MUCILAGE, OMEGA-3 AND -6 FATTY ACIDS, PROTEIN

✓ ANTI-COUGH, LOWERS CHOLESTEROL, IMMUNO-STIMULANT, LAXATIVE

Flaxseeds (*Linum usitatissimum*) can help treat coughs, bronchitis, chronic constipation, and psoriasis. They also help maintain healthy blood-fat levels and may be protective against cardiovascular disease and cancer.

RECIPES *muesli (page 103)*

HAZELNUT

★ VITAMINS E, B1, B2, B3, B5, B6, BIOTIN, FOLATE; CALCIUM, MAGNESIUM, MANGANESE, PHOSPHORUS, POTASSIUM; BORON, COPPER, IRON, ZINC; FIBER, PROTEIN, UNSATURATED FAT

✓ ANTIOXIDANT, LOWERS CHOLESTEROL

! SOME PEOPLE ARE ALLERGIC TO HAZELNUTS

Hazelnuts (*Corylus avellana*) help regulate blood fats and aid cell renewal and repair. They help protect cells against free-radical damage and benefit skin, hair, nails, glands, nerves, bone marrow, and mucous membranes.

RECIPES *toasted nuts and seeds (page 108)*

MACADAMIA NUT (QUEENSLAND NUT)

★ VITAMINS B1, B3, B5, B6, BIOTIN; MAGNESIUM, MANGANESE, PHOSPHORUS; COPPER, IRON, SELENIUM, ZINC; FIBER, PROTEIN, UNSATURATED FAT

✓ ANTIOXIDANT, LOWERS CHOLESTEROL

Research shows that the unsaturated fat in macadamia nuts (*Macadamia ternifolia*) has a favorable effect on blood cholesterol.

RECIPES *spring greens and macadamia nuts (page 118)*

MELON SEED

★ VITAMINS B2, B3, FOLATE; CALCIUM, MAGNESIUM, MANGANESE, POTASSIUM; COPPER, IRON, ZINC; PROTEIN, UNSATURATED FAT

✓ ANTIOXIDANT, LOWERS CHOLESTEROL

Melon (*Cucumis melo*) seeds support the immune and cardiovascular systems, help regulate healthy blood-fat levels, and provide the nutrients necessary to aid wound healing and help maintain healthy skin, nails, and nerves.

RECIPES *toasted nuts and seeds (page 108)*

PECAN NUT

★ VITAMINS E, B1, B2, B3, B5, FOLATE; CALCIUM, MAGNESIUM, MANGANESE, PHOSPHORUS, POTASSIUM; COPPER, SELENIUM, ZINC; FIBER, PROTEIN, UNSATURATED FAT (MAINLY OLEIC ACID)

✓ ANTIOXIDANT, LOWERS CHOLESTEROL

! SOME PEOPLE ARE ALLERGIC TO PECAN NUTS

Pecan nuts (*Carya illinoensis*) are high in monounsaturated fat and health-protective vitamins and minerals, helping to prevent cancer and heart disease. Eating pecans regularly also lowers blood cholesterol and improves blood lipid balance, emphasizing the importance to health of the type of fat contained in the diet.

RECIPES *muesli (page 103)*

PISTACHIO

★ VITAMINS E, B1, B2, B3, FOLATE; CALCIUM, MAGNESIUM,
PHOSPHORUS, POTASSIUM; COPPER, IRON, SELENIUM, ZINC;
FIBER, PROTEIN, UNSATURATED FAT

✓ ANTIOXIDANT, LOWERS CHOLESTEROL

Pistachio (*Pistacia vera*) nuts protect against heart disease and
some cancers, aid liver function and metabolism, boost energy,
and improve the health and function of blood cells, muscles,
nerves, mucous membranes, and skin.

RECIPES muesli (page 103), toasted nuts and seeds (page 108)

PINE NUT

★ VITAMINS E, B1, B2, B3; MAGNESIUM, MANGANESE, POTASSIUM;
COPPER, IRON, ZINC; FIBER, PROTEIN, UNSATURATED FAT

Pine (*Pinus spp.*) nuts protect against heart disease and some
cancers. They aid liver function and metabolism, boost energy, and
benefit the blood, muscles, nerves, mucous membranes, and skin.

RECIPES pasta, pesto, and shiitake (page 75)

PUMPKIN SEED

★ VITAMINS B1, B2, B3; MAGNESIUM, PHOSPHORUS, POTASSIUM;
COPPER, IRON, SELENIUM, ZINC; FIBER, OMEGA-3 FATTY ACIDS,
PROTEIN, UNSATURATED FAT

✓ ANTI-INFLAMMATORY, ANTIOXIDANT, DETOXIFYING, IMMUNO-STIMULANT

Pumpkin (*Cucurbita maxima*) seeds are highly nutritious, and a
valuable aid in the prevention and treatment of cardiovascular,
autoimmune, and immunodeficiency disorders. They can also
benefit the prostate gland.

RECIPES carrot 'n' beet salad (page 119)

SESAME SEED/TAHINI

★ VITAMINS E, B1, B2, B3; CALCIUM, MAGNESIUM, MANGANESE,
PHOSPHORUS, POTASSIUM; COPPER, IRON, ZINC; COMPLEX
CARBOHYDRATES, FIBER, OMEGA-6 FATTY ACIDS, PROTEIN,
UNSATURATED FAT

✓ ANTIOXIDANT, LOWERS CHOLESTEROL, NUTRIENT-RICH

Sesame (*Sesamum indicum*) seeds are an excellent natural food
supplement, aiding tissue repair and renewal and helping the body
cope with stress. Tahini is a paste made from ground sesame and
adds interest and nutritional value to many different dishes.

RECIPES oriental salad with tempeh (page 63), lemon tahini dressing
(page 111), green lentil salad (page 120)

SUNFLOWER SEED

★ VITAMINS E, B1, B2, B3; CALCIUM, MAGNESIUM, MANGANESE,
PHOSPHORUS, POTASSIUM; COPPER, IRON, SELENIUM, ZINC;
COMPLEX CARBOHYDRATES, FIBER, OMEGA-6 FATTY ACIDS,
PROTEIN, UNSATURATED FAT

✓ ANTIOXIDANT, NUTRIENT-RICH

Sunflower (*Helianthus annuus*) seeds improve skin health, help
regulate blood-fat levels, and aid tissue repair. They may also
be beneficial in treating eczema.

RECIPES muesli (page 103), toasted nuts and seeds (page 108)

SWEET CHESTNUT (SPANISH CHESTNUT)

★ VITAMINS B3, B5, B6; MAGNESIUM, MANGANESE, PHOSPHORUS,
POTASSIUM; COPPER, ZINC; COMPLEX CARBOHYDRATES, FIBER,
SUGARS, PROTEIN

✓ ENERGY-BOOSTING, IMMUNO-STIMULANT, NUTRIENT-RICH

Sweet chestnuts (*Castanea sativa*) are versatile and nutritious.
Their energy is released slowly and steadily in the body, helping
to stabilize blood-sugar levels and boosting energy and strength.

RECIPES sweet chestnuts and kumquats (page 117)

WALNUT

★ VITAMINS E, B1, B2, B3, B5, B6, BIOTIN, FOLATE; CALCIUM,
MAGNESIUM, MANGANESE, PHOSPHORUS, POTASSIUM; COPPER,
IRON, SELENIUM, ZINC; FIBER, OMEGA-3 FATTY ACIDS, PROTEIN

✓ ANTIOXIDANT, ANTI-INFLAMMATORY, LOWERS CHOLESTEROL

Walnuts (*Juglans sp.*) reduce the risk of heart disease and cancer,
benefit blood cells, muscles, and nervous system, aid brain
function, boost energy and strength, and help us cope with stress.

RECIPES florence fennel salad (page 120), arugula salad (page 119)

brazil nut

THIS DELICIOUS SOUTH AMERICAN KERNEL IS ONE OF THE RICHEST NATURAL SOURCES OF SELENIUM AND VITAMIN E—TWO POWERFUL ANTIOXIDANTS WITH ANTI-AGEING PROPERTIES THAT CAN HELP GUARD AGAINST MANY DISORDERS INCLUDING HEART DISEASE AND CANCER.

The origin of the Brazil nut

The Brazil nut, also called the para nut, cream nut and castanea, is the edible seed of a giant tree (*Bertholletia excelsa*) that grows in the Amazon rainforest. It is an important source of nutrition—and income—to the local population. Most Brazil nuts are collected from wild trees. They grow in clusters of 8 to 24 nuts enclosed in a woody, fibrous fruit capsule that looks like a cross between a coconut and a cooking pot with a lid. The nut is enclosed in a hard, dark-brown, wedge-shaped shell. From January to June, the capsules ripen and fall to the ground, where they are collected. The kernels are taken out, sun-dried and washed before being sold and exported, mainly to North America and Europe. (After the nuts have been removed, the dried capsules are used as animal traps, a practice that has given them the name "monkey-pots.")

Immune-boosting properties

The Brazil nut is extremely nutritious with high levels of protein, unsaturated fat, selenium, zinc, and other minerals, plus substantial quantities of vitamins E and B-complex. It is the combination of vitamin E with selenium that gives the Brazil nut its special immune-enhancing properties. These two important antioxidants work synergistically, each improving the performance of the other to boost immune-system function. Antioxidants prevent cell damage by mopping up free radicals and thus preventing the "oxidative" chain reactions that can damage DNA. Some oxidation is normal and vital for health (the immune system actually uses oxidative reactions to destroy micro-organisms), but if the level of oxidation outstrips the body's own defensive capabilities, the resulting excess of free radicals can cause cellular damage.

Accumulated damage by free radicals is known to be an important factor in ageing and disease, and the role of antioxidants in the prevention and treatment of illness is well recognized. Antioxidants play a preventive role in many conditions including asthma, heart disease, immunodeficiency disorders, and cancer.

Selenium enhances immunity by activating an enzyme in the body called glutathione peroxidase, which inhibits the formation of free radicals and suppresses tumor growth. Infection depletes the body's selenium levels. This, in turn, suppresses the immune system because a low level of selenium affects the normal antibody response to infection and cell damage. Thus even a moderate increase in selenium intake is beneficial to the body's self-defense mechanisms, and can help to reduce the risk of cancer, heart disease, and fungal infections such as candidiasis. However, it is possible to get too much of a good thing. Taking excess selenium as a food supplement can result in selenium toxicity, which causes hair loss,

dizziness, fatigue, and skin problems. Fortunately, the Brazil nut–selenium "package" provides a natural safety limit because Brazil nuts satisfy hunger long before selenium intake reaches toxic limits. Selenium is found in many other foods of plant origin—the amount depending on the plant's ability to absorb it from the soil. Unfortunately, in many parts of the world, modern agricultural practices have depleted the soil of selenium, providing yet another good reason for preserving the Amazon rainforest—Brazil nuts.

IMMUNE-BOOSTING PROFILE

★ VITAMINS E, B1, B3, B5, B6, BIOTIN; CALCIUM, MAGNESIUM, MANGANESE, PHOSPHORUS, POTASSIUM; COPPER, IODINE, IRON, SELENIUM, ZINC; FIBER, OMEGA-6 AND OLEIC FATTY ACIDS, PROTEIN

✓ ANTI-CANCER, ANTIOXIDANT, IMMUNO-STIMULANT

! SOME PEOPLE ARE ALLERGIC TO BRAZIL NUTS

! GENETICALLY MODIFIED SOY BEANS MAY CONTAIN GENES FROM BRAZIL NUTS, AND SO MAY TRIGGER AN ALLERGIC REACTION

brazil nuts and sun-dried tomatoes with beans (above)

1 lb French beans, topped and tailed	3½ oz sun-dried tomatoes, sliced
7 oz Brazil nuts, chopped	1 tbs olive oil
	salt and pepper

Steam the beans till tender. Place the rest of the ingredients in a bowl, add the beans while still hot, mix well, and serve.

broiled endive and brazil nut salad

4 endives, halved lengthwise	2 oz Brazil nuts
3 tbs olive oil	Salt and pepper

Brush the endives with olive oil, then broil a few minutes on each side until they begin to char and soften. Brush with more oil as you turn them, if necessary. Place on a serving dish, scatter with Brazils nuts and season to taste. Serve with vinaigrette.

spicy brazil nut pâté

2 oz Brazil nuts, roughly chopped	Pinch of cayenne
Soy sauce	1 tsp thyme
1 lb 2 oz mushrooms, chopped	3 tbs olive oil
7 oz tofu, crumbled	Salt and pepper
2 garlic cloves, chopped	to taste
1 tsp garam masala	2 tsp fresh parsley

Roast the Brazil nuts in a dry skillet, add a little soy sauce, stir, and remove from the pan. Sauté the mushrooms and the tofu in the oil with the garlic, thyme, and the spices until soft. Blend all the ingredients (except the parsley) to a coarse pâté. Place in a serving dish, garnish with parsley, and serve.

grains

BULGUR WHEAT

★ VITAMINS B1, B2, B3; MAGNESIUM, PHOSPHORUS; COPPER, IRON; COMPLEX CARBOHYDRATES, PROTEIN

✓ EASILY DIGESTIBLE, ENERGY-BOOSTING

! AVOID IF ALLERGIC OR SENSITIVE TO GLUTEN IN WHEAT

Bulgur is the cracked kernels of boiled and dried durum wheat (*Triticum durum*). Fine grains are used for salads and need very little cooking—cover with boiling water and leave for a few minutes to expand and soften. Larger grains are cooked like rice (but need less cooking time and water).

RECIPES bulgur wheat salad (page 119)

CORN (SWEETCORN, MAIZE)

★ VITAMINS B3, B5, FOLATE; MAGNESIUM, PHOSPHORUS; ZINC; COMPLEX CARBOHYDRATES, FIBER, OMEGA-6 FATTY ACIDS, PROTEIN

✓ ANTI-STRESS, AIDS DIGESTION

💡 CORN SILK (FINE THREAD ON FRESH CORN COBS) CAN BE USED IN A TISANE TO SOOTHE IRRITATIONS OF THE BLADDER AND URETHRA

Corn (*Zea mays*) aids wound healing, strengthens the immune system by boosting antibody production, and keeps the skin and mucous membranes in good condition. It helps the body cope with stress, stabilizes blood sugar, and maintains a healthy level of blood fats.

RECIPES sweet potato curry (page 116), tempeh kebabs (page 63)

MUESLI (SWISS STYLE, NO ADDED SUGAR)

★ VITAMINS E, B1, B2, B3, B5, B6, BIOTIN, FOLATE; CALCIUM, MAGNESIUM, PHOSPHORUS, POTASSIUM; IRON, ZINC; COMPLEX CARBOHYDRATES, FIBER, PROTEIN, SUGARS

✓ ANTI-CANCER, ANTIOXIDANT, ANTI-STRESS, LOWERS CHOLESTEROL

Muesli contains a potent mixture of highly nutritious, vitality-enhancing ingredients.

RECIPES muesli (page 103)

OATS

★ VITAMINS E, B1, B2, B3, B5; MAGNESIUM, MANGANESE, PHOSPHORUS, POTASSIUM; IRON, SELENIUM, ZINC; COMPLEX CARBOHYDRATES, FIBER, PROTEIN

✓ ANTI-CANCER, ANTI-STRESS, LOWERS CHOLESTEROL, ENERGY-BOOSTING

Oats (*Avena sativa*) are high in protein, iron, and soluble fiber. They lower blood cholesterol, ease stress, and soothe tired nerves.

RECIPES muesli (page 103), oatmeal with dried fruit and quinoa (page 102), blackberry crumble (page 123), pick-me-up (page 130)

PASTA (MADE FROM DURUM WHEAT)

★ VITAMINS B1, B3; MAGNESIUM, MANGANESE, PHOSPHORUS, POTASSIUM; IRON, ZINC; COMPLEX CARBOHYDRATES, FIBER, PROTEIN

✓ ENERGY-BOOSTING

! AVOID IF ALLERGIC OR SENSITIVE TO GLUTEN IN WHEAT

Durum wheat (*Triticum durum*) is high in protein. When ground to flour and mixed with water, it is ideal for rolling into pasta shapes.

RECIPES pasta, pesto, and shiitake (page 75)

QUINOA

★ VITAMINS E, B2, B3; CALCIUM, MAGNESIUM, PHOSPHORUS, POTASSIUM; COPPER, IRON, ZINC; SAPONINS; COMPLEX CARBOHYDRATES, FIBER, PROTEIN, SUGARS, UNSATURATED FAT

✓ ANTI-CANCER, ANTIOXIDANT, LOWERS CHOLESTEROL, ENERGY-BOOSTING

💡 CONTAINS NO GLUTEN

Quinoa (*Chenopodium quinoa*) is arguably the most nutritious of all grains. It is rich in protein and minerals, and can be used to add nutritional value to breakfast cereals, biscuits, and casseroles.

RECIPES oatmeal with dried fruit and quinoa (page 102)

RICE

★ VITAMINS B1, B3, FOLATE; MAGNESIUM, MANGANESE, PHOSPHORUS; COPPER, IRON, ZINC; COMPLEX CARBOHYDRATES, FIBER, PROTEIN

✓ ENERGY-BOOSTING, LOWERS CHOLESTEROL

💡 CONTAINS NO GLUTEN

Brown rice (*Oryza sativa*) is a rich source of energy, fiber, protein and B vitamins. It helps protect the cardiovascular system, nerves, digestion, muscles, mucous membranes, skin, hair, glands, and bone marrow. Rice milk is a good alternative to cow's milk—ideal for those with irritable bowel syndrome and other gastro-intestinal disorders.

RECIPES rice: paella (page 112), khichuri—rice with lentils (page 117), rice milk: heart chai (page 129), muesli (page 103)

WHEATGRASS

★ VITAMINS A, E; ZINC; CHLOROPHYLL; ESSENTIAL FATTY ACIDS, FIBER, PROTEIN

✓ ANTIOXIDANT, DETOXIFYING

Wheatgrass (*Triticum sp.*) comes from newly sprouted wheat kernels. It is a highly concentrated source of immune-enhancing nutrients, and is a powerful liver detoxifier. It stimulates hemoglobin production, lowers cholesterol, and helps regulate blood-fat levels.

RECIPES grow your own to eat in sandwiches or salads, or, buy wheatgrass juice, or add wheatgrass powder to other juices

WHEAT BRAN

★ VITAMINS B2, B3, B5, B6; CALCIUM, MAGNESIUM, MANGANESE, PHOSPHORUS, POTASSIUM; COPPER, IRON, ZINC; FIBER, COMPLEX CARBOHYDRATES

✓ ANTIOXIDANT, DETOXIFYING, LAXATIVE

! THE PHYTATES IN BRAN INHIBIT ABSORPTION OF NUTRIENTS INCLUDING IRON, CALCIUM, AND ZINC; HOWEVER, AS BRAN ALSO CONTAINS LARGE AMOUNTS OF THESE MINERALS, THE NET EFFECT OF EATING IT IN MODERATE AMOUNTS IS STILL HIGHLY BENEFICIAL

! ALWAYS DRINK PLENTY OF FLUIDS WHEN EATING BRAN TO AVOID INTESTINAL BLOCKAGE

Wheat bran, the outer layer of wheat (*Triticum sp.*) grain, is the richest source of insoluble fiber. It absorbs large amounts of water and increases in bulk, aiding the passage of waste through the bowel and relieving constipation. This helps prevent diseases such as diverticulitis and bowel cancer. Bran also helps regulate blood-fat and blood-sugar levels.

RECIPES muesli (page 103)

WHEATGERM

★ VITAMINS B1, B2, B3, B5, B6; MAGNESIUM, MANGANESE, PHOSPHORUS, POTASSIUM; COPPER, IRON, SELENIUM, ZINC; COMPLEX CARBOHYDRATES, FIBER, PROTEIN, SUGARS, UNSATURATED FAT

✓ ANTIOXIDANT, ANTI-STRESS

! AVOID IF ALLERGIC OR SENSITIVE TO GLUTEN IN WHEAT

Wheatgerm is the inner (embryo) layer of wheat (*Triticum sp.*) grain. It is a delicious natural source of zinc, vitamin E, folate, biotin, and other B-complex vitamins. It helps the body maintain energy levels, enhances fat metabolism, and helps protect against heart disease, immunodeficiency disorders, and some cancers.

RECIPES muesli (page 103), try sprinkling on salads and desserts

WILD RICE

★ VITAMIN B1, B2, B3; PROTEIN; UNSATURATED FAT

✓ ENERGY-BOOSTING, LOWERS CHOLESTEROL

💡 WILD RICE IS A NATIVE AMERICAN GRASS, UNRELATED TO COMMON RICE BUT EQUALLY NUTRITIOUS

Wild rice (*Zizania aquatica*) aids metabolism, improves the release of energy from food and helps the body to maintain optimum energy levels. It enhances the health of nerves, muscles, skin, and mucous membranes, and helps prevent cardiovascular disease.

RECIPES provençal-style kidney beans (page 115), sweet chestnuts and kumquats (page 117), wild rice salad (page 121)

pulses

ADUKI BEAN (ADZUKI BEAN, AZUKI BEAN)

★ VITAMINS B1, B2, B3; CALCIUM, MAGNESIUM, MANGANESE, PHOSPHORUS, POTASSIUM; COPPER, IRON, ZINC; COMPLEX CARBOHYDRATES, FIBER, PROTEIN

✓ HEALING, ENERGY-BOOSTING

Aduki beans (*Phaseolus angularis*) are small red beans with a sweet, nutty flavor. Their nutrients help release energy from food and keep skin and mucous membranes in good condition.

RECIPES add to stews, casseroles and salads

BLACK-EYE PEA (BLACK-EYE BEAN, COWPEA)

★ VITAMINS B1, B2, B3, BIOTIN, FOLATE; CALCIUM, MAGNESIUM, MANGANESE, PHOSPHORUS, POTASSIUM; COPPER, IRON, SELENIUM, ZINC; COMPLEX CARBOHYDRATES, FIBER, PROTEIN

✓ AIDS DIGESTION, LOWERS CHOLESTEROL, IMMUNO-STIMULANT

Black-eye peas (*Vigna sinensis*) are savory and are used like haricot beans and butterbeans. Rich in energy and micro-nutrients, they enhance the body's ability to make amino acids and D.N.A.

RECIPES beans and tomatoes on toast (page 102), black-eye pea and wild marjoram soup (page 105)

BUTTERBEAN

★ VITAMINS B3, B5, FOLATE; POTASSIUM, PHOSPHORUS, MAGNESIUM, MANGANESE; IRON, ZINC; COMPLEX CARBOHYDRATES, FIBER, PROTEIN

✓ ANTI-STRESS, LOWERS CHOLESTEROL

Butterbeans (*Phaseolus vulgaris sp.*) help the body to release energy from food and promote normal function of the immune and nervous systems. They also help maintain healthy skin, glands, hair, and bone marrow.

RECIPES italian butterbean soup (page 105)

FAVA BEAN

★ VITAMINS C, B3, B5, BIOTIN, FOLATE; POTASSIUM, PHOSPHORUS; IRON, ZINC; COMPLEX CARBOHYDRATES, FIBER, PROTEIN

✓ ANTI-STRESS, LOWERS CHOLESTEROL, DETOXIFYING

The high level of vitamin B5 and folate (the plant form of folic acid) in fava beans (*Vicia faba*) makes them a useful support for the body's defence against stress.

RECIPES artichoke hearts, fava beans, and shiitake (page 112)

GARBANZO BEAN (CHICKPEA)

★ VITAMINS E, B2, B3, B5, FOLATE; CALCIUM, MAGNESIUM, MANGANESE, PHOSPHORUS, POTASSIUM; ZINC; COMPLEX CARBOHYDRATES, FIBER, PROTEIN

✓ ANTI-CANCER, ANTIOXIDANT, ANTI-STRESS, LOWERS CHOLESTEROL

One of the most nutritious and delicious of the pulses, garbanzos (*Cicer arietinum*) aid the absorption of nutrients and protect the cells from free radical damage. They support the function of nerves, muscles, enzymes, and hormones and may help protect the body against heart disease and cancer.

RECIPES spicy moroccan soup (page 106), hummus with crudités and warm pitta bread (page 106), winter hot pot (page 116)

HARICOT BEAN/GREEN BEAN

★ VITAMINS A, B3, FOLATE; IRON; FIBER

✓ ANTI-CANCER, ANTIOXIDANT, LOWERS CHOLESTEROL

Haricot beans and green beans (*Phaseolus vulgaris sp.*) help keep cells well oxygenated and in good condition, particularly those of the skin and mucous membranes. They also enhance energy levels, support the nervous system, and aid liver function.

RECIPES beans and tomatoes on toast (page 102); okra in sweet and sour tamarind sauce (page 116), salad niçoise (page 119)

LENTIL

★ VITAMINS B3, B5, B6, FOLATE; CALCIUM, MAGNESIUM, MANGANESE, PHOSPHORUS, POTASSIUM; COPPER, IRON, SELENIUM, ZINC; COMPLEX CARBOHYDRATES, FIBER, PROTEIN

✓ ANTIOXIDANT, ENERGY-BOOSTING, LOWERS CHOLESTEROL

Lentils (*Lens culinaris*) are an excellent source of antioxidants, and so can protect against heart disease and cancer. They improve the function of red blood cells and the integrity of cell membranes, and also help regulate blood-fat levels.

RECIPES spicy moroccan soup (page 106), casserole de puy (page 112), shepherdess' pie (page 116), winter hot pot (page 116), khichuri—rice with lentils (page 117), green lentil salad (page 120)

MANGETOUT PEA

★ VITAMINS A, B1, B2, B3, B5, BIOTIN; CALCIUM; IRON; FIBER, PROTEIN

✓ **ANTI-CANCER, ANTIOXIDANT**

Mangetout peas (*Pisum sativum sp.*) are good for the skin, hair, glands, nerves, and muscles. They aid metabolism, liver function, and antibody production, and help maintain energy levels.

RECIPES chinese salad (page 120)

MUNG BEAN SPROUTS

★ VITAMINS B3, B5, FOLATE; PHOSPHORUS; IRON; FIBER, PROTEIN

✓ **ANTI-STRESS, LOWERS CHOLESTEROL**

Mung bean sprouts (*Phaseolus aureus*) help the body maintain optimum energy levels during stressful situations. They also aid antibody production and enhance liver function.

RECIPES asparagus asian-style (page 113), carrot 'n' beet salad (page 119), chinese salad (page 120), grapefruit salad (page 49), oriental salad with tempeh (page 63)

PINTO BEAN

★ VITAMINS B1, B2, B3, B5, B6, FOLATE; CALCIUM, MAGNESIUM, MANGANESE, PHOSPHORUS, POTASSIUM; COPPER, IRON, SELENIUM, ZINC; COMPLEX CARBOHYDRATES, FIBER, PROTEIN

✓ **ANTIOXIDANT, ENERGY-BOOSTING, LOWERS CHOLESTEROL**

Pinto beans (*Phaseolus vulgaris sp.*) help keep the skin, mucous membranes, and muscles (including the heart) in good condition, maintain optimum energy levels, and aid the nervous system, helping to ease stress.

RECIPES spicy moroccan soup (page 106)

SOY BEAN

★ VITAMINS E, B1, B3, B6, BIOTIN, FOLATE; CALCIUM, MAGNESIUM, MANGANESE, PHOSPHORUS, POTASSIUM; COPPER, IRON, SELENIUM, ZINC; ISOFLAVONES, PROTEASE INHIBITORS, SAPONINS; COMPLEX CARBOHYDRATES, FIBER, PROTEIN, UNSATURATED FAT

✓ **ANTI-CANCER, ANTIOXIDANT, ENERGY-BOOSTING, LOWERS CHOLESTEROL, NUTRIENT-RICH**

! **SOME PEOPLE ARE ALLERGIC TO SOY**

! **MUCH OF THE WORLD SOY CROP HAS BEEN GENETICALLY MODIFIED: BUY ORGANIC**

! **SOME GENETICALLY MODIFIED SOY BEANS CONTAIN GENES FROM BRAZIL NUTS, AND SO MAY TRIGGER AN ALLERGIC REACTION**

Soy beans (*Glycine max*) are a versatile and extremely nutritious food that can be eaten sprouted or cooked, and as tempeh, tofu, soy milk, flour, yogurt, sauce, or miso. They contain numerous phytochemicals beneficial to human health, some of which halt the growth of hormone-sensitive tumor cells. In particular, soy bean products are believed to reduce the risk of prostate and breast cancer, and can help both prevent and treat cardiovascular disease. Soy milk, which is made from soy beans, is a nutritious alternative to dairy milk.

RECIPES see tofu (below) and tempeh (page 62)

SOY YOGURT

★ AS FOR SOY BEAN, PLUS LACTOBACILLI

✓ **ANTI-CANCER, ANTIOXIDANT, IMMUNO-STIMULANT, LOWERS CHOLESTEROL**

! **AS FOR SOY BEAN**

Live yogurt contains lactobacilli, beneficial bacteria that help prevent the colonization of the gut by harmful micro-organisms. Live yogurt is especially helpful after antibiotic treatment (which kills off beneficial bacteria in the digestive tract). It also helps in the treatment of urinary-tract infections, gastroenteritis, infection by *helicobacter pylori* (the bacterium that causes stomach ulcers), inflammatory bowel disease, and colon cancer.

RECIPES yogurt with fruit (page 103), potato salad (page 120), raspberry gateau (page 122), blackberry cream (page 124), passion and lime (page 127), avocado smoothie (page 53)

TOFU (BEANCURD)

★ VITAMIN B3, FOLATE; CALCIUM, MAGNESIUM, MANGANESE, PHOSPHORUS; COPPER, IRON, ZINC; ISOFLAVONES, PROTEASE INHIBITORS, SAPONINS; PROTEIN, UNSATURATED FAT

✓ **ANTI-CANCER, LOWERS CHOLESTEROL, CALCIUM-RICH**

! **AS FOR SOY BEAN**

Tofu is an extremely versatile food that is made from soy beans (*Glycine max*) in a process similar to cheese-making. It is high in protein, free from saturated fat, easy to digest and, like all soy products, has many health benefits. Soft tofu has a delicate texture and is generally mixed with other ingredients before being used in recipes. Firm tofu can be cut, sliced, chopped, or crumbled and added to a wide variety of dishes. Both soft and firm types have a neutral taste and absorb flavors readily when marinated or cooked with herbs and spices. See also tempeh (page 62).

RECIPES scrambled tofu (page 102), tofumasalata (page 108), tofu balls (page 110), amaranth and tofu puffs (page 112), spicy tofu burgers (page 117), vegetable kebabs (page 107)

tempeh

TEMPEH IS A VERSATILE AND NUTRITIOUS PRODUCT MADE FROM SOY BEANS. PACKED WITH PHYTOCHEMICALS, IT IS ONE OF THE BRIGHTEST STAR FOODS FOR BOOSTING IMMUNITY, AND PREVENTING CANCER, HEART DISEASE, AND HORMONE-RELATED PROBLEMS.

The origin of tempeh

Tempeh is a form of beancurd, originally produced in Indonesia but now popular all over the world. It is a near-perfect source of protein. Unlike animal meat, it contains no saturated fats, and it is also one of the few vegetable products to contain vitamin B12.

Tempeh is made by mixing dehulled, split, and precooked soy beans (Glycine max) with a yeast culture in a process similar to cheese-making. The beans are packed tightly into perforated containers (traditionally banana leaves, but nowadays usually plastic bags) and molded into flat cakes or sausages. These are set to incubate, in ovens or in the sun, at a temperature of 60–100°F until the process of fermentation transforms the mixture into a tight lump. The finished product is delicious, with a nutty taste resembling chicken or fish. Tempeh can be sliced and fried, or cut into cubes and added to stews and other dishes. The fermentation process initiates the partial breakdown of the beans, which makes tempeh easier to digest than other cooked beans, with less tendency to cause flatulence.

Immune-boosting properties

Tempeh is packed with health-enhancing carbohydrates, fiber, and protein and also contains a wealth of minerals, B vitamins, phytoestrogens (isoflavonoids), protease inhibitors and saponins that have anti-microbial and anti-cancer properties. Phytoestrogens are active against viruses, and are known to inhibit the growth of cancers and halt the spread of malignant cells into surrounding tissues, reducing the risk of breast and prostate cancers in particular. They also appear to be protective against many other hormone-related health problems, such as fibrocystic breast disease, osteoporosis, endometriosis, and uterine fibroids.

Protease inhibitors are believed to prevent cancer-causing agents from entering cells and so help to keep cellular DNA intact. They have also been found to inhibit the growth of some cancers and to stop the spread of tumor cells. Saponins support the immune system, reduce the growth rate of some cancer cells, and help control blood cholesterol. Tempeh protein improves the efficiency of cell-mediated immunity.

Heart protector

Heart disease is much less common in regions where soy bean protein is eaten in preference to animal protein. Like other soy products, tempeh helps lower blood cholesterol. It contains a protein that inhibits intestinal absorption of dietary cholesterol and helps remove cholesterol from the blood, thereby reducing the risk of cardiovascular disorders. Tempeh also contains antioxidants and genistein, which may help prevent cardiovascular disorders such as atherosclerosis. The nutrients in tempeh boost energy levels and make the body better able to cope with stress by supporting both the nervous and immune systems. They also keep hair, glands, blood cells, bone, bone marrow, skin, and mucous membranes in good condition, and act as building blocks for proteins, carbohydrates and fats. The nutrients in tempeh aid in the production of hemoglobin (the chemical that transports oxygen in the blood), as well as supporting liver function and fat metabolism, and may also protect against high blood pressure, allergy, asthma, migraine, depression, and prostate disorders.

IMMUNE-BOOSTING PROFILE

★ VITAMINS B2, B3, B5, B6, B12, BIOTIN; CALCIUM, MAGNESIUM, MANGANESE, PHOSPHORUS, POTASSIUM; COPPER, IRON, ZINC; ISOFLAVONES, GENISTEIN, PROTEASE INHIBITORS, SAPONINS; COMPLEX CARBOHYDRATES, FIBER, PROTEIN

✓ ANTI-CANCER, ANTI-STRESS, ANTI-VIRAL, LOWERS CHOLESTEROL, ENERGY-BOOSTING, IMMUNO-STIMULANT

! SOME PEOPLE ARE ALLERGIC TO SOY PRODUCTS

! MUCH OF THE WORLD'S SOY BEAN CROP HAS BEEN GENETICALLY MODIFIED: BUY ORGANIC

oriental salad with tempeh *(above)*

1-in piece fresh ginger root, finely chopped	8 tempeh rashers, cut into chunks
1 garlic clove, finely chopped	1 tbs sesame oil
4-in stalk of lemongrass, finely chopped	1 bunch of scallions, thinly sliced
4 tbs lemon juice	8 baby corn cobs, steamed
1 tbs balsamic vinegar	3½ oz bean sprouts
1 tbs maple syrup	6 leaves of chinese cabbage, shredded
½ cup orange juice	salt and pepper
4 tbs soy sauce	2 tbs sesame salt

Mix the ginger, garlic, lemongrass, lemon juice, vinegar, maple syrup, orange juice, and soy sauce in a bowl. Add the tempeh and leave to marinate for 1 hour. Remove the tempeh (keeping the marinade in the bowl), and fry it in the oil. Sprinkle with salt. Mix the scallions, baby corns, bean sprouts and chinese cabbage in a salad bowl, mix in the marinade, add the tempeh and sprinkle with sesame salt.

tempeh kebabs

7 oz tempeh, cubed	For the marinade:
1 zucchini, in thick slices	2 tbs lemon juice
1 lime, in wedges	2 tbs sherry
8 garlic cloves	2 tbs olive oil
2 corns, cut into chunks	1 tbs soy sauce
16 cherry tomatoes	2 garlic cloves, crushed
1 eggplant, diced	4 tbs tomato ketchup
1 lb small new potatoes, cooked	*(see page 111)*

Place the kebab ingredients in a bowl. Add the marinade ingredients and mix well. Leave covered for a couple of hours, stirring occasionally. Divide the different ingredients between 8 barbecue skewers. Brush with the leftover marinade and place on a hot barbecue for about 10 minutes, turning from time to time.

herbs and spices

HERBS

BORAGE (BEEPLANT, TALEWORT)

★ VITAMINS A, C, B3; CALCIUM, MAGNESIUM, PHOSPHORUS, POTASSIUM; ZINC; MUCILAGE, SAPONINS, TANNIN, VOLATILE OIL; FIBRE

✓ ANTI-INFLAMMATORY, ANTIOXIDANT, DIAPHORETIC, EXPECTORANT

The leaves of borage (*Borago officinalis*) can be used to treat inflammation, fevers, and coughs, and help the body recover from the effects of stress. They taste like cucumber and are delicious chopped finely and added to salads.

RECIPES immuni-tea (page 129), stress relief (page 130), tea for fever (page 131), tea for glands (page 131), cough mixture (page 128)

CATNIP (CATMINT, CATNEP)

★ CALCIUM, MAGNESIUM, PHOSPHORUS, POTASSIUM; ZINC; BITTER PRINCIPLE, TANNIN, VOLATILE OILS

✓ ANTISPASMODIC, ASTRINGENT, CIRCULATORY AND DIGESTIVE STIMULANT, DIAPHORETIC, FEBRIFUGE

Catmint (*Nepeta cataria*) leaves and flowering tops are particularly useful in treating childhood fevers and respiratory-tract infections, and help settle stomach upsets and diarrhea.

RECIPES sleepy time (page 130), tea for fever (page 131)

CHAMOMILE (CAMOMILE—WILD, GERMAN, ANNUAL)

★ COUMARINS, MUCILAGE, RUTIN, SALICYLIC ACID, TANNIN, VALERIANIC ACID, VOLATILE OIL

✓ ANTI-ALLERGIC, ANTI-INFLAMMATORY, ANTISEPTIC, ANTISPASMODIC, SEDATIVE

Chamomile (*Matricaria recutita*) flowers relieve restlessness and tension, and are useful for headache, anxiety, and sleeplessness. They also help relieve digestive upsets, and are particularly suitable for children.

RECIPES calming tea (page 128), hay fever relief (page 129), sleepy time (page 130), tea for fever (page 131), chamomile tonic (page 128)

CALENDULA (MARIGOLD)

★ VITAMIN C; BITTERS, CAROTENOIDS, LUTEIN, LYCOPENE, QUERCETIN, MUCILAGE, RESIN, RUTIN, SALICYLIC ACID, SAPONINS, VANILLIC ACID

✓ ANTI-MICROBIAL, ANTI-INFLAMMATORY, ANTIOXIDANT, WOUND HEALING

Calendula or marigold (*Calendula officinalis*) flowers are a natural antibacterial, antifungal, and antiviral treatment for mouth and skin infections, inflammation, and ulcers (both internal and external). Calendula helps relieve gall-bladder disorders, and may have a role in the management of cancer.

RECIPES tea for fungal infections (page 131), tea for ear infections (page 131), tea for glands (page 131), tea for the skin (page 131)

CLEAVERS (CLIVERS, GOOSEGRASS)

★ BIOFLAVONOIDS, CITRIC ACID, COUMARINS, GLYCOSIDES, TANNIN

✓ ANTI-CANCER, ANTI-INFLAMMATORY, DETOXIFYING

Cleavers (*Galium aparine*) is a tonic for the lymphatic system, useful for treating swollen glands, eczema, psoriasis, joint problems, edema, ulcers, tumors, infections of the urinary tract, and urinary stones.

RECIPES immuni-tea (page 129), tea for ear infections (page 131), tea for glands (page 131), tea for the skin (page 131)

ECHINACEA

★ ECHINACEIN, GLYCOSIDE (ECHINACOSIDE), RESIN, VOLATILE OIL

✓ ANTI-ALLERGIC, ANTI-CANCER, ANTI-INFLAMMATORY, ANTI-MICROBIAL, ANTISEPTIC, IMMUNO-STIMULANT

Echinacea (*Echinacea angustifolia*) enhances the body's natural resistance to infection, and is one of the most important natural remedies against colds and influenza and other infectious diseases (including H.I.V.) and cancer.

RECIPES tea for fungal infections (page 131), hay fever relief (page 129), immuni-tea (page 129), tea for glands (page 131)

ELDERFLOWER (BLACK, EUROPEAN)

★ CHOLINE; BIOFLAVONOIDS (INCLUDING RUTIN AND KAEMPFEROL), CYANOGLYCOSIDE; MUCILAGE, OMEGA-3 AND -6 FATTY ACIDS, PECTIN, TANNIN, VOLATILE OIL

✓ **ANTI-MUCUS, ANTI-INFLAMMATORY, CIRCULATORY AND IMMUNE STIMULANT, DIAPHORETIC, EXPECTORANT**

Elderflower (*Sambucus nigra*) enhances natural resistance to disease and promotes perspiration—excellent for colds, influenza and high temperature, as well as allergic symptoms and mucus.

RECIPES cold buster (page 128), elderflower spritzer (page 128), hay fever relief (page 129), lung-cleansing tea mix (page 130), tea for ear infections (page 131)

FEVERFEW (MIDSUMMER DAISY)

★ **BITTERS, VOLATILE OIL**

✓ **ANTI-INFLAMMATORY, DIGESTIVE STIMULANT, PAINKILLING, VASODILATOR**

! **CHEWING FRESH FEVERFEW LEAVES MAY CAUSE MOUTH ULCERS**

! **STIMULATES UTERUS AND SO BEST AVOIDED DURING PREGNANCY**

The leaves of fresh feverfew (*Tanacetum parthenium/ Chrysanthemum parthenium*) are used to relieve headache. They offer an effective way of preventing migraine, and can help relieve the pain of rheumatoid arthritis.

RECIPES tea for headache (page 131)

LAVENDER

★ **TANNIN, VOLATILE OIL**

✓ **ANTIDEPRESSANT, ANTISPASMODIC, RELAXING, SEDATIVE**

Lavender (*Lavandula angustifolia*) is an effective treatment for headaches, and for nervous exhaustion, depression, and skin irritations. Soothing and relaxing, it promotes healing by bringing body and mind into balance.

RECIPES calming tea (page 128), pick-me-up (page 130), sleepy time (page 130), stress relief (page 130)

LEMON BALM

★ **BITTERS, ROSMARINIC ACID, TANNIN, VOLATILE OIL**

✓ **ANTI-DEPRESSANT, ANTI-VIRAL, LOWERS BLOOD PRESSURE, MILD SEDATIVE, RELAXANT**

Lemon balm (*Melissa officinalis*) is a sweet-tasting herb that can help prevent and treat cold sores, and is thought to reduce the growth rate of tumors. It has a calming effect on the nerves and the digestion, and is useful in the management of heart problems.

RECIPES calming tea (page 128), immuni-tea (page 129), pick-me-up (page 130), stress relief (page 130), stuffed grapefruit (page 49)

PEPPERMINT

★ **VITAMINS A, C, E, B2, B3, FOLATE; CALCIUM, MAGNESIUM, POTASSIUM, PHOSPHORUS; IRON; BITTERS, PECTIN, RUTIN, TANNIN, VOLATILE OILS (INCLUDING MENTHOL)**

✓ **ANTI-CANCER, ANTIMICROBIAL, ANTIOXIDANT, ANTISEPTIC, ANTISPASMODIC, CARMINATIVE, COOLING, DIGESTIVE STIMULANT**

Peppermint (*Mentha x piperita*) is an effective treatment for colds and coughs, helping to clear airways and make breathing easier. It also stimulates the secretion of digestive juices and helps to relieve symptoms of indigestion, ulcerative colitis, and Crohn's disease.

RECIPES mint and melon soup (page 105), nectarine surprise (page 123), green tea with mint (page 129), lung-cleansing tea mix (page 130), grapefruit and peppermint fizz (page 49)

ROSEMARY

★ **VITAMIN A; CALCIUM, MAGNESIUM; IRON, ZINC; BIOFLAVONOIDS, BITTERS, SAPONINS, VOLATILE OILS (INCLUDING CAMPHOR)**

✓ **ANTI-MICROBIAL, ANTIOXIDANT, ANTISPASMODIC, ASTRINGENT, CARMINATIVE, CIRCULATORY AND DIGESTIVE STIMULANT, TONIC**

Rosemary (*Rosmarinus officinalis*) stimulates the circulation and the nervous system. It is a traditional tonic for the heart, and it has a calming effect on the digestion. It is also an effective treatment for tension headaches.

RECIPES scrambled tofu (page 102), pick-me-up (page 130), tea for aches and pains (page 131), tea for headache (page 131)

SAGE (RED, GARDEN)

★ VITAMIN A; CALCIUM, MAGNESIUM, MANGANESE, POTASSIUM; ZINC; BIOFLAVONOIDS, GLYCOSIDES, PHYTOESTROGENS, SAPONINS, TANNIN, VOLATILE OIL

✓ ANTI-MICROBIAL, ANTIOXIDANT, DIGESTIVE, DRYING, PERIPHERAL VASODILATOR

! AVOID DURING PREGNANCY

Sage (*Salvia officinalis*) is an antiseptic herb that improves the health of mucous membranes. It can also reduce perspiration.

RECIPES mushrooms with sage and thyme stuffing (page 116), pan bread (page 118), eucalyptus mix (page 129), sage mix for sore throats (page 130), tempeh kebabs (page 63)

ST. JOHN'S WORT (HYPERICUM)

★ VITAMIN C; BIOFLAVONOIDS, CAROTENOIDS, GLYCOSIDES, PECTIN, RESIN, TANNIN

✓ ANTIDEPRESSANT, ANTISEPTIC, ASTRINGENT, ANTI-INFLAMMATORY, ANTIOXIDANT, EXPECTORANT, HEALING, PAINKILLING

! MAY INHIBIT THE EFFECT OF PRESCRIPTION DRUGS: IF RECEIVING MEDICATION, SEEK YOUR DOCTOR'S ADVICE BEFORE TAKING

St. John's wort (*Hypericum perforatum*) is helpful in the management of post-viral disorders. It is an effective remedy for mild depression and can also be used as a mild painkiller.

RECIPES calming tea (page 128), tea for aches and pains (page 131), tea for joints (page 131)

THYME (COMMON, GARDEN)

★ VITAMIN A; CALCIUM, MAGNESIUM, MANGANESE; ZINC; BITTERS, BIOFLAVONOIDS, RESIN, VOLATILE OIL (INCLUDING THYMOL AND CAMPHOR); OMEGA-3 AND -6 FATTY ACIDS

✓ ANTIMICROBIAL, ANTIOXIDANT, ANTISEPTIC, ANTISPASMODIC, ASTRINGENT, CARMINATIVE, EXPECTORANT

Thyme (*Thymus vulgaris*) contains the volatile oil thymol, a powerful antiseptic and one of the most effective of all herbal antibiotics. It is particularly useful in the treatment of respiratory-tract infections, such as bronchitis, laryngitis, and whooping cough, and helps relieve the symptoms of asthma. Thyme is also beneficial in the treatment of gastro-intestinal disorders including colic and diarrhea.

RECIPES beans and tomatoes on toast (page 102), italian butterbean soup (page 105), marinated olives (page 108), mushrooms with sage and thyme stuffing (page 116), catalan salad (page 120), cough mixture (page 128), eucalyptus mix (page 129)

VIOLET (BLUE, SWEET)

★ ALKALOID, METHYL SALICYLATE, RUTIN, SAPONINS, VOLATILE OIL

✓ ANTI-CANCER, ANTI-INFLAMMATORY, EXPECTORANT

Violet (*Viola odorata*) leaves and flowers have a role in the management of malignant tumors and may help inhibit the spread of cancer. They are also useful in the treatment of chronic bronchitis, chronic nasal mucus, skin problems, and arthritis.

RECIPES yogurt with fruit (page 103), lung-cleansing tea mix (page 130), tea for the skin (page 131), cough mixture (page 128)

WILD MARJORAM (EUROPEAN OREGANO)

★ VITAMIN A; CALCIUM, MAGNESIUM, MANGANESE, PHOSPHORUS, POTASSIUM; COPPER, IRON, ZINC; BIOFLAVONOIDS, BITTERS, PHYTOSTEROLS, TANNINS, VOLATILE OILS; OMEGA-3, -6 AND OLEIC FATTY ACIDS

✓ ANTIMICROBIAL, ANTIOXIDANT, DIAPHORETIC, EXPECTORANT, STIMULANT, WARMING

Wild marjoram (*Origanum vulgare*) is an excellent warming remedy for coughs (including whooping cough), colds, and influenza. It can also be used to relieve headache and indigestion.

RECIPES black-eye pea and wild marjoram soup (page 105), cold buster (page 128), tea for headache (page 131), cough mixture (page 128), scandinavian beet burgers (page 37)

YARROW (MILFOIL)

★ BIOFLAVONOIDS, BITTERS, RESIN, SALICYLATES, TANNIN, VOLATILE OILS (INCLUDING CINEOL, AZULENE AND CAMPHOR)

✓ ANTI-INFLAMMATORY, ANTISEPTIC, ASTRINGENT, BLOOD PRESSURE LOWERING, DIAPHORETIC, DIGESTIVE TONIC, PERIPHERAL VASODILATOR

! EXCESS YARROW INTAKE CAN CAUSE HEADACHE

Yarrow (*Achillea millefolium*) has a long tradition as a remedy for colds and influenza but in fact this versatile herb has a multitude of beneficial effects on health. As an anti-inflammatory and diaphoretic it helps to relieve mucus, bronchitis, cystitis, and gastro-intestinal inflammation, and enables the body to deal more effectively with infections. As a cardiovascular restorative, it improves peripheral circulation and lowers blood pressure. As an external remedy, it has a longstanding reputation for stopping bleeding and healing wounds.

RECIPES circulation booster (page 128), cold buster (page 128), cystitis relief (page 128), tea for ear infections (page 131)

garlic

THIS AROMATIC HERB DOESN'T JUST KEEP VAMPIRES AT BAY! GARLIC
PROTECTS AGAINST A WIDE RANGE OF BACTERIAL, FUNGAL, AND VIRAL
INFECTIONS. IT ALSO STRENGTHENS THE HEART AND BLOOD VESSELS
AND HELPS PREVENT CANCER.

The origin of garlic

Garlic (*Allium sativum*) is a plant so ancient that no one is really
sure of its origins. It is thought to have evolved from the wild garlic
of central Asia (*Allium longicuspis*), and is known to have been
cultivated in Egypt and Mesopotamia before 2000BCE. According
to Pliny, it had a semi-divine status in the ancient world, and was
called upon in the swearing of oaths. Now one of the world's most
popular herbs, it is cultivated and used worldwide as both a food
and medicine.

Immune-boosting properties

Garlic grows best where warm and dry summers prevail, and is
itself a warming and drying herb. It is also one of the most effective
natural anti-microbials, stimulating the production of white blood
cells and acting against a wide range of bacteria, fungi, parasites,
and viruses. Even with the development of modern antibiotics and
a more sophisticated understanding of microbiology, garlic is still
regarded by many health practitioners as first-line treatment for
infectious disease. Garlic fights various gastro-intestinal infections
and infestations such as dysentery, typhoid, threadworm, and
tapeworm. It contains a volatile oil that is mostly excreted through
the lungs, making it an excellent remedy for
respiratory disorders such as bronchitis,
mucus, influenza, and whooping
cough. This oil is also active against
tuberculosis, and plays a role in
the management of asthma.
Garlic combats fungal

infections such as yeast infections, athlete's foot, and ringworm,
and is a standard ingredient in anti-candida diets, encouraging the
growth of beneficial bacteria and inhibiting pathogens. It may also
reduce the virulence of the H.I.V. virus.

One of the most popular modern uses for garlic is in dealing
with cardiovascular disease. It acts on the circulatory system to
reduce the level of blood fat and cholesterol, and decreases the
tendency of the blood to clot.

Over time, garlic will also lower blood pressure significantly,
and it prevents the formation of atheroma (fat deposits on artery
walls). Recent studies have also shown that garlic reduces the
arteriosclerotic changes (hardening of arteries) that appear with
age. These changes are accelerated by smoking, and eating a
typical Western diet high in saturated fats and sugar.

Allicin is one of the active ingredients responsible for garlic's
ability to suppress the formation of cancer cells and enhance the
immune system's ability to slow the spread of malignant tumors.
This corresponds with epidemiological findings that cancer is less
common in areas with high garlic consumption.

Even the idea that garlic keeps vampires away may be based
on fact, not fiction. In Central
Asia, a rare variety of the
disease porphyria

was once relatively common. Symptoms included extreme paleness and a complete intolerance to sunlight. Relief from some of these might have been found in garlic's medicinal properties.

IMMUNE-BOOSTING PROFILE

★ VITAMIN B6; MAGNESIUM, PHOSPHORUS, POTASSIUM; IRON, ZINC; BIOFLAVONOIDS, GLUCOKININ, MUCILAGE, PHYTOHORMONES, VOLATILE OILS (INCLUDING ALLICIN)

✓ ANTIBACTERIAL, ANTICOAGULANT, ANTI-MUCUS, ANTIOXIDANT, ANTISEPTIC, DETOXIFYING, EXPECTORANT, LOWERS BLOOD PRESSURE AND CHOLESTEROL

! THE SULFUR COMPOUNDS IN GARLIC CAN IRRITATE ULCERS

! HIGH DOSES OF GARLIC CAN EXAGGERATE THE EFFECTS OF ANTICOAGULANT AND BLOOD-PRESSURE-LOWERING DRUGS

💡 EAT WITH PARSLEY TO AVOID GARLIC ON THE BREATH

tomato, wild marjoram, and garlic salad (above)

2 lb ripe tomatoes, sliced
4 tbsp fresh wild marjoram, chopped
2 garlic cloves, finely chopped

6 tbsp olive oil
2 tbsp balsamic vinegar
Salt and pepper to taste

Arrange the tomatoes on a large plate and sprinkle with marjoram, garlic, oil, vinegar, and salt and pepper.

garlic and savoy cabbage

3 tbsp olive oil
1 tsp curry powder
1 tbsp black mustard seeds
1 medium savoy cabbage, finely shredded

3 garlic cloves, finely chopped
2 tbsp desiccated coconut
1 tbsp maple syrup
2 tbsp lemon juice
Salt and pepper to taste

Heat the oil in a large skillet or wok. Add the spices and stir-fry until the mustard seeds begin to pop. Add the cabbage and the garlic and stir-fry until the cabbage begins to wilt. Add the coconut and stir-fry for 1 minute more, then add the maple syrup and lemon juice. Mix well and season with salt and pepper. Serve hot.

rich garlic dressing

4 tbsp balsamic vinegar
1 tbsp maple syrup
1 tbsp Dijon mustard

2 garlic cloves, crushed
½ cup olive oil (approximately)
Salt and pepper to taste

Whisk or hand-blend the vinegar, maple syrup, mustard, garlic, salt, and pepper with a little oil. Add the oil very slowly, a little at a time until the dressing starts to emulsify. Then add more oil, still a little at a time, until the taste is right. Adjust seasoning.

SPICES

BLACK CUMIN

★ VITAMINS A, B1, B2, B3; CALCIUM, MAGNESIUM, MANGANESE, PHOSPHORUS, POTASSIUM; COPPER, IRON, ZINC; OMEGA-3 AND -6 FATTY ACIDS

✓ ANTI-ALLERGIC, ANTI-INFLAMMATORY, ANTIMICROBIAL, ANTIOXIDANT

Black cumin (*Nigella sativa*) has been used for centuries in Asia and the Middle East as a treatment for allergy, eczema and upper respiratory-tract disorders such as asthma and bronchitis. It may also help in the prevention of immunodeficiency disorders.

RECIPES beans and tomatoes on toast (page 102), spicy moroccan soup (page 106), baba ganoush (page 108), garlic oxymel (page 129), heart chai (page 129), spicy chai (page 130)

CARAWAY

★ VITAMINS B1, B2, B3; CALCIUM, MAGNESIUM, PHOSPHORUS, POTASSIUM; COPPER, IRON, ZINC; BIOFLAVONOIDS, VOLATILE OIL

✓ ANTIBACTERIAL, ANTIOXIDANT, ANTISPASMODIC, CARMINATIVE, EXPECTORANT, TONIC

Caraway (*Carum carvi*) seeds are used to alleviate upper respiratory-tract problems such as asthma and bronchitis and in a gargle to treat laryngitis. They can also be chewed to alleviate gastro-intestinal disorders, including indigestion, colic, diarrhea, and trapped gas.

RECIPES healing soup (page 104), spicy moroccan soup (page 106), pan bread (page 118), spicy chai (page 130)

CAYENNE

★ VITAMINS A, B2, B3; CALCIUM, MAGNESIUM, PHOSPHORUS, POTASSIUM; IRON, ZINC; BIOFLAVONOIDS, CAPSAICIN, VOLATILE OIL

✓ ANTIBACTERIAL, ANTI-CANCER, ANTI-MUCUS, ANTIOXIDANT, DIAPHORETIC, STIMULANT, TONIC

! CAYENNE IRRITATES MUCOUS MEMBRANES: HANDLE WITH CARE, AND AVOID IN CASES OF GASTRITIS OR STOMACH ULCER.

Cayenne (*Capsicum anuum*) is a powerful circulatory stimulant that increases the blood supply to all parts of the body, thus creating a feeling of heat. It is useful for preventing colds, and to deal with general debility in convalescence.

RECIPES spicy moroccan soup (page 106), cold buster (page 128), spicy chai (page 130), tea for fever (page 131)

CELERY SEED

★ CALCIUM, MAGNESIUM, PHOSPHORUS, POTASSIUM; COPPER, IRON, ZINC; BIOFLAVONOIDS, VOLATILE OIL

✓ ANTIOXIDANT, DETOXIFYING, DIGESTIVE TONIC, URINARY ANTISEPTIC

! SHOULD BE AVOIDED DURING PREGNANCY

Celery (*Apium graveolens*) seeds enhance the elimination of uric acid from the body making them useful in arthritic conditions, particularly gout. They also help in the treatment of urinary-tract infections and stones.

RECIPES tea for joints (page 131)

EUCALYPTUS

★ BIOFLAVONOIDS, VOLATILE OIL

✓ ANTIBACTERIAL, ANTIFUNGAL, ANTIOXIDANT, ANTISEPTIC, ANTISPASMODIC, EXPECTORANT, FEBRIFUGE, STIMULANT

Eucalyptus (*Eucalyptus globulus*) is a well-known ingredient in cough remedies, and is useful in treating upper respiratory-tract infections in general. It also acts against urinary-tract infections, and has broad-spectrum antibiotic properties.

RECIPES eucalyptus mix (page 129), lung-cleansing tea mix (page 130)

GINGER

★ ZINC; MUCILAGE, PHENOLS, RESIN, VOLATILE OILS

✓ ANTISEPTIC, ANTISPASMODIC, CARMINATIVE, DETOXIFYING, DIAPHORETIC, EXPECTORANT, VASODILATOR

Ginger (*Zingiber officinale*) is a warming and comforting remedy for colds and chills. It stimulates peripheral circulation and helps the body rid itself of toxins.

RECIPES korean kimchi-style salad (page 107), apricot and ginger (page 124), circulation booster (page 128), heart chai (page 129)

HORSERADISH

★ VITAMIN C; CALCIUM, MAGNESIUM; ZINC; ASPARAGIN, RESIN, VOLATILE MUSTARD OIL

✓ ANTI-ALLERGIC, ANTIBACTERIAL, ANTI-CANCER, ANTIOXIDANT, ANTISEPTIC, DETOXIFYING, DIAPHORETIC, EXPECTORANT, TONIC

! AVOID IN CASES OF UNDERACTIVE THYROID

Horseradish (*Armoracia rusticana*) is a circulatory stimulant, useful for chronic rheumatic conditions, urinary-tract infections, and upper respiratory-tract disorders, such as asthma, bronchial mucus, whooping cough, and hay fever. It also stimulates digestion.

RECIPES beet and horseradish salad (page 37)

JUNIPER

★ BITTER PRINCIPLES, GLYCOSIDE, TANNIN, VOLATILE OIL

✓ ANTIBACTERIAL, ANTI-MUCUS, ANTIFUNGAL, CARMINATIVE, DIURETIC, URINARY ANTISEPTIC

! SHOULD BE AVOIDED DURING PREGNANCY AND BY THOSE WITH KIDNEY DISEASE

A digestive stimulant, juniper (*Juniperus communis*) helps detoxify the body and relieves arthritis and gout. It is also used to treat urinary-tract disorders.

RECIPES swiss chard and juniper berries (page 119)

LICORICE ROOT

★ CALCIUM, PHOSPHORUS; BIOFLAVONOIDS, TANNIN, BITTER PRINCIPLES, COUMARINS, GLYCOSIDES, PHYTOESTROGEN, VOLATILE OILS

✓ ANTI-INFLAMMATORY, ANTIOXIDANT, ANTISPASMODIC, ANTI-STRESS, EXPECTORANT, GENTLE LAXATIVE, IMMUNO-STIMULANT

Licorice (*Glycyrrhiza glabra*) helps the body to cope better in stressful conditions, and has a beneficial effect on the adrenal glands (useful for recovery after steroid therapy). It also relieves bronchial mucus and coughs, and is a specific treatment for gastro-intestinal ulcers. It has been found to inhibit tumor growth.

RECIPES cough mixture (page 128), immuni-tea (page 129), licorice mix (page 130), lung-cleansing tea mix (page 130)

MUSTARD SEED (BLACK)

★ VITAMINS B1, B2, B3; CALCIUM, MAGNESIUM, PHOSPHORUS, POTASSIUM; IRON, ZINC; MUCILAGE, SINIGRIN, VOLATILE OIL

✓ CARMINATIVE, DIAPHORETIC, DIURETIC, STIMULANT, TONIC

! MUSTARD SEED CAN CAUSE IRRITATION—USE SPARINGLY

Black mustard (*Brassica nigra*) stimulates the circulation and relieves colds, bronchitis, fevers, and influenza.

RECIPES sweet potato curry (page 116), tea for joints (page 131)

TURMERIC

★ VITAMIN B3; CALCIUM, PHOSPHORUS, POTASSIUM, MAGNESIUM; COPPER, IRON, ZINC; CURCUMINOIDS, VOLATILE OIL

✓ ANTIBACTERIAL, ANTI-INFLAMMATORY, ANTIOXIDANT

Turmeric (*Curcuma longa*) aids immunity by enhancing the health of the liver. It also mops up free radicals and so helps fight degenerative diseases.

RECIPES casserole de puy (page 112), paella (page 112)

other foods and drinks

EVENING PRIMROSE OIL

★ VITAMIN E; PHYTOSTEROLS; OMEGA-3 AND -6 FATTY ACIDS

✓ ANTIOXIDANT, HEALING, IMMUNO-STIMULANT

! THIS OIL IS RATHER EXPENSIVE

Evening primrose (*Oenothera biennis*) oil improves the health of body cells, aids normal blood clotting, and tissue repair. It is a remedy for eczema and psoriasis, and helpful for multiple sclerosis. It also helps protect against heart disease and some cancers.

RECIPES *use in marinades and dressings, or sprinkle on to food*

GREEN TEA

★ BIOFLAVONOIDS, CATECHINS, THEOPHYLLINE

✓ ANTI-ALLERGIC, ANTI-ASTHMATIC, ANTIOXIDANT, LOWERS BLOOD FATS, LOWERS BLOOD PRESSURE, PREVENTS ABNORMAL CLOTTING

! GREEN TEA CONTAINS CAFFEINE

Green tea is made from the fresh leaves of the tea bush (*Camellia sinensis sp.*). However, unlike the black tea made from the same plant, green tea is unfermented and does not contain the tannins and polyphenolic compounds that inhibit absorption of micronutrients such as iron.

RECIPES *green tea with mint (page 129), heart chai (page 129)*

MISO

★ VITAMINS B2, B3, FOLATE; CALCIUM, MAGNESIUM, PHOSPHORUS; COPPER, IRON, ZINC

✓ ANTIOXIDANT, HEALING, LOWERS BLOOD FATS

Miso is a paste made from fermented soy beans. It can be used as the basis of stews, soups, marinades, and sauces. There are several different types, each with a different degree of sweetness and saltiness. It helps keep heart, nerves, and muscles healthy, aids liver and red blood cell function, and regulates blood-fat levels.

RECIPES *shiitake mushroom soup (page 105)*

OYSTER MUSHROOM

★ VITAMINS B2, B12; MAGNESIUM, MANGANESE, PHOSPHORUS; IRON, SELENIUM

✓ ANTIOXIDANT

♡ ADD SOY SAUCE TO ENHANCE FLAVOR

Oyster mushroom (*Pleurotus ostreatus*) enables the body to make full use of the energy stored in the tissues, and helps red blood cells to function properly. It aids liver function, and may help protect against heart disease, cancer, and rheumatism.

RECIPES *use in recipes in place of shiitake or button mushrooms*

POLENTA

★ VITAMINS B1, B3; MAGNESIUM, PHOSPHORUS; IRON, ZINC; COMPLEX
CARBOHYDRATES, FIBER, OMEGA-6 FATTY ACIDS, PROTEIN

✓ ANTIOXIDANT, ENERGY-RICH

Polenta is an important energy-rich, savory, course-ground cornmeal that boosts the body's natural healing capacity. It can taste rather bland on its own, but is an excellent accompaniment to many Mediterranean dishes and a familiar ingredient in Italian country cooking. It is particularly popular as polenta cakes. To make, add boiling water, *herbes de Provence*, sea salt and pepper to pre-cooked polenta to form a stiff dough. Shape the dough into small rissoles and fry in olive oil until golden brown.

RECIPES serve as an accompaniment in place of potatoes or rice

SAFFLOWER AND SUNFLOWER OILS

★ VITAMIN E; PHYTOSTEROLS; OMEGA-6 FATTY ACIDS

✓ ANTIOXIDANT, IMMUNO-STIMULANT

Safflower (*Carthamus tinctorius*) and sunflower (*Helianthus annuus*) oils enhance the body's ability to react to injury and repair tissue damage. The omega-6 fatty acids and vitamin E they contain are important for healthy cell membranes, and help ensure normal blood clotting. They also have a beneficial influence on blood pressure, and help lower blood-cholesterol levels.

RECIPES safflower oil: tropical sunshine salad (page 121), baked beet salad (page 37); sunflower oil: samosa parcels (page 108), hasselbach potatoes (page 118), carrot 'n' beet salad (page 119), raspberry gateau (page 122), filled avocados (page 53)

SEA VEGETABLE (HIJIKI, IZIKI)

★ VITAMINS A, B12; CALCIUM, MAGNESIUM, PHOSPHORUS; COPPER,
IODINE, IRON, ZINC; FIBER

✓ ANTIOXIDANT, IMMUNO-STIMULANT

♀ IODINE IN THE DIET PROTECTS AGAINST THE ABSORPTION OF
RADIOACTIVE IODINE FROM THE ENVIRONMENT

Most of the iodine in the body is found in the thyroid gland. It is an essential component of thyroid hormones, which influence nearly all biochemical reactions in the body and regulate growth, metabolic rate, and tissue health. The most reliable sources of iodine in the diet come from the sea, and one of the easiest to use (and most tasty) of the edible seaweeds is sea vegetable (also known as hijiki or iziki).

RECIPES shiitake with sea vegetable (iziki) (page 75)

SUN-DRIED TOMATO

★ VITAMINS A, E; POTASSIUM; COPPER, IODINE, IRON, ZINC;
LYCOPENE; ESSENTIAL FATTY ACIDS, PROTEIN, SUGARS

✓ ANTI-CANCER, ANTIOXIDANT

Sun-dried tomatoes (*Lycopersicon esculentum*) promote the health of all body cells (especially the nerves, muscles, skin, and mucous membranes). They help prevent the formation of cancer cells and protect against heart disease.

RECIPES corn and sun-dried tomato salad (page 120), brazil nuts and sun-dried tomatoes with beans (page 57)

VEGETABLE MARGARINE

★ VITAMIN E; PHYTOSTEROLS; ESSENTIAL FATTY ACIDS

✓ ANTIOXIDANT, LOWERS BLOOD PRESSURE, LOWERS CHOLESTEROL

! CHOOSE UNSATURATED, NON-HYDROGENATED PLANT MARGARINES

Like the oils it is made from, vegetable margarine helps keep cell membranes healthy, lowers blood cholesterol, and has a beneficial influence on blood pressure.

RECIPES scrambled tofu (page 102), welsh leek and potato soup (page 106), french onion tart (page 115), pear tart (page 123)

WHEATGERM OIL

★ VITAMIN E; PHYTOSTEROLS; OMEGA-3 AND -6 FATTY ACIDS

✓ ANTIOXIDANT, HEALING

Wheatgerm (*Triticum sp.*) oil increases the efficiency of the immune response and helps to prevent the immune system from over-reacting to allergens. It increases the health of all cell membranes and may protect against heart disease and cancer. It is also good for skin problems and rheumatoid arthritis.

RECIPES use in salad dressings, and as a replacement for butter or margarine on vegetables

YEAST EXTRACT

★ VITAMINS B1, B2, B3, B6, B12, FOLATE; CALCIUM, MAGNESIUM,
PHOSPHORUS, POTASSIUM; IODINE, IRON, ZINC

! SOME YEAST EXTRACTS ARE HIGH IN SALT

Yeast extract is a concentrated source of minerals and vitamins, particularly B vitamins. It can help the body to maintain optimum energy levels and improve the health of the blood, bone marrow, nervous system, skin, muscles, mucous membranes, and heart. It can be spread on bread or added to soups and stews.

RECIPES italian butterbean soup (page 105)

shiitake mushroom

DELICIOUS AND NUTRITIOUS, SHIITAKE MUSHROOMS HAVE LONG BEEN PRIZED IN THE EAST FOR THEIR ABILITY TO COMBAT INFECTION AND PROTECT AGAINST HEART DISEASE. NOW THE WEST IS DISCOVERING THE AMAZING PROPERTIES OF THIS "FOOD OF EMPERORS."

The origin of shiitake

Shiitake mushrooms (*Lentinus edodus*) are native to Japan, China, and Korea. Shiitake has a long history of medicinal use in the East, useful in the prevention and treatment of infectious diseases and gastro-intestinal problems, and as a remedy to improve circulation and increase vitality. In China, shiitake mushrooms were once reserved for the emperor and his family. Today, shiitake is one of the most widely produced edible mushrooms in the world.

Immune-boosting properties

As well as being delicious, shiitake mushrooms are an excellent source of immune-boosting minerals and vitamins, essential amino acids, and enzymes. Recent scientific research has concentrated on shiitake's immune-stimulating properties, but Japanese studies have long confirmed its beneficial properties against other common health problems such as atherosclerosis and cancer. Shiitake's ability to stimulate resistance to disease and enhance the immune response is thought to be owing to the fact that the fungus causes the release of interferon and, at the same time, increases the number of

macrophages in the blood, enhances phagocytosis, and increases the activity and number of blood lymphocytes. (Lymphocytes and macrophages are two of the most important blood cell types involved in immunity—see page 16.) This combination of actions means that shiitake strengthens the body's first line of defense against infection, by encouraging blood cells to destroy harmful organisms and share information about them with the rest of the immune system, and to clear up cellular debris and waste. In particular, eating shiitake increases resistance to viral infection.

Shiitake's powerful stimulation of immune reaction has kindled interest in the West because of its potential use in the treatment of H.I.V. infections and A.I.D.S. Research suggests that shiitake increases resistance to H.I.V. by blocking initial stages of infection. It is also active against viral encephalitis infection.

The polysaccharide compound lentinan contained in shiitake has a lowering effect on blood pressure and blood cholesterol, and is beneficial to the whole cardiovascular system, making shiitake a useful remedy in the prevention and treatment of heart disease. It has also attracted considerable attention for its strong tendency to inhibit the growth of tumor cells, and to prevent the spread of metastases (secondaries). However, rather than attacking tumors directly, it works by stimulating the immune system, and boosting the body's own ability to deactivate and eliminate malignant cells.

Shiitake mushrooms are more expensive than the common white field mushrooms, but also very filling—so you need fewer of them in meals. They are widely available, and can be bought fresh, dried, or pickled. Fresh or pickled shiitake are prepared and eaten in the same way as white mushrooms. However, dried mushrooms should be rinsed and then soaked for half an hour before use. The stems are hard and should be removed before cooking.

IMMUNE-BOOSTING PROFILE

★ VITAMINS B1, B2, B3; MAGNESIUM, PHOSPHORUS, POTASSIUM; IRON; BIO-ACTIVE ENZYMES; LENTINAN (POLYSACCHARIDE), PROTEIN

✓ ANTIBACTERIAL, ANTI-CANCER, ANTIVIRAL, LOWERS CHOLESTEROL, IMMUNO-STIMULANT

! SHIITAKE MAY CAUSE DIARRHEA IF EATEN IN LARGE QUANTITIES

shiitake with sea vegetable *(above)*

½ cup dried sea vegetable (iziki)
1 bunch of scallions
3 tbsp olive oil
8 oz fresh shiitake mushrooms, cut into strips

4 oz asparagus
4 carrots, cut into julienne strips
1 cup basic vegetable bouillon
1 tbsp dry sherry
2 tbsp soy sauce
2 tbsp toasted sesame seeds

Rinse the iziki, soak in warm water for 30 minutes, then rinse again. Finely chop the scallions. Heat the oil in a wok, add the iziki, then the mushrooms, asparagus, carrots, and scallions. Stir-fry for a few minutes, then add the bouillon, sherry and soy sauce. Simmer gently for 10 minutes. Season to taste. Top with toasted sesame seeds.

shiitake salad

9 oz smoked tofu, cubed
3 tbsp olive oil
8 oz fresh shiitake
2 tbsp fresh tarragon, finely chopped

1 tbsp lime juice
Salt and pepper to taste
1 little gem lettuce
1 handful arugula
1 handful sorrel leaves

Stir-fry the tofu in oil for a few minutes. Add the shiitake; fry till tender. Add tarragon and lime juice; season. Serve on a bed of green leaves.

pasta, pesto, and shiitake

14 oz pasta spirals
4 carrots, finely chopped
Kernels of 2 corn cobs
4 tbsp green peas
10 oz fresh shiitake
1 tsp soy sauce
4 tbsp lemon juice

For the pesto:

4 tbsp pine nuts, ground
2 garlic cloves, crushed
1 bunch fresh basil, chopped
1 tsp coarse sea salt
4 tbsp olive oil

Mix the pesto ingredients and set aside. Cook the pasta in salted water and a splash of oil. After 5 minutes, add the carrots, kernels and peas and cook for 2 more minutes. Drain, place in a bowl and mix in the pesto. Fry the shiitake (halved) until golden; add a little soy sauce as you turn off the heat. Add the mushrooms to the bowl and mix. Sprinkle with lemon juice and freshly ground black pepper.

coping with
common ailments

Making the right food choices not only keeps your immune system in tip-top condition but also helps you target specific diseases. The following pages feature some of the common ailments that can develop when the immune system is operating below par, and the steps you can take to avoid or manage such disorders. There is advice on which superfoods to include in your meals, along with page references directing you to mouthwatering recipes that present these foods at their best. There is also advice on problematic products you should avoid, and other simple ways to ensure your immune system is ready for anything that the modern world might have in store.

colds & influenza

SUPERFOODS FOR COLDS AND INFLUENZA: BLACK MUSTARD, CARROT, CATNIP, CAYENNE, ECHINACEA, ELDERBERRY AND FLOWER, FLAXSEED, GARLIC, GINGER, GRAPEFRUIT, GREEN LEAVES, GUAVA, HORSERADISH, LEMON, MELON SEED, NASTURTIUM, NUTS, ONION, ORANGE, PEPPERMINT, ROSEHIP, SUNFLOWER SEED, SWEET POTATO, WILD MARJORAM, YARROW

Cold and influenza (flu) are viral infections. Both cause runny nose, sore throat, headache, fever, and general malaise. Cold symptoms are usually mild at first and develop relatively slowly. In contrast, flu symptoms start abruptly and include aching joints and limbs, high fever, shivering, severe headache, and often persistent dry cough. Most flu symptoms last only a few days, but a cough may persist, and depression, lethargy, and tiredness often follow and may be long-lasting. Influenza can be accompanied by secondary bacterial infections, such as bronchitis or pneumonia (especially among the elderly), that take advantage of the body's weakened state.

Prevention

We are constantly surrounded by cold viruses, but if your immune system is strong you are less likely to catch a cold. To strengthen your resistance to colds and flu, ensure good nutrition, manage your stress levels, and try to avoid alcohol, tobacco, recreational drugs, chemicals, excess sugar intake, high levels of dietary cholesterol and other fats, dehydration, or over-exposure to hot

or cold. Flu is highly infectious and usually occurs in epidemics that peak in winter. Flu vaccination is only partially effective since the vaccine does not give resistance to all possible strains of the virus. Adverse reactions to the vaccine are common.

Management

Support the body and let the infection take its course rather than suppressing symptoms that show that the body's defenses are at work. The best treatment in the acute phase is sleep and rest, eating very little and drinking lots of liquid in the form of water, weak herbal tea, and soup.

Good hydration creates a less favorable environment for the virus while improving the function of the immune system. Because of their natural sugar content, fruit juices and sweetened drinks are not beneficial once the disease gets hold, but thanks to their high antioxidant content, fruit juices are excellent cold and influenza preventives. Dairy products are "mucus forming" and should be avoided altogether.

SUGGESTED RECIPES FOR COLDS AND INFLUENZA

Sunrise—left (page 127), tea for fever (page 131), cough mixture (page 128), syrup of onion—make in the same way as garlic oxymel (page 129), lung-cleansing tea mix (page 130), cold buster (page 128), eucalyptus mix (page 129), immuni-tea (page 129), si c (page 130), sage mix for sore throats (page 130), tea for headache (page 131), cool tomato soup (page 104), healing soup (page 104), mint and melon soup (page 105), shiitake mushroom soup (page 105), spicy moroccan soup (page 106).

Cold remedy (tea mixture): Infuse 1 tsp each of elderflowers and chamomile flowers in ½ pint of boiling water for 10 minutes; drink hot.

ear, nose, & throat infections

SUPERFOODS FOR E.N.T. INFECTIONS: ADUKI BEAN, ASPARAGUS, BEET, BILBERRY, BLACKBERRY, CALENDULA, CARROT, CHERRY, CLEAVERS, CURLY KALE, ECHINACEA, ELDERFLOWER, EUCALYPTUS, GARBANZOS, GARLIC, GRAPE, GRAPEFRUIT, GREEN LEAVES, GUAVA, HORSERADISH, LEEK, LEMON, MANGO, MUESLI, ONION, PEPPERMINT, PUMPKIN, SAGE, SHIITAKE, SPRING GREENS, TAHINI, TEMPEH

The ear, nose, and throat are closely linked by a labyrinth of tubes and passages. This allows infection to spread quickly from one to another. Common ear, nose, and throat (E.N.T.) disorders include middle ear and throat infections (including tonsillitis) and sinusitis.

Middle ear infection is especially common in children and often follows colds, flu, tonsillitis, or childhood fevers. It can lead to a build-up of fluid that puts pressure on the eardrum, causing severe earache. The eardrum may perforate, which relieves pressure and pain. Recurrent middle ear infection can lead to otitis media ("glue ear"), a chronic condition causing deafness and learning difficulties.

Sinusitis is inflammation of the cavities in the bones around the nose, causing headache, facial pain, and stuffy nose. It is a common complication of colds and flu, and may also be caused by allergy, injury, tooth infection, or poor drainage of the sinuses.

Throat infection can be viral or bacterial, and cause fever, malaise, sore throat, and difficulty swallowing associated with inflammation of the lymphoid tissues (tonsils and adenoids) at the back of the throat. Swollen adenoids can cause difficulty breathing, and a tendency to repeated ear or upper respiratory tract infection.

Prevention

The best way to prevent ear, nose, and throat infections is to strengthen the immune system by eating lots of vegetables and fruit—particularly those high in vitamins A and C, bioflavonoids, and zinc. Avoid common allergens, such as dairy foods (including cow's milk in baby formulas), eggs, shellfish, wheat, and peanut butter. Avoid repeated upper respiratory tract infections by following the guidelines on page 78. If you do catch a cold or suffer a bout of influenza, take plenty of time to convalesce after the symptoms subside, and do not go out and about too early.

Management

Seek professional help in cases of suspected middle ear infection or if a nose or throat disorder leads to breathing difficulties. Drink lots of fluids (water, herb tea, diluted vegetable juices, and soups). Get plenty of rest, including bed rest if necessary. Avoid suspected allergens and concentrated sources of sugar such as dried fruit, honey, syrups, and concentrated fruit juice. Gentle facial massage helps alleviate sinusitis. Herbal gargles can ease throat infections.

SUGGESTED RECIPES FOR E.N.T. INFECTIONS

Ear infections: beet and apple (page 124), green party (page 124), shiitake mushroom soup (page 105), tea for ear infections (page 131), cold buster (page 128), green leafy salad (page 41).

Sinusitis: elderflower spritzer (page 128), carrot and lemon with garlic (page 124), beet and horseradish salad (page 37), eucalyptus mix (page 129), curly kale, tomato and fava beans (page 41), spiced nettle soup (page 45).

Throat infection: sage mix for sore throats (page 130), tea for glands (page 131), pumpkin soup (page 105), welsh leek and potato soup (page 106), mint and melon soup (page 105), garlic oxymel (page 129), cool cucumber (page 124), si c (page 130).

Sinusitis remedy (horseradish poultice): Grate fresh horseradish root into a portion of oatmeal, wrap the mixture in a tea towel and place the compress over the nose, cheeks, and forehead (taking care to avoid the eyes).

childhood fevers

SUPERFOODS FOR CHILDHOOD FEVERS: BLACK MUSTARD, BORAGE, CARROT, CATNIP, CAYENNE, ECHINACEA, ELDERBERRY AND FLOWER, GARLIC, GINGER, GRAINS, GRAPEFRUIT, GREEN LEAVES, GUAVA, HORSERADISH, LEMON, NUTS, ONION, ORANGE, PEPPERMINT, ROSEHIP, SEEDS, STRAWBERRY, SWEET POTATO, WILD MARJORAM, YARROW

Childhood fevers are common, especially those arising from colds and other simple upper respiratory tract infections. They are part of the immune system's natural development and should be managed rather than suppressed. While most childhood fevers resolve quickly, it is vital to exclude serious disorders such as meningitis, so never hesitate to seek medical help in cases of high fever, or if you are worried about a child's condition.

The diseases chickenpox, rubella (German measles), measles, mumps, and whooping cough are also common causes of fever in childhood. Chickenpox causes sore throat, headache, and rash. Rubella causes runny nose, sore throat, swollen lymph nodes (glands), rash, and sometimes joint pain. (Rubella infection in pregnancy may lead to birth-defects.) Measles causes sore eyes, runny nose, dry cough, white spots in the mouth, and rash. It may be complicated by middle ear infection, bronchitis, pneumonia, or, less commonly, febrile convulsions (fits). Mumps causes sore throat and painful swelling of the salivary glands. Whooping cough causes distressing bouts of coughing.

Prevention

A healthy diet aids the proper development and functioning of the immune system and is the mainstay of prevention of childhood fevers. Encourage your children to eat fresh and dried fruit, carrot and cucumber sticks, grapes, tomatoes, grains, nuts, and seeds, and restrict the availability of candies, sodas, burgers, and other junk foods. Give children the chance to eat organic foods whenever possible.

Management

During the acute phase of the fever, bed rest, tender loving care, and plenty of fluids (water and weak herbal teas) are the most important steps. When the child's appetite starts to return, offer freshly prepared juices (diluted with water). During convalescence, fruit salads and soups are beneficial, and children love pasta dishes, Scandinavian beet burgers (page 37), and fruity pancakes (page 103). Avoid sugar, dairy produce, and junk foods, as well as common allergens (wheat, eggs, peanut butter, additives).

SUGGESTED RECIPES FOR CHILDHOOD FEVERS

Si c—left (page 130), tea for fever (page 131), cough mixture (page 128), caribbean smoothie (page 124), cool cucumber (page 124), creamy mango (page 124), apricot and ginger (page 124), blackberry cream (page 124), nirvana (page 127), pink pineapple (page 127), soft tutti fruity (page 127), fresh fruit salad (page 102), tropical fruit salad (page 123), yogurt with fruit (page 103), fruity pancakes (page 103), mint and melon soup (page 105), tibetan dumpling soup (page 106), black-eye pea and wild marjoram soup (page 105), italian butterbean soup (page 105), scandinavian beet burgers (page 37), pasta, pesto, and shiitake (page 75), raspberry gateau (page 122).

bronchitis

SUPERFOODS FOR BRONCHITIS: ADUKI BEAN, AMARANTH LEAVES, ASPARAGUS, BLACK CURRANT, BUTTERNUT SQUASH, CARROT, CHERRY, CLEAVERS, CURLY KALE, ELDERFLOWER, GARBANZOS, GARLIC, GRAPEFRUIT, GRAPE, GREEN LEAVES, GUAVA, HORSERADISH, LEEK, LEMON, LENTILS, MANGO, MUESLI, NASTURTIUM, ONION, SPRING GREENS, SWEET POTATO, TAHINI, THYME, TOFU, SWEET VIOLET, YARROW

Bronchitis is inflammation of the lining of the bronchial tubes in the lungs. The acute form of bronchitis is usually caused by a viral or bacterial infection and often follows a bout of cold or influenza. The symptoms are cough (initially harsh and dry, later with yellow or green sputum), shortness of breath and fever. Pneumonia is a potentially serious complication of bronchitis, and is particularly dangerous for elderly people. Chronic bronchitis causes persistent or recurrent cough and breathing difficulties, and is most common in people with lowered immune function, particularly smokers, drug and alcohol abusers, patients taking immuno-suppressive drugs, and those suffering immunodeficiency disorders and cancer. Chronic bronchitis goes hand in hand with structural damage within the lungs called emphysema, which decreases the amount of lung tissue available to absorb oxygen and get rid of carbon dioxide and other waste products. The lungs also develop a rough, thickened lining making breathing very difficult.

Prevention

The most important step you can take to avoid chronic bronchitis is to quit smoking—or not start in the first place! Keep your weight within optimum limits and eat plenty of foods rich in vitamins A and C, and bioflavonoids and zinc to enhance your immune function. Avoid noxious fumes and immuno-suppressive drugs wherever possible, and breathe fresh air every day. Avoid eating dairy products, which encourage the production of excess mucus.

Management

Drink large amounts of fluid (water, herbal tea, juice, soup), and drink juices rich in vitamin C—the immune system needs a lot of this nutrient when fighting infection. Garlic, onion, and leek have natural antibacterial properties and help avoid the development of complications such as pneumonia. Limit your sugar consumption, particularly added sugar, candies, sodas, and concentrated fruit juices, and cut out dairy products altogether. Try to avoid suppressing the cough. Herbal expectorants make the cough more "productive" and make it easier to get rid of excess mucus from the airways. A warm poultice (see below) applied to the chest eases breathing. Rest is important but avoid lying flat in bed, which may make breathing more difficult and exacerbate the cough. Use extra pillows or a bolster to prop up your head and upper body.

SUGGESTED RECIPES FOR BRONCHITIS

Si c (page 130), blackberry cream (page 124), carrot and lemon with garlic (page 124), cold buster (page 128), lung-cleansing tea mix (page 130), tea for fever (page 131), yogurt with fruit (page 103), provençal mesclun salad (page 119), tropical sunshine salad (page 121), green leafy salad (page 41), spicy moroccan soup (page 106), amaranth and tofu puffs (page 112), garlic oxymel (page 129).

Cough mixture: Pour 1 cup of boiling water over 2–3 tsp flaxseeds and leave to infuse for 10 to 15 minutes.

Inhalation: Add 1 tbsp each of chamomile, thyme, eucalyptus and wild marjoram to 1 pint of boiling water and infuse for 5 minutes, covered. Wrap a blanket around you and put a big towel over your head. Take the lid off the infusion and gently inhale the steam for about ten minutes. Afterwards, splash your face with cool water.

Mustard poultice: Mix 5 tsp crushed black mustard seeds with a large portion of hot oatmeal. Wrap the mixture in a tea towel and place this on the chest for 20 minutes; make sure it is not so hot as to cause discomfort, and check from time to time that the mustard is not causing skin irritation.

cystitis

SUPERFOODS FOR CYSTITIS: ADUKI BEAN, ASPARAGUS, BELL PEPPER, BLACKBERRY, BLACK CURRANT, BRUSSELS SPROUT, BUTTERNUT SQUASH, CARROT, CELERY SEED, CHERRY, CLEAVERS, CRANBERRY, CURLY KALE, EUCALYPTUS, GARBANZOS, GARLIC, GRAPE, GREEN LEAVES, GUAVA, HORSERADISH, LENTIL, MANGO, MUESLI, NETTLE, PASTA, RICE, SPRING GREENS, SWEET POTATO, TAHINI, TEMPEH, YARROW

Cystitis is inflammation of the bladder, most often caused by an infection. The disorder triggers various symptoms including lower abdominal pain, painful and frequent urination, a feeling of urgency to urinate and that the bladder is never completely empty. The urine smells fishy and looks cloudy (maybe with traces of blood).

Cystitis is more common in women than in men (probably because the urethra—the tube that carries urine out of the body—is shorter in women and close to the openings of the vagina and anus, making infection more likely). Cystitis is often associated with pregnancy, sex, sensitivity to cold, and mechanical injury (such as catheterization, a medical procedure).

Classical cystitis is caused by bacterial infection, but other organisms, such as chlamydia, are frequently involved. However, many people suffer recurrent symptoms of cystitis without any obvious infective cause, and are given a diagnosis of "urethral syndrome." Some cases of urethral syndrome can be explained by an allergy or sensitivity to materials such as nylon, washing powder, soaps, and bubble baths. In bacterial cystitis, serious complications can occur if the infection spreads to the kidneys including acute glomerulonephritis (the symptoms of which are severe malaise, high fever, and intense back pain), and chronic reflux nephropathy, which can cause permanent kidney damage.

Prevention

Eat plenty of fresh foods, mainly of plant origin, and avoid eating too much sugar or drinking too much alcohol or coffee. Keep your meat and dairy intake to a minimum, and avoid junk food and food additives altogether. Include foods that contain plenty of vitamins A and C, and bioflavonoids and zinc. Garlic has natural antibiotic properties and helps the body to deal with urinary-tract infections. In severe cases, try the detox diet on page 132.

Above all, avoid dehydration and get plenty of rest. Replace coffee and tea with lots of fresh juices, smoothies, herbal teas, and water. Avoid acidic foods and drinks (including citrus fruits). Pay attention to personal hygiene, and make sure that you are not allergic to the soaps or soap powders you are using. Avoid douches and intimate deodorants, because they may disrupt the natural bacterial flora and allow harmful micro-organisms to flourish. If you have a tendency to cystitis, it is also important to empty your bladder and wash your genitals before and after sex.

Management

Cranberry juice can be a highly effective treatment for cystitis. Otherwise, the conventional treatment for cystitis is a course of antibiotics together with high fluid intake, regular bladder emptying, and scrupulous hygiene. However, many cases do not respond to this regimen, and repeated or long-term use of antibiotics can bring other problems (such as candidiasis and disturbance of intestinal flora). If you do take antibiotics it is important to allow the body to rebuild its natural defenses afterward. Live yogurt helps the bowel to recolonize with beneficial micro-organisms. Antioxidants including vitamins A, C, and E, and zinc, selenium, and bioflavonoids help to restore immune function.

SUGGESTED RECIPES FOR CYSTITIS

Cystitis relief (page 128), cranberry spritzer (page 124), asparagus with ravigote (page 106), asparagus asian-style (page 113), catalan salad (page 120), pasta salad (page 120), beet and horseradish salad (page 37), swiss chard and juniper berries (page 119), immuni-tea (page 129), nettle and sweet potato mash (page 45), korean kimchi-style salad (page 107), tzaziki (page 111), mushrooms with sage and thyme stuffing (page 116), pasta, pesto, and shiitake (page 75), vegetable cocktail (page 127), yogurt with fruit (page 103), avocado smoothie (page 53).

fungal infections

SUPERFOODS FOR FUNGAL INFECTIONS: ADUKI BEAN, AVOCADO, BRAZIL NUT, BUTTERNUT SQUASH, CALENDULA, CARROT, CHAMOMILE, CINNAMON, COCONUT, CURLY KALE, ENDIVE, EUCALYPTUS, FAVA BEAN, GARLIC, GINGER, GRAPEFRUIT, LEEK, LEMON BALM, LENTIL, LIVE SOY YOGURT, PAPAYA, PINTO BEAN, PSYLLIUM SEED, PUMPKIN, RICE, ROSEMARY, SPINACH, SPRING GREENS, SWISS CHARD, THYME, TOFU

Common fungal infections include candidiasis or "thrush" (yeast infection caused by *Candida albicans*); athlete's foot (*Tinea pedis*); and ringworm (*Tinea corporis*). There are two forms of candidiasis—oral and vaginal. Oral thrush produces thin, white, moist, cottage-cheesy plaques inside the mouth, which rub off to leave red, sore patches. It mainly affects sick babies, the immuno-compromized and the elderly. Vaginal thrush causes abnormal vaginal discharge, irritation, and soreness. In managing the disease it is important to treat sexual partners to avoid a cycle of re-infection. Candida is a common yeast that forms part of our normal gut flora. Drugs (particularly antibiotics and steroids), stress, and poor diet can lead to candida overgrowth that affects absorption of nutrients as well as general health, and can lead to serious illness if it spreads to the rest of the body.

Fungal skin infections affect warm, damp places, such as groin creases, and produce clearly demarcated, moist, itchy dark red patches with a few smaller lesions scattered around. Infected finger nails appear thick and brownish. Ringworm appears as a scaly, red patch that enlarges and becomes a raised, scaly circle with a pale center. It looks as though it has been caused by a burrowing worm, hence the name. It may spread and form more circles, and can cause bald patches if it affects the scalp. Athlete's foot often develops between the fourth and fifth toes with the skin becoming itchy, pale, damp, flaky, cracked, and mushy.

Prevention and management

Factors that suppress immunity can increase the risk of fungal infections. These include a diet high in sugar and saturated fat, drugs (antibiotics, steroids, chemotherapy, oral contraceptives, anti-ulcer medication), environmental chemicals, alcohol, and stress. Avoiding these is the mainstay of prevention. Papaya contains enzymes that can inhibit yeast proliferation. Cut down on dairy products and, if you have to take antibiotics, eat live yogurt to help restore a healthy balance of intestinal flora. To manage fungal infection, take plenty of rest and limit your consumption of foods containing yeast (such as bread and yeast extract) and fermented foods (such as cheese, tempeh, and vinegar). Avoid known food allergens, alcohol, dairy products, and foods high in refined sugar, such as sucrose, fructose, syrup, fruit juice, honey, and dried fruits. Take a teaspoon of psyllium seeds in a glass of water after meals.

SUGGESTED RECIPES FOR FUNGAL INFECTIONS

Carrot and lemon with garlic—above (page 124), tea for fungal infections (page 131), green leafy salad (page 41), eucalyptus mix (page 129), calming tea (page 128), guacamole (page 110), chinese salad (page 120), apricot and ginger (page 124), stuffed grapefruit (page 49), avocado smoothie (page 53), korean kimchi-style salad (page 107), spicy chai (page 130), khichuri—rice with lentils (page 117), spicy brazil nut pâté (page 57), stress relief (page 130), scrambled tofu (page 102), beet and horseradish (page 37), tzaziki (page 111).

herpes simplex

SUPERFOODS FOR HERPES SIMPLEX: ADUKI BEAN, AVOCADO, BEET, BRAZIL NUT, CALENDULA, CARROT, GARBANZOS, GARLIC, HAZELNUT, LEMON BALM, LENTIL, LICORICE ROOT, MACADAMIA NUT, MUESLI, PINE NUT, PUMPKIN SEED, SHIITAKE, SPINACH, ST. JOHN'S WORT, SUN-DRIED TOMATO, SAFFLOWER AND SUNFLOWER OILS, SWEET POTATO, TEMPEH, TOFU, TOMATO, WALNUT, WHEATGERM, YAM

Herpes simplex is a virus that causes blisters on skin and mucous membranes known as cold sores. The sores commonly appear on the face, fingers, mouth, lips, and genitals, and are often accompanied by swollen lymph nodes, itching, stinging pain, fatigue, and fever. The virus is transmitted through direct contact with an active cold sore, for example via saliva or sexual fluids.

After the initial infection, the virus lies dormant and may remain unnoticed for long periods of time, until the body's resistance is lowered by colds (hence the name) and other infections, stress, trauma, menstruation, or exposure to sun. Cold sores recur near or at the primary site of infection whenever the body is feeling run down. Infection lasts for one or two weeks. Men are generally more prone to cold sores than women.

Herpes simplex infection is a common cause of genital ulcers, but it is important to exclude other, more serious causes such as syphilis and lymphoma. Genital cold sores are also associated with an increased risk of developing cervical dysplasia (abnormal changes in cervical cells that may be a prelude to cancer). However, it is unclear whether the herpes virus is a direct cause of the condition or simply a symptom of a run-down immune response failing to keep cell changes in check.

Prevention

The best way to avoid infection is to avoid direct contact with active cold sores. The likelihood of infections and the frequency of recurrence are both reduced by maintaining good general health. Resistance to infection depends on having a strong immune system, which in turn depends on good nutrition and having sufficient rest, fresh air, and exercise. People suffering from immunodeficiency syndromes, or whose immunity is suppressed by drugs, stress, poor nutrition, or chronic disease, are at greater risk of infection. People with eczema are also more susceptible to cold sores and other viral skin conditions.

Management

Eat foods containing vitamins A and C, and bioflavonoids and carotenoids, which all enhance resistance and inhibit viral attack. Foods rich in zinc reduce the time it takes for sores to heal. Vitamin E-rich foods speed up healing and help reduce pain. Foods with anti-viral properties, such as shiitake, garlic, lemon balm, calendula (marigold), St. John's wort, spinach, sweet potato, tempeh, yam, and tomato should also be included in the diet. Following a detox diet (see page 132) is a good way to help the body avoid recurring cold sores. Managing stress, avoiding exposure to allergens and limiting refined carbohydrate intake are also important factors.

Carrot, beet, licorice root, and lemon balm are all efficient anti-cold-sore remedies. Licorice root reduces the cell damage caused by herpes simplex infection, and inhibits the growth of the sores. A tisane made of licorice root and lemon balm may decrease the severity and duration of an outbreak if taken regularly (3–4 cups per day) as soon as the first signs of a sore appear. However, licorice causes an increase in the rate at which potassium is eliminated from the body. So, when taking licorice, you should also include in your diet plenty of foods that are high in potassium, such as banana, avocado, sweet potato, dried apricot, beans and peas, and green leaves.

SUGGESTED RECIPES FOR HERPES SIMPLEX

Calming tea (page 128), carrot 'n' beet salad (page 119), muesli (page 103), oatmeal with dried fruit and quinoa (page 102), blackberry crumble (page 123), pick-me-up (page 130), winter hot pot (page 116), shiitake salad (page 75), tofumasalata (page 108), pan amb oli (page 111), tea for glands (page 131), green leafy salad (page 41), oriental salad with tempeh (page 63), sweet potato curry (page 116).

eczema

SUPERFOODS FOR ECZEMA: ASPARAGUS, BEANS, BELL PEPPER, BILBERRY, BUTTERNUT SQUASH, CHAMOMILE, CARROT, CLEAVERS, CURLY KALE, ECHINACEA, ELDERBERRY, EVENING PRIMROSE OIL, FLAXSEED, GRAPEFRUIT, GRAPES, HAWTHORN, LENTILS, MANGO, NETTLE, PEAS, PINE NUTS, PUMPKIN SEED, SPINACH, SUNFLOWER OIL AND SEED, SWEET POTATO, SWISS CHARD, TEMPEH, TOFU, VIOLET, WALNUT OIL

Eczema (also called dermatitis) is a very common skin condition characterized by red, itchy, weeping skin patches, which are prone to infection. As time goes by, the skin becomes progressively harder, drier, and more brittle because of repeated scratching.

Atopic eczema causes an itchy, sometimes weeping and scaly rash on the face, and in body creases. It is common in infants and tends to run in families—two-thirds of eczema sufferers have a family member with the condition, and many also develop hay fever and/or asthma. There is also an increased susceptibility to skin infections, including cold sores and warts. Seborrheic eczema causes a crusty rash on hairy skin—especially in the armpits and groin creases and on the face in men. When it occurs on the scalp in babies it is called "cradle cap."

Irritant eczema is caused by direct contact with strong chemicals and usually develops within 24 hours of initial exposure. It causes redness, blisters, and cracks in the skin, but does not spread beyond the area exposed to the irritant. Allergic contact dermatitis develops after a second exposure to an allergen such as lanolin, skin cream additives, antibiotic ointments, and nickel in jewelery or buttons. The rash is most prominent over the area of initial contact, but can spread all over the body.

Prevention

Food allergy is a common cause of eczema, and dairy products are the most likely culprits. Stress is also a common factor, and tension can provoke itching. Identifying and eliminating allergens, and dealing with stress, are thus the mainstays of prevention.

Management

It is necessary to eliminate known food allergens. Animal fats and dairy products should be limited in the diet until symptoms subside. Deficiency of essential fatty acids is sometimes a factor in the development of eczema and can be avoided by eating more polyunsaturated oil. Walnut oil is particularly useful because it is both anti-inflammatory and anti-allergic. Evening primrose oil, sunflower oil and seeds, and flaxseed also help dampen inflammation. Foods containing bioflavonoids are important for controlling inflammation and allergic reactions and enhance the action of vitamin C. Foods containing high levels of zinc and vitamin A are excellent for skin healing and repair.

SUGGESTED REMEDIES FOR ECZEMA

Licorice mix (page 130), natural beauty (page 126), tea for the skin (page 131), calming tea (page 128), toasted nuts and seeds (page 108), tomato and cucumber canapés (page 110), asparagus asian-style (page 113), fresh fruit salad (page 102), tofu balls (page 110), spring greens and macadamia nuts (page 118), spinach bouillabaisse (page 115), orange mango salad (page 120), toasted nuts and seeds (page 108), grapefruit salad (page 49), spicy moroccan soup (page 106), arugula salad (page 119).

Steroid creams and tablets are common orthodox treatments for eczema, but can carry a risk of side effects after prolonged use. Try a calendula (marigold) ointment or make this compress to reduce inflammation. Pour 1 pint of boiling water on to 3 tbsp of calendula flowers. Cover and allow to cool. Strain and use the liquid to soak a compress before placing it on the affected area. Keep the compress moist and leave in place for 1 hour.

Detoxifying herbs such as nettle, cleavers, violet, chamomile, and echinacea aid the digestive system and are an important part of the treatment. Oily ointments can ease discomfort, and barrier creams and gloves can prevent contact with allergens.

psoriasis

SUPERFOODS FOR PSORIASIS: APPLE, AVOCADO, BANANA, BEANS, BEET, BELGIAN ENDIVE, BERRIES, BRAZIL NUT, BROCCOLI, CHAMOMILE, CARROT, CLEAVERS, CURLY KALE, DRIED FRUIT, GLOBE ARTICHOKE, GRAPE, GREEN LEAVES, LENTIL, LICORICE ROOT, MELON, MUSHROOMS, NETTLE, NUTS, OKRA, PAPAYA, PARSNIP, PEAS, PINEAPPLE, PUMPKIN, SPINACH, SQUASH, SWEET POTATO, SUN-DRIED TOMATO, WHEATGRASS

Psoriasis is a relatively common skin condition that tends to run in families. It is characterized by red, silvery, scaly "plaques" of thickened skin, especially on the scalp, and on the outside of the knees and elbows. These are caused by skin cells dividing at a much faster rate than normal. The scaly plaques can be itchy and may join up to cover large areas of skin. Some sufferers also develop arthritis. Problems with protein digestion, impaired liver function, excess alcohol and animal fats, and psychological factors are all thought to be associated with the development of psoriasis.

Prevention and management

Both ultraviolet light (from sunlight) and seawater are beneficial—so relaxing on a sunny beach is an excellent preventive and curative measure. Protein digestion can be enhanced by eating foods containing digestive enzymes and vitamin A, such as papaya and pineapple. Detoxing is also important, and is encouraged by eating plenty of fruits and vegetables, and foods that encourage liver function such as beet, globe artichoke, Belgian endive, turmeric,

and wheatgrass. Foods high in the trace elements chromium and zinc are beneficial. Chromium helps regulate blood-sugar levels and zinc is necessary for skin repair. Foods high in vitamins A, E, folate, and selenium are helpful too. Essential fatty acids found in flaxseed, walnut and walnut oil, fatty fish, and fish oil inhibit production of inflammatory leukotrienes in the skin. However, avoid animal fats, found in dairy products and meat, which contain substances such as arachidonic acid that increase leukotriene production. Avoid alcohol and high-protein foods, limit sugar intake and try excluding gluten (found in wheat, barley, rye, and oats).

Exercise improves circulation and contributes to skin and blood cleansing. Heat therapy in the form of a warm flaxseed poultice on the affected area may help. Mix a portion of crushed seeds with hot water to make a mushy paste. Spread the paste on to folded muslin or a thin flannel. Wrap the material well around the paste to stop it oozing out. Place the poultice on the affected area and cover with a piece of plastic to keep the moisture in. Leave it in place until it no longer feels pleasantly warm.

SUGGESTED RECIPES FOR PSORIASIS

Beet and apple—left (page 124), tea for the skin (page 131), calming tea (page 128), tomato and cucumber canapés (page 110), immuni-tea (page 129), nettle and sweet potato mash (page 45), okra in sweet and sour tamarind sauce (page 116), butternut squash with bell pepper and tomato (page 113), broiled endive and brazil nut salad (page 57), spicy moroccan soup (page 106), spicy brazil nut pâté (page 57), papaya power (page 127), pink pineapple (page 127), arugula salad (page 119), casserole de puy (page 112).

Remedy: Pour a cup of boiling water on to 2 to 3 tsp of flaxseeds; leave to infuse for 10 minutes. Drink a cup morning and evening.

hay fever

SUPERFOODS FOR HAY FEVER: ARTICHOKE, AVOCADO, BEANS, BEET, BELL PEPPER, BERRIES, BROCCOLI, BUTTERNUT SQUASH, CALENDULA, CARROT, CAULIFLOWER, CORN, GREEN TEA, GUAVA, HORSERADISH, LENTIL, MUSTARD CRESS, OKRA, PAPAYA, SEA VEGETABLE, SHIITAKE, SPINACH, SUN-DRIED TOMATO, SWEET POTATO, SWISS CHARD, TEMPEH, VEGETABLE OIL, WHEATGERM OIL, YEAST EXTRACT

Hay fever is an allergic condition that causes inflammation of the mucous membranes lining the nasal cavity. It is often seasonal. Allergy to tree pollen is worst in spring, allergy to grass and weed pollen is worst in the summer, and allergy to molds occurs mainly in the fall. Allergy to dust mites and animal dander tends to be worse in the winter when sufferers spend more time indoors with the windows closed. The tendency to develop hay fever often runs in families. When inhaled antigens come into contact with the mucous membranes of the upper respiratory tract, the immune system releases histamine and other chemicals that cause a variety of unpleasant symptoms. These include runny nose, sneezing, and itchy eyes. It is also common to feel lethargic.

Allergic reactions are much more frequent and severe if you are over-tired, under stress, recovering from infection, or your immune system is compromised. Common food allergens (such as dairy foods) can lower the threshold for developing hay fever symptoms.

Prevention

To prevent attacks, aim to strengthen and detoxify the immune system, and minimize exposure to allergens. It is beneficial to avoid additives, such as colorings and preservatives, and common food allergens including eggs, fish, shellfish, nuts (especially peanuts), dairy products, chocolate, wheat, and citrus fruits. At the same time you should include some of the foods and herbs listed above in your daily diet. For the prevention to be effective, start at least a month before the season that your hay fever symptoms occur.

Management

Eat lots of foods containing vitamins B5, B6, B12 and E, trace elements such as selenium and magnesium, and bioflavonoids and carotenoids. Follow an elimination diet (see page 132) to discover which foods and drinks aggravate your allergy. To strengthen and detoxify your immune system, avoid animal products, coffee, tea, chocolate, and refined sugar, and limit your intake of potatoes and citrus fruits. Consider excluding wheat during the hay fever season.

Keep your house as dust-free as possible. For example, consider having wooden or tiled floors with rugs instead of carpets, which trap dust and animal dander. Exclude pets from bedrooms and main living areas. Wash all bedding regularly, using washing powder or perfume-free washing liquid and choose non-feather and low-allergy mattresses, duvets, and pillows, and open the windows at least once a day in winter.

SUGGESTED RECIPES FOR HAY FEVER

Elderflower spritzer—above (page 128), hay fever relief (page 129), syrup of onion (see recipe for garlic oxymel—page 129), beet and horseradish salad (page 37), immuni-tea (page 129), green lentil salad (page 120), artichoke hearts, fava beans, and shiitake (page 112), okra in sweet and sour tamarind sauce (page 116), provençal mesclun salad (page 119), tropical sunshine salad (page 121), height of passion (page 126), elderberry cordial (page 128), pick-me-up (page 130), green tea with mint (page 129).

asthma

SUPERFOODS FOR ASTHMA: AVOCADO, BEANS, BEET, BELL PEPPER, BERRIES, BLACK CUMIN, BROCCOLI, BUTTERNUT SQUASH, CARAWAY, CARROT, CAULIFLOWER, CAYENNE, CORN, CURLY KALE, DRIED FRUIT, EUCALYPTUS, GARLIC, GREEN TEA, GUAVA, HORSERADISH, LENTILS, LICORICE ROOT, NETTLE, OKRA, ONION, PAPAYA, POTATO, SEA VEGETABLE, SHIITAKE, SORREL, SWEET POTATO, TEMPEH, THYME, YARROW

Asthma is a common respiratory disorder causing wheezing, difficulty breathing, and dry cough. It is caused by a narrowing of the airways in the lungs as a result of spasm in the bronchial tubes and excess production of thick, sticky mucus. There are two main types: one begins in childhood (especially in families with a history of asthma or allergy) and often clears up with age; the other starts later in life and is often preceded by infection. "Late onset" asthma tends to be chronic and is often harder to treat. Asthma attacks can be triggered by an allergic reaction to dust, pollen, foods, drugs, bacteria, and by exhaustion, excitement, tension, anxiety, exercise, over-exposure to cold air, colds and influenza, or certain drugs (such as beta-blockers). In cases of mild asthma, sufferers usually have no breathing problems between attacks. However, those who have frequent, severe attacks over many years can suffer from constant breathing difficulty.

During an attack it takes tremendous effort to breathe, and severe, prolonged attacks can be fatal unless treated with bronchodilators, steroids, oxygen, and, if necessary, artificial ventilation. At times like this, most sufferers find they can breathe more easily when sitting up rather than lying down.

Prevention

Finding and avoiding the underlying causes and trigger factors is the most important preventive measure. For example, keeping the home as dust-free as possible and washing bedding regularly in perfume-free detergents can help eliminate house-dust mites. Elimination diets are useful for identifying potential food allergens and avoiding them. The most common offenders are: eggs, fish, shellfish, nuts (especially peanuts), milk, chocolate, wheat, citrus fruits, apples, and food additives and coloring such as tartrazine, benzoates, sulfur dioxide, and sulfites.

Management

Exclude all meat, fish, eggs, and dairy products from the diet, as elimination of animal products has been shown to significantly reduce susceptibility to attacks. Other potential trigger factors that should be avoided include known allergens such as food additives, and also aspirin and other non-steroidal anti-inflammatory drugs, chlorinated tap water, and coffee, tea, refined sugar, and added salt. Limiting the amount of grains in the diet can also be beneficial. Eat plenty of foods containing vitamins B5, B6, B12, C, and E, magnesium, trace elements such as selenium, and carotenoids.

SUGGESTED RECIPES FOR ASTHMA

Eucalyptus mix—above (page 129), lung-cleansing tea mix (page 130), curly kale, tomato, and fava beans (page 41), filled avocados (page 53), shiitake with sea vegetable (page 75), salad with sorrel and tempeh (page 121), curly kale parcels (page 41), butternut squash with bell pepper and tomato (page 113), casserole de puy (page 112), italian butterbean soup (page 105), potato salad (page 120), beet and horseradish salad (page 37), nettle and sweet potato mash (page 45), carrot 'n' beetroot salad (page 119), vegetable cocktail (page 127).

migraine

SUPERFOODS FOR MIGRAINE: ADUKI BEAN, BRAZIL NUT, CALENDULA FLOWER, CHAMOMILE, CAYENNE, CORN, FAVA BEAN, FEVERFEW, GARLIC, LAVENDER, MELON SEED, MUESLI, MUSHROOMS, OATS, OKRA, ONION, PASSION FLOWER, PEAS, RICE, ROSEMARY, SWISS CHARD, TAHINI, TEMPEH, WALNUT AND WALNUT OIL, WILD MARJORAM

Migraine is a recurrent and particularly intense form of headache, often accompanied by visual and gastro-intestinal disturbances. The pain always begins on one side of the head, and attacks may start with a visual "aura" (thought to be caused by constriction of cerebral blood vessels). Subsequent dilation of the blood vessels causes a characteristic throbbing headache, often accompanied by nausea, vomiting, and sensitivity to light. Migraine often runs in families, and may be associated with a childhood tendency to symptoms such as stomach ache, colic, vomiting, dizziness, or travel sickness. Migraine is more common in women than men, and can be triggered by many factors including food allergy. Chronic stress is thought to cause changes to the nervous system that make attacks more likely. Hormonal changes associated with menstruation and the menopause may be a factor in some women. Musculoskeletal disorders such as whiplash injury may be other important triggers.

Prevention

It may help to keep a diary and make a note of any factors that seem to be linked to an attack, such as particular foods and your emotional state just prior to an attack. Identifying and avoiding allergens can often reduce the number and severity of migraines you suffer. Common offenders include red meat (especially pork), dairy products, wheat, chocolate, eggs, cheese, alcohol (especially red wine, sherry, and port), tobacco, coffee, strong tea, tomato, oranges, white sugar, shellfish, and food additives (such as nitrates, benzoic acid, tartrazine, and monosodium glutamate).

Eating a leaf of fresh feverfew each day over a long period of time may reduce the frequency and/or intensity of the attacks. However, some people are sensitive to the bitter principles in feverfew and can develop small blisters in the mouth after eating the fresh leaves. If you are susceptible to this problem, you can take feverfew in the form of a tisane (place a couple of fresh leaves in a cup, pour boiling water over the top and leave to infuse). Calendula (marigold) flowers offer some protection from the effects of food allergens because they contain quercetin, which dampens down the body's responses to allergens. Foods containing vitamin B3 (niacin) may also be useful in preventing migraine attacks. These include soy products such as tempeh and tofu, muesli, fava bean, brown rice, aduki bean, corn, and mushrooms.

Management

Many people find the condition is improved by a change of diet such as a reduction in intake of animal produce and increased consumption of fresh fruits and vegetables. Important foods and drinks to eliminate are those containing alcohol, caffeine, cheese, chocolate, shellfish, and oranges. Vegetable oils (particularly walnut), cayenne, garlic, and onion are all beneficial. Foods high in magnesium (such as Brazil nut, okra, melon seed, tahini paste, Swiss chard, and brown rice) may also help in the long-term treatment of migraines.

SUGGESTED RECIPES FOR MIGRAINE

Muesli (page 103), green leafy salad (page 41), khichuri—rice with lentils (page 117), spicy brazil nut pâté (page 57), florence fennel salad (page 120), nettle and sweet potato mash (page 45), tea for headache (page 131), tea for aches and pains (page 131).

Following a detox and elimination diet (see page 132) can be very useful for identifying and avoiding some of the causes of migraine attacks. After completing the diet, alcohol, cheese, oranges, and shellfish should still be avoided until symptom-free for six months. Foods high in animal fats should be kept to a minimum; vegetable oils, garlic, and onion should form a regular part of the diet.

rheumatoid arthritis

SUPERFOODS FOR ARTHRITIS: ADUKI BEAN, ALFALFA, ASPARAGUS, BEET, BELGIAN ENDIVE, BERRIES, CARROT, CELERY, CLEAVERS, CURLY KALE, FENNEL, FEVERFEW, GARLIC, GRAPE, HARICOT BEAN, HAWTHORN, JUNIPER, LENTIL, LICORICE ROOT, MANGO, NETTLE, NUTS, ONION, PAPAYA, PEAS, PINEAPPLE, RICE, SEA VEGETABLE, SUNFLOWER SEED AND OIL, SWISS CHARD, TAHINI, TEMPEH, VIOLET

Rheumatoid arthritis is a chronic, generalized inflammatory disease that attacks the membranes surrounding joints and tendons, causing pain, swelling, stiffness, and loss of movement. It mostly affects adults but can occur in childhood. It commonly begins with weeks of feeling generally unwell, perhaps with weight loss, mild fever, stiffness, and pain. The joint symptoms often start in the hands or feet, and are worse in the morning. The inflammation may spread to affect all of the joints, leading to increased pain, swelling, stiffness and—in severe cases—deformity. Most sufferers also have some degree of anemia and vitamin C deficiency.

The condition is an autoimmune disease in which antibodies attack the lining of the joints. What triggers the process is unclear, although it may be associated with genetic factors, nutrition, and lifestyle. There is also an association with poor digestion and waste elimination, which can lead to an accumulation of antigenic toxins.

SUGGESTED RECIPES FOR ARTHRITIS

Tea for joints (page 131), immuni-tea (page 129), licorice mix (page 130), heart warmer (page 126), green tea with mint (page 129), yogurt with fruit (page 103), toasted nuts and seeds (page 108), florence fennel salad (page 120), spiced nettle soup (page 45), asparagus asian-style (page 113), broiled endive and brazil nut salad (page 57), toasted tempeh with herb salad (page 108), artichoke hearts, fava beans, and shiitake (page 112), curly kale parcels (page 41), nettle and sweet potato mash (page 45), garlic and savoy cabbage (page 69), swiss chard and juniper berries (page 119), spring greens and macadamia nuts (page 118), tropical sunshine salad (page 121).

Prevention and management

Rheumatoid arthritis is virtually non-existent in cultures where the diet consists mainly of fresh, unadulterated fruits, vegetables, nuts, and grains. However, it is relatively common in communities that eat a diet high in sugar, meat, dairy products, saturated fat, and refined carbohydrates. Different fats influence inflammation in different ways. Arachidonic acid (from meat and dairy products) increases inflammation but a diet high in polyunsaturated fats and low in saturated fat inhibits inflammation and improves symptoms.

Free radicals are responsible for much of the inflammatory damage caused in arthritis. So eating foods high in antioxidants can be beneficial. Improving digestion with foods such as papaya and pineapple, which contain proteolytic enzymes, alleviates the effect of food allergy and reduces the inflammatory process in the joints. Bioflavonoids block release of histamine and leukotrienes, which are both active inflammatory agents. Foods containing copper reduce arthritic inflammation. Foods high in niacin and tryptophan (components of vitamin B3) dampen arthritic pain.

To aid the elimination of toxins, include natural diuretics in the diet (celery seed, nettle, and cleavers), and support the liver with foods containing bitter principles (globe artichoke, endive, and chicory). Taking psyllium seeds helps detoxify the gut and a traditional grape fast (see page 133) can aid general detoxification. Eliminating food allergens can have a beneficial effect on rheumatoid arthritis. Common offenders are dairy products, red meat, pork, wheat, vegetables of the solinacea family (tomato, eggplant, bell peppers, tobacco—although potatoes are usually fairly well tolerated), shellfish, alcohol (especially red wine and port), oranges, and coffee. Other foods to avoid are strawberries, sorrel, currants (red and black), rhubarb, beet leaves, and spinach.

inflammatory bowel disease

SUPERFOODS FOR I.B.D.: APRICOT, ASPARAGUS, AVOCADO, BANANA, BEANS, BEET, BELGIAN ENDIVE, BERRIES, BRUSSELS SPROUT, BUTTERNUT SQUASH, CABBAGE, CAULIFLOWER, CORN, FLAXSEED, GARBANZOS, GRAPE, LEMON, LENTIL, LIVE SOY YOGURT, MANGO, NUTS, MUESLI, OKRA, PAPAYA, PARSLEY, PEAS, RICE, SEEDS, SPINACH, SPRING GREENS, SWISS CHARD, TAHINI, TEMPEH

Inflammatory bowel disease (I.B.D.) is a general term for two important digestive disorders, ulcerative colitis and Crohn's disease. Ulcerative colitis involves recurrent inflammation of the large intestine. There is ulceration, leading to bouts of profuse and bloody diarrhea, fever, abdominal pain, dehydration, and often weight loss. There is a risk of life-threatening perforation of the bowel. Crohn's disease involves chronic patchy inflammation of the bowel resulting in diarrhea (without blood) and fever. It may lead to abscesses, poor absorption of nutrients, bowel obstruction, and perforation. I.B.D. may develop at any age, but most often starts between the ages of 15 and 35. Ulcerative colitis is currently the more common of the two, but the incidence of Crohn's disease is rising. The cause is not well understood, but the Western lifestyle and diet, infection, allergy, autoimmune disorders, and heredity, psychosomatic, and emotional factors have all been implicated.

Prevention and management

A balanced diet containing sufficiently good quality calories is one of the most important factors in the prevention and management of I.B.D. The diet should include foods high in calcium, magnesium, potassium, and trace elements such as zinc and iron. Folate and vitamin B12 are important for the health of the intestinal mucosa and vitamins A, C, and E are powerful antioxidants able to inhibit inflammation. Bioflavonoids found in most medicinal herbs have a powerful effect on enzymes involved in the inflammatory response. Inflammation can also be reduced by cutting consumption of animal fats in favor of omega-3 oils found in walnut oil, flaxseed oil and fish oils. Aim to re-establish the natural gut flora by adding live soy yogurt and complex carbohydrates to the diet. But avoid wheat bran, sugar, and refined carbohydrates, and common food allergens such as wheat, corn, and dairy products.

SUGGESTED RECIPES FOR INFLAMMATORY BOWEL DISEASE

Spicy chai—left (page 130), healing soup (page 104), muesli (page 103), yogurt with fruit (page 103), toasted tempeh with herb salad (page 108), artichoke hearts, fava beans, and shiitake (page 112), green lentil salad (page 120), green leafy salad (page 41), nettle and sweet potato mash (page 45), oatmeal with dried fruit and quinoa (page 102), creamy cauliflower soup (page 105), pumpkin soup (page 105), tzaziki (page 111), winter hot pot (page 116), khichuri— rice with lentils (page 117), lemon rice (page 117), carrot 'n' beet salad (page 119), florence fennel salad (page 120), wild rice salad (page 121), tropical fruit salad (page 123), apricot and ginger (page 124), caribbean smoothie (page 124), calming tea (page 128).

H.I.V. & A.I.D.S.

SUPERFOODS FOR H.I.V. AND A.I.D.S.: BEANS, BEET, BELL PEPPER, BLACK CUMIN, BORAGE, BROCCOLI, BUTTERNUT SQUASH, CALENDULA, CARROT, CATECHIN, CITRUS FRUITS, CURLY KALE, ECHINACEA, EVENING PRIMROSE OIL, GARBANZOS, GRAPEFRUIT, GREEN LEAVES, GREEN TEA, GUAVA, LENTIL, LICORICE ROOT, MANGO, MUESLI, NETTLE, NUTS, OKRA, PAPAYA, PASTA, PEANUT BUTTER, PUMPKIN SEED, SAFFLOWER AND SUNFLOWER OILS, SEA VEGETABLE, SEEDS, SHIITAKE, SPINACH, STRAWBERRY, SWEET POTATO, TEMPEH, TOFU, TOMATO, YAM

Acquired immune deficiency syndrome (A.I.D.S.) is a group of disorders apparently related to previous infection by the human immunodeficiency virus (H.I.V.). The virus is transmitted via body fluids, during sexual contact, or contaminated blood products. Everyone is potentially at risk of infection, but the most vulnerable groups are people with multiple sexual partners, intravenous drug users who share needles and syringes, and recipients of blood products in countries that do not employ scrupulous screening procedures. The incubation period is 1 to 6 months after infection by the virus. Progression from infection to being "antibody positive" is not well understood. Even though 98 per cent of sufferers have H.I.V. antibodies in their blood, 2 per cent do not! Furthermore, being H.I.V.-positive does not necessarily lead to full-blown A.I.D.S. There are four recognized A.I.D.S.-related states:

● antibodies in the blood but no symptoms;

● persistent generalized lymph node enlargement (P.G.L.);

● A.R.C. (A.I.D.S.-related complex), which involves the clinical features of chronic disease plus abnormal blood test results;

● full-blown A.I.D.S., involving opportunistic lung infections, skin cancer (Kaposi's sarcoma), and lymphatic cancer.

Prevention

The most important preventive measure you can take is to use safer sexual practices if your partner's sexual history is unknown to you. This involves taking steps to prevent contact with sexual fluids—for example, by using condoms or avoiding penetrative sex. Intravenous drug users should never share injecting materials. When traveling in developing countries, it is advisable to carry disposable syringes and needles with you, in case of emergency.

Your diet should include plenty of foods that help prevent viral infection, such as garlic, Brazil nut, and echinacea, and that strengthen the immune system, such as shiitake and beet.

Management

A.I.D.S. is a growing problem all over the world and, although a cure remains elusive, there are simple nutritional and lifestyle changes that are proven to make life easier for sufferers. H.I.V. infection, nutritional status and immune function are intimately connected. The relationship between H.I.V. infection and food is important because strategies that improve nutritional status have a beneficial effect on the course of the disease. The outcome with drug therapy is less hopeful in people with compromized nutrition, whereas good nutrition greatly improves the chances of survival.

In Africa, A.I.D.S. was first known as "slim disease" because the condition caused rapid weight loss, leading to early death. The wasting associated with A.I.D.S. is caused by inefficient absorption of food, excessive loss of nutrients (mainly through chronic diarrhea), and less efficient use of nutrients that are absorbed.

Once the disorder has been diagnosed, it is possible to maintain the weight of the patient through intensive feeding regimes. When the condition has been stabilized, patients can regain some of the weight they have lost and start to build up the reserves that will make it easier to cope with the condition. Avoiding, reversing, or delaying the wasting process requires adopting measures involving all the ways in which food is converted into energy and body mass.

Food intake H.I.V.-positive individuals often have a poor appetite, because of inefficient absorption of nutrients, secondary infections, the side effects of certain drugs, fungal infections of the mouth or esophagus (which makes eating and swallowing difficult), and enlargement of the liver or spleen (which gives a false feeling of fullness). Depression may also be a factor. Therefore, the quality of the food that the patient eats is of vital importance to compensate for the lack of quantity.

Absorption The food we eat is broken down in the small intestine, and nutrients are absorbed through the gut wall. This important process can be hampered by H.I.V. infection, and is also disturbed by diarrhea, which causes food to pass through the digestive system too quickly. Antibiotics used to destroy harmful bacteria may also kill friendly bacteria that live in the gut and support the digestive process by aiding absorption and manufacturing vitamins.

To boost nutrient absorption, it is best to avoid dairy produce and include foods such as apple, grapefruit, garbanzos, amaranth leaves, potatoes, fennel, arugula, globe artichoke, Belgian endive, and the medicinal herbs peppermint, thyme, catnip, and calendula.

Metabolism Our metabolic rate determines how quickly we expend the energy we obtain from food. It is often raised in H.I.V. infection and is responsible for much of the fatigue and lethargy felt by people with A.I.D.S. H.I.V. infection alters metabolism, with less protein being manufactured by the liver and more being broken down and used for energy. The result is muscle wasting and a decline in "lean body mass." To maintain energy and stabilize metabolism, the diet should be high in complex carbohydrates, vegetable proteins, and fiber, and low in fat. All produce should be fresh, organic, and unprocessed.

Foods rich in zinc, vitamins A and C, and bioflavonoids are beneficial because they inhibit the activity of viruses and bacteria. Licorice root and echinacea both support the immune system and enhance many aspects of immune function, as well as inhibiting the spread of viral infection. Grapefruit, pumpkin seed, Brazil nut, nettle, black cumin, borage, sweet potato, yam, tomato, and shiitake act specifically against immunodeficiency. Important immuno-stimulants include okra, beet, spinach, curly kale, guava, safflower and sunflower oils, evening primrose oil, sea vegetable, peanut butter, and calendula.

The stress factor

The psychological and emotional stress following a diagnosis of H.I.V. may contribute to the progression of the disease because negative emotions have a detrimental effect on the immune response. However, positive emotions enhance appropriate immune responses, so involvement in pleasurable, creative activity, and spending more time in the company of close friends and loved ones are both positive ways of improving immune function.

SUGGESTED RECIPES FOR H.I.V. AND A.I.D.S.

Vegetable cocktail—above (page 127), immuni-tea (page 129), grapefruit and peppermint fizz (page 49), grapefruit salad (page 49), avocado smoothie (page 53), carrot 'n' beet salad (page 119), broiled endive and brazil nut salad (page 57), tofu balls (page 110), brazil nuts and sun-dried tomatoes with beans (page 57), nettle and lime tisane (page 45), nettle and sweet potato mash (page 45), avocado, watercress, and cumin salad (page 53), stress relief (page 130), shiitake salad (page 75), artichoke hearts, fava beans, and shiitake (page 112), okra in sweet and sour tamarind sauce (page 116), heart warmer (page 126), tropical sunshine salad (page 121), healing soup (page 104), shepherdess' pie (116), wild rice salad (page 121).

stress & chronic fatigue syndrome

SUPERFOODS FOR STRESS: BEANS, BORAGE, BROCCOLI, CABBAGES, CARROT, GRAPEFRUIT, GREEN LEAVES, LAVENDER, LEMON BALM, LENTIL, LICORICE ROOT, MANGO, MUESLI, NUTS, OATS, ORANGE, PAPAYA, RICE, STRAWBERRY, TEMPEH, TOFU; SUPERFOODS FOR C.F.S.: AVOCADO, BANANA, BEANS, BEET, BELL PEPPER, BLACK CURRANT, BORAGE, CHAMOMILE, CLEAVERS, ECHINACEA, GRAPEFRUIT, GREEN LEAVES, LICORICE ROOT, LIVE SOY YOGURT, MUESLI, NUTS, OKRA, PAPAYA, PEAS, RICE, TEMPEH, TOFU, WHEATGRASS

STRESS

The relationship between stress and ill health is well documented, but stress levels vary enormously from person to person, as does each individual's ability to cope. To deal effectively with stress, it is necessary to take account of these variations, and to remember that the immune system does not work in isolation. It is affected by thoughts, actions, and emotional responses as well as by disease, environment, general lifestyle, age, and genetic predisposition.

Stress hormones such as epinephrine and cortisol enable the body to cope with stressful situations, but if they are released in excess or over too long a period, they inhibit (and can damage) the immune response. This means that during periods of chronic stress, exposure to pathogens is more likely to cause disease.

Prevention and management

Like rest and relaxation, good nutrition can reduce the effects of stress in our lives and enhance immune function. Foods high in vitamins A and C, and zinc and selenium are particularly helpful. Other foods and herbs for stress relief include Belgian endive, cauliflower, artichoke, banana, sesame seed, oats, corn, wheatgerm, borage, lemon balm, lavender, and licorice root.

CHRONIC FATIGUE SYNDROME (C.F.S.)

This poorly understood syndrome is also known as myalgic encephalomyelitis (M.E.) or post-viral syndrome, and may relate to the immune system's difficulty in handling viral infections when already overburdened by "environmental" stress. It does not seem to be related to any specific viral infection, but can persist for months or even years. Common symptoms include severe fatigue after minimal exertion that is not relieved by rest, generalized aches and pains, depressed mood, recurrent sore throats, swollen lymph nodes, headache, mild fever, difficulty adjusting to changes in temperature, and gastro-intestinal disturbance. There may also be a variety of inexplicable neurological symptoms.

Prevention and management

The best way to prevent or manage the condition is through detoxification, and following a diet rich in foods that enhance resistance to disease and support immune function. To boost the immune system drink plenty of pure water and eat a variety of fresh fruit and vegetables. Choose foods rich in vitamins B6 and C, essential fatty acids, calcium, magnesium, and zinc.

SUGGESTED RECIPES FOR STRESS AND C.F.S.

Stress: stress relief (page 130), scrambled tofu (page 102), muesli (page 103), creamy cauliflower soup (page 105), spiced nettle soup (page 45), samosa parcels (page 108), toasted nuts and seeds (page 108), amaranth and tofu puffs (page 112), artichoke hearts, fava beans, and shiitake (page 112), broiled endive and brazil nut salad (page 57), provençale-style kidney beans (page 115), blackberry cream (page 124), creamy mango (page 124).

C.F.S.: sleepy time (page 130), shiitake with sea vegetable (page 75), grapefruit salad (page 49), carrot 'n' beet salad (page 119), tomato cocktail (page 127), sweet chestnuts and kumquats (page 117), immuni-tea (page 129).

depression & anxiety

SUPERFOODS FOR DEPRESSION: AVOCADO, BANANA, BEANS, BELL PEPPER, BORAGE, ENDIVE, GREEN LEAVES, LICORICE ROOT, MANGO, MUESLI, PEAS, RICE, SOY PRODUCTS, ST. JOHN'S WORT, TAHINI, YEAST EXTRACT; SUPERFOODS FOR ANXIETY: APRICOT, ARTICHOKE, BEANS, BUTTERNUT SQUASH, CAULIFLOWER, CHAMOMILE, GRAPEFRUIT, GREEN LEAVES, LAVENDER, LEMON BALM, OATS, OKRA, PASSION FLOWER, POTATO, RED BELL PEPPER, ROSEMARY, ST. JOHN'S WORT, SWEET POTATO, TEMPEH, TOFU, WALNUT, YEAST EXTRACT

DEPRESSION

There are two forms of depression: psychotic (endogenous) and neurotic (reactive). Psychotic depression is a severe emotional disturbance more common in middle age. The sufferer may become agitated, or profoundly withdrawn and lethargic, and may experience hallucinations and delusions. There are disturbances in bowel habit, appetite and sleep, and a real risk of suicide. Neurotic depression is a reaction to traumatic events such as bereavement and may be accompanied by anxiety, and disturbed appetite and sleep. The underlying causes are not completely understood but contributing factors include physical disorder (such as underactive thyroid), diet, food allergy, smoking, drugs, and lifestyle.

Prevention and management

Measures to prevent or manage depression include taking regular exercise; avoiding cigarettes, alcohol, and drinks containing caffeine; using alternatives to oral contraception; eliminating food allergens and additives (particularly aspartame); and eating regular meals with plenty of fresh fruits and vegetables (to stabilize blood-sugar levels). To optimize your nutritional state, eat foods high in B and C vitamins, and magnesium and tryptophan. St. John's wort is an effective antidepressant, and herbs that support the adrenal glands, such as borage and licorice root, are also valuable.

ANXIETY

Anxiety states are dominated by fast pulse, sweating, butterflies in the stomach, light headedness, and feelings of apprehension and fear. Chronic anxiety takes a toll on the immune system and can lead to physical illness, such as irritable bowel syndrome. The cause can be hormonal, or linked to overactive thyroid and premenstrual syndrome, or a traumatic event. It can also be a symptom of psychiatric illness, such as depression or dementia.

Prevention and management

Once hormonal imbalance (which needs medical attention) has been ruled out, anxiety states can often be managed with foods that strengthen the nervous system, such as oats, potato, sweet potato, butternut squash, okra, bell pepper, Brussels sprout, cauliflower, artichoke, spring greens, curly kale, apricot, grapefruit, walnut, tempeh, butterbean, haricot bean, pinto bean, and yeast extract. Herbs to calm the nerves include chamomile, lemon balm, rosemary, St. John's wort, lavender, and passion flower.

SUGGESTED RECIPES FOR DEPRESSION & ANXIETY

Depression: pick-me-up (page 130), stress relief (page 130), licorice mix (page 130), calming tea (page 128), pasta, pesto, and shiitake (page 75), paella (page 112), chinese salad (page 120), italian butterbean soup (page 105), baba ganoush (page 108), hummus with crudités and warm pitta bread (page 106), baked apples (page 122).

Anxiety: chamomile tonic (page 128), oatmeal with dried fruit and quinoa (page 102), apricot and ginger (page 124), creamy cauliflower soup (page 105), spicy moroccan soup (page 106), arugula salad (page 119), ruby red melon salad (page 102), curly kale parcels (page 41), sleepy time (page 130).

cancer

SUPERFOODS FOR CANCER: AVOCADO, BEET, BEANS, BELL PEPPER, BERRIES, BRAZIL NUT, BROCCOLI, BUTTERNUT SQUASH, CABBAGE, CALENDULA, CARROT, CELERY SALT, CLEAVERS, CURLY KALE, ECHINACEA, GARBANZOS, GARLIC, GRAPEFRUIT, GRAPE, GRAPESEED, GREEN LEAVES, GUAVA, LEMON, LENTILS, MANGO, MUNG BEAN SPROUT, NETTLE, NUTS, OLIVE, ORANGE, PAPAYA, PASTA, POTATO, PULSES, RICE, SEEDS, SHIITAKE, SPICES, SUN-DRIED TOMATO, SWEET POTATO, TEMPEH, TOFU, VEGETABLE OILS, VIOLET, WHOLEMEAL BREAD, WILD RICE

Research into the nature of cancer has not yet clarified exactly what it is that turns a normal cell into a cancer cell. Although we know that carcinogens such as chemicals, radiation, tobacco, asbestos, and viruses can cause tumors, it is not known precisely how or why. But there is growing evidence that nutritional, social, psychological, and environmental factors play a role in cancer.

Evidence linking food and nutrition to cancer risk is growing and has been collected over a number of years by comparing different diets with cancer rates. There are big differences in incidence and death from cancer in different parts of the world, but specialists have identified general patterns. Developing countries tend to have high rates of cancers of the upper digestive tract, liver and cervix, whereas developed countries have relatively high rates of hormone-related cancers, and cancers of the colon and rectum.

There is great variation in the length and intensity of exposure to particular environmental carcinogens that will trigger cancerous changes. It is also possible that simultaneous exposure to a combination of carcinogens produces cancer where one alone would have been relatively harmless, and that exposure to stress may alter the body's response to different carcinogens. Genetic factors play a role in some cancers, and some carcinogens—such as free radicals—can originate within the body. Some tumors are benign (non-spreading), but malignant tumors invade surrounding tissues and spread via blood and lymph to form metastases

(secondary tumors). There is controversy surrounding the role of viruses in cancer formation. In other mammals (such as chickens, rabbits, mice, and cats) several tumors are known to be caused by viruses, but the picture in humans is less clear. However, there is good evidence that viruses may cause some cancers in humans (such as cervical and liver cell cancer, lymphoma, and leukemia).

There are many different types of cancer, each one with its individual features, but all cancers sooner or later disturb normal body function. The danger signals for malignant disease include a change in bowel or bladder habit, sores that won't heal, unusual bleeding or discharge, newly discovered lumps, obvious changes in skin moles or warts, a persistent cough and/or hoarseness, coughing up blood, and, very importantly, loss of appetite and unexplained weight loss.

Prevention

It has been estimated that in the U.S. 30 per cent of all cancer deaths are related to dietary factors, and that 30 to 40 per cent of cancer cases throughout the world are potentially preventable with simple changes to diet and lifestyle. It is now beyond doubt that the most effective way to reduce cancer risk is to stop smoking, eat plenty of fresh fruit and vegetables, and limit exposure to occupational and environmental carcinogens. Environmental carcinogens are usually man-made and fall into five distinct groups—additives, dyes and coal tar, pollutant chemicals, fumes, and radiation. Not all of these will inevitably trigger cancer in all cases, but it is worth remembering that many carcinogens cause damage by weakening the immune system and so may be indirectly responsible for causing cancerous changes. Therefore, in cancer prevention and management it is very important to keep the immune system as strong as possible by adopting a healthy lifestyle, and eating a diet rich in energy and vital nutrients.

For cancer prevention, choose a plant-based diet that includes a rich variety of vegetables, fruits, nuts, pulses, and minimally processed starchy foods. Eat at least five portions of seasonal, organic fresh fruit and vegetables daily, all year round, and at least five portions a day of grains, pulses, roots, and tubers. Use modest amounts of vegetable oils (mainly olive, walnut, grapeseed, and safflower and sunflower oils), and avoid animal fats altogether. Use herbs, spices, celery salt, and soy sauce to season foods, and limit consumption of salted and pickled foods and table salt.

Choose organic foods free of additives, pesticides, and other chemicals. Avoid alcohol, meat, and dairy products, and if animal protein is eaten, choose fish, organic poultry, or meat from non-domesticated animals. Choose minimally processed foods and limit your consumption of refined sugar. Avoid being over- or underweight, stop smoking and take an hour's exercise daily.

Immune system boosters to guard against cancer include garlic, beet, grapefruit, curly kale, nettle, avocado, Brazil nut, cleavers, calendula, violet, echinacea and shiitake mushroom, among many others. Also important are foods that contain vitamins A (sweet potato, carrot, red bell pepper, green leaves, mango, papaya, butternut squash), C (guava, red and green bell peppers, green leaves, black currant, papaya, mango, lemon, orange, cabbage, broccoli), E (avocado, nuts, sun-dried tomato, sweet potato, sunflower seed), zinc (aduki bean, tofu, tempeh, lentil, muesli, garbanzos, tahini, pumpkin seed) and selenium (beans, Brazil nuts, lentils, pasta, sunflower seed, mushrooms, wholemeal bread), carotenoids (yellow and orange fruits and vegetables), bioflavonoids (especially anthocyanin in dark-colored berries such as red grape, blueberry, cranberry, and hawthorn berry, and quercetin in calendula) and the fatty acids found in walnuts.

Management

In the early stages of cancer, the most effective dietary approach is to detoxify the system (see detox diet, page 132). Later on in the course of the disease, freshly made juices, smoothies, and tisanes are particularly helpful because they contain a high concentration of nutrients (together with antioxidants and other immune system boosters), but are nevertheless easy to digest. Half of the diet should be fresh fruits, especially grape, which are detoxifying and also contain immune-enhancing anthocyanin. The diet should also be rich in complex carbohydrates—for example, from potato, sweet potato, rice, and wild rice, and essential fatty acids, such as from walnut. Good sources of protein are pulses, mung bean sprouts, tofu, mushrooms (especially shiitake), and tempeh.

SUGGESTED RECIPES FOR CANCER

Guava and apple—left (page 126), baked tomatoes on toast (page 102), carrot 'n' beet salad (page 119), grapefruit salad (page 49), oriental salad with tempeh (page 63), green leafy salad (page 41), spiced nettle soup (page 45), black-eye pea and wild marjoram soup (page 105), guacamole (page 110), tofu balls (page 110), shiitake mushroom soup (page 105), tropical fruit salad (page 123), wild rice salad (page 121), tomato and cucumber canapés (page 110), arugula salad (page 119), tea for glands (page 131), tea for the skin (page 131), green party (page 124), caribbean smoothie (page 124), avocado smoothie (page 53), nettle and lime tisane (page 45), artichoke hearts, fava beans, and shiitake (page 112), casserole de puy (page 112), greek casserole (page 115).

ischemic (coronary) heart disease

SUPERFOODS FOR ISCHEMIC HEART DISEASE: ALFALFA, ALMOND, APRICOT, BELL PEPPER, BLACK-EYE PEA, BRAZIL NUT, BROCCOLI, BUTTER BEAN, CANTALOUPE MELON, FLAXSEED, GARBANZOS, GARLIC, GINGER, GREEN LEAVES, GUAVA, HARICOT BEAN, HAWTHORN BERRY, HAZELNUT, LEMON, LENTIL, MACADAMIA NUT, MANGETOUT PEAS, MANGO, MELON, MUESLI, OKRA, ONION, ORANGE, PAPAYA, PINEAPPLE, PINE NUT, PINTO BEAN, PUMPKIN SEED, RICE, SESAME SEED, SOY BEAN, SUNFLOWER SEED, SWISS CHARD, TAHINI, TEMPEH, TOFU, YAM

Ischemic heart disease is the partial blockage of the coronary arteries by atherosclerosis and thrombosis, leading to poor blood supply to the heart muscle. It is one of the commonest causes of illness and disability and the main cause of death in the Western world. Its major symptom is angina (a crushing pain in the chest spreading up into the neck and down the left arm), and the worst outcome is myocardial infarction (heart attack).

Risk factors include smoking, high blood pressure, high blood cholesterol, a diet high in saturated fats and salt and low in fiber, obesity, diabetes, gout, emotional stress, lack of exercise, social deprivation, oral contraception, genetic predisposition, and age.

Prevention

It is important to avoid smoking, alcohol, and coffee completely. Daily gentle exercise, such as walking, is beneficial. Stress is dangerous and should be avoided where possible (or counteracted by allowing plenty of time and space for relaxation). High blood cholesterol, triglyceride (fat) and low- and very low-density lipoproteins (L.D.L.s and V.L.D.L.s) are associated with the build-up of fatty deposits in the blood vessels that can lead to coronary artery blockage. Saturated fats (such as animal fats) make things worse, but monounsaturated (mostly oleic acid from olive oil) and polyunsaturated fats (from nuts, seeds, and kernels) are associated with more favorable blood-fat levels and thus reduced risk of heart disease. "Trans-fats" (hardened unsaturated fatty acids in meat, dairy, and manufactured foods such as margarine) have the same negative effect on blood-fat levels as saturated fats. Obesity, alcohol, and refined sugar also contribute to raised blood-fat levels.

Avoiding red meat, eggs, milk, and cheese is desirable, and a decrease in overall fat intake by avoiding "table fats" (such as butter) and foods containing invisible fat (such as mayonnaise, cakes and rich sauces and soups) can make a major contribution to long-term cardiac health. The diet should be high in complex carbohydrates and fiber (including oats, flaxseed, and foods high in pectin) and include plenty of fresh fruits and vegetables.

Management

Angina and heart attack are serious conditions that require professional medical attention. Orthodox management is to encourage gentle exercise and maintain a normal lifestyle while reducing relevant risk factors, and taking drugs such as oral nitrates, beta-blockers, and nifedipine. People at high risk of myocardial infarction may be offered a coronary bypass operation.

However, there are a number of changes that people can make for themselves to reduce risk and make management easier. The therapeutic goal is to improve blood supply and nutrition to the heart muscle. Healthy eating plays a vital role in the management of heart disease. The aim is to create a diet that provides beneficial nutrients without clogging up the tissues and blood vessels with sugars, fats, and additives. Processed and convenience foods are usually high in these but low in nourishment. Making a gradual change and exchanging them for fresh fruits, vegetables, nuts, seeds, pulses, and whole grain foods reduces blood-cholesterol

SUGGESTED RECIPES FOR HEART DISEASE

Green tea with mint—above (page 129), circulation booster (page 128), heart chai (page 129), si c (page 130), papaya power (page 127), oatmeal with dried fruit and quinoa (page 102), baked beet salad (page 37), oriental salad with tempeh (page 63), chinese salad (page 120), italian butterbean soup (page 105), shiitake mushroom soup (page 105), spicy moroccan soup (page 106), vegetable cocktail (page 127), provençal mesclun salad (page 119), french onion tart (page 115), okra in sweet and sour tamarind sauce (page 116), orange mango salad (page 120), brazil nuts and sun-dried tomatoes with beans (page 57), paella (page 112), baked apples (page 122), tropical fruit salad (page 123), muesli (page 103), mango and lime (page 126).

levels and improves the blood-fat balance. Alfalfa sprouts and leaves decrease blood-cholesterol levels and reduce fatty plaque formation in blood vessels. Bromelain from pineapple inhibits blood clot formation and also breaks down fatty plaques in the arteries. Onions, garlic, and ginger have the same effect, and ginger and garlic also lower levels of blood cholesterol and fat. Magnesium deficiency causes coronary artery spasm and irregular heart beat. Good sources of this mineral include Brazil nut, okra, melon and sunflower seed, tahini, Swiss chard, brown rice, muesli, tempeh, tofu, and other soy bean products.

Carnitine is a vitamin-like compound made in the liver, kidney, and brain. It is made from the amino acid lysine (with the help of iron and vitamin C), and is effective in treating heart disease because of its ability to boost the metabolism of saturated fats and cholesterol. The heart normally stores more carnitine than it needs but lack of oxygen in ischemic heart disease causes depletion of carnitine stores. Foods rich in lysine and iron (such as tempeh, lentils, muesli, peas, tahini, garbanzos, beans, nuts, and seeds) help to replenish carnitine. Good sources of vitamin C include guava, bell pepper, green leaves, mangetout pea, broccoli, papaya, mango, and citrus fruits.

People with heart disease often have a deficiency of coenzymes because their nutritional intake does not keep pace with the increased needs of their tissues. Coenzymes CoA and Q10 are particularly beneficial to the heart because they are involved in the transport of fatty acids to and from cells and in the conversion of fat into energy. Coenzymes have many components in their structure that cannot be synthesized in the body, and which must therefore be supplied in the diet. B-complex vitamins are particularly important in this regard, and good sources of B vitamins include muesli, yeast extract, beans, peas, tahini, soy products such as tempeh, and green leaves.

Hawthorn berries and flowering tops are valuable herbal remedies for heart and circulation disorders. They strengthen the heart muscle and lower blood pressure and blood cholesterol levels. They contain anthocyanoid bioflavonoids, which relax the smooth muscle of the artery walls, thus dilating the blood vessels that feed the heart muscle, and increasing the supply of nutrients and oxygen. Garlic is an excellent blood cleanser and thinner, and, if used regularly over a period of time, guards against the formation of fatty deposits in the blood vessels. It can also help to keep blood-cholesterol levels under control.

part four

immune
foods in practice

Eating is not only the most important route to good health, it is highly enjoyable, too! The most nutritious plant foods are usually also the tastiest. On the following pages we have created a host of delicious recipes that you can enjoy for breakfast, dinner, supper, or as tasty snacks. They comprise foods that are packed with vitamins, minerals, and other vital nutrients, combined in ways that maximize their health-giving properties. With the exception of the juices, herbal drinks, and syrups, the following recipes serve four people unless otherwise stated. Where possible, harvest your own ingredients or use fresh, organic produce. Take care to wash ingredients thoroughly.

breakfasts

baked tomatoes on toast

4 large ripe beef tomatoes
3½ ounces mushrooms, finely chopped
2 garlic cloves, crushed
1 bunch of fresh basil, finely chopped
Breadcrumbs
Sea salt and freshly ground pepper
Olive oil
4 thick slices of bread, toasted

Preheat the oven to 350°F. Cut off the bottom of the tomatoes and scoop out the flesh into a bowl. Mix with the mushrooms, garlic, and basil. Add enough breadcrumbs to make the mixture hang together. Season with salt and pepper. Fill the tomato shells with the mixture. Sprinkle with a little olive oil. Bake in the oven for about 20 minutes, until the tomatoes are quite soft. Spread a little olive oil on each slice of toast, place a tomato on each and serve immediately.

scrambled tofu

8 ounces marinated tofu
4 tablespoons soy milk
Sea salt and freshly ground pepper
1 ounce polyunsaturated vegetable margarine
4 slices of wholemeal bread, toasted
Fresh chopped rosemary

Crumble the tofu and mix with the milk. Add salt and pepper to taste. Melt the margarine gently in a saucepan, add the tofu and stir continuously over a low heat until you have a thick, creamy consistency. Meanwhile make the toast. Divide the scrambled tofu on each piece, garnish with rosemary. Serve immediately.

ruby red melon salad *(far right)*

2 cantaloupe melons, peeled and deseeded
1 pink grapefruit, peeled
12 cherries, halved and depipped
1-inch piece fresh ginger root, finely chopped
Maple syrup (optional)

Cut the melon into cubes and divide the grapefruit into segments. Place on individual serving bowls. Garnish with the cherries and the ginger (and add a splash of maple syrup to taste—if liked).

beans and tomatoes on toast

14 ounces cooked black-eye peas (or navy beans or haricots)
2 tablespoons olive oil
1 red onion, sliced
1 garlic clove, sliced
½ teaspoon Florence fennel, finely chopped
1 teaspoon turmeric
1 teaspoon ground black cumin seed (or ground cumin)
½ teaspoon cayenne
2 teaspoons thyme, plus sprigs for garnish
Sea salt and freshly ground pepper
4 slices of bread, to toast
8 thick tomato slices

Rinse, drain, and mash the beans. Stir-fry the onion, garlic, and fennel in the oil for 1 minute. Add the turmeric, cumin, cayenne, and thyme. Mix in the beans and heat through. Season to taste. Toast the bread and spread the bean mixture on top. Garnish with 2 tomato slices on each and a little thyme and black pepper. Serve hot.

fresh fruit salad

1 banana
1 kiwi or 2 passion-fruits
1 papaya
1 small bunch of grapes
2 peaches or nectarines
Seasonal berries to garnish
1 cup unsweetened fruit juice

Peel, deseed and slice the fruit. Place in serving bowl. Add fruit juice and serve.

oatmeal with dried fruit and quinoa

2 cups rolled oats
4 tablespoons quinoa
5 ounces dried, unsulfured apricots
5 ounces raisins
5 ounces each of dried mango, pineapple, and apple
8 tablespoons plain soy yogurt

Soak the oats and the quinoa overnight in a saucepan with ¾ cup of water. Place the dried fruit in another small saucepan, cover with water and soak overnight too. In the morning, bring both to the boil (stirring the oats continuously), then cover and simmer each gently for 10–15 minutes. Serve the oatmeal in separate breakfast bowls, topped with the dried fruit (and liquid), and garnished with two spoonfuls of soy yogurt.

muesli

1¾ cups rolled oats
2 tablespoons each dried apricots, raisins, dates, chopped
1 tablespoon pecan nuts, chopped
1 tablespoon almonds, chopped
1 tablespoon sunflower seeds
1 tablespoon flaxseed
2 tablespoons wheatgerm
1 tablespoon wheat bran
Soy, rice, or almond milk
4 tablespoons plain soy yogurt
4 tablespoons fresh seasonal fruit

Combine all the muesli ingredients and serve with your choice of milk. Garnish each serving with a spoonful of yogurt and a spoonful of seasonal fruit. Serve.

fruity pancakes

1⅓ cups wheat flour
3 tablespoons gram flour
2 teaspoons baking powder
½ teaspoon salt (optional)
1¼ cups soy milk
1¼ cups water
3 tablespoons olive oil
Grapeseed oil for frying

For the filling:
5 ounces dried apricots, chopped
1 cup soy milk
10 strawberries, chopped
3½ ounces raspberries
1–2 guavas (or peaches), peeled and sliced
1 banana, chopped
Cinnamon, ground
Maple syrup (optional)

Soak the apricots for the filling in the soy milk overnight. Next day, sift the flours with the baking powder and salt and mix well. Add the soy milk and the water a little at a time, stirring continuously with a whisk. Slowly add the oil, continuing to stir. Refrigerate for 15 minutes while you combine the filling ingredients. First place the creamed apricots in a bowl and then carefully fold in the other fruit. Cook the pancakes and place a couple of spoonfuls of the fruit filling in the center of each. Sprinkle with cinnamon and maple syrup. Serve immediately.

yogurt with fruit

2½ cups plain soy yogurt
1 apple, cored and finely chopped
1 mango, deseeded, peeled, and finely chopped
4 tablespoons blackberries (or other seasonal berries)
1 banana, peeled and finely chopped
Candied sweet violets (optional)

Divide the yogurt into individual serving bowls. Then divide the fruit between each and decorate with candied violets.

soups, appetizers, snacks, and sauces

SOUPS

basic vegetable bouillon

2 tablespoons olive oil
2 onions, chopped
3 garlic cloves, crushed
2 carrots, chopped
1 parsnip or parsley root, chopped
2 carrots, chopped
½ celery root, chopped
3 cups of greens, chopped
2 leeks (including green tops), sliced
10 cups water
5 tomatoes, chopped
2 teaspoons thyme
2 tablespoons fresh lovage, chopped
2 bay leaves
2 tablespoons fresh parsley, chopped
Sea salt and black pepper to taste

Stir-fry the vegetables. Add water and tomatoes. Bring to the boil and add herbs and salt and pepper. Simmer for 1½ hours. Skim from time to time. Strain, cool, refrigerate, and use diluted within a few days to add flavor to soups and stews.

cool tomato soup *(below)*

2 pounds fresh ripe tomatoes, quartered and stalks removed
2 scallions, finely chopped
4 tablespoons fresh (or 4 teaspoons dried) basil, finely chopped
Sea salt and black pepper to taste

Blend the tomatoes. Heat gently in a saucepan. Add scallions and basil. Season. Leave to cool and then chill well before serving.

healing soup

7½ cups water
1½ pounds potatoes, chopped
1 pound carrots, chopped
1 tablespoon fresh lovage or 1 teaspoon dried
1 tablespoon miso
1 teaspoon caraway seeds
1 teaspoon herbes de Provence
Sea salt and freshly ground black pepper to taste

Bring the water to the boil and add the vegetables, lovage, miso, and caraway seeds. Simmer gently for 20 minutes. Add the herbes de Provence, blend, and heat through. Season to taste and serve with pan bread *(see page 118)*.

mint and melon soup

Flesh from 2 cantaloupe melons, chopped
1 cucumber, chopped and peeled
1 teaspoon maple syrup
1 tablespoon lemon rind, grated
1 cup water
3 tablespoons fresh mint, finely chopped
Sea salt and freshly ground black pepper to taste
Juice from 1 lemon
Lemon wedges (to garnish)

Heat the melon and the cucumber in a saucepan with the maple syrup, lemon rind, and water. Stir from time to time and simmer for 10 minutes. Add the mint. Blend, season and then add the lemon juice. Allow to cool, then refrigerate for 2 hours before serving. Serve with wedges of lemon.

black-eye pea and wild marjoram soup

2 tablespoons olive oil
2 shallots, chopped
1 garlic clove, crushed
1 teaspoon fennel seeds
2 teaspoons ground cilantro (coriander) seeds
1 small fennel, chopped
1 small zucchini, chopped
14 ounces black-eye peas, cooked
1 pound tomatoes, skinned and blended
5 cups diluted basic vegetable bouillon *(see page 104)*
2 tablespoons tomato paste
3 tablespoons fresh (or 3 teaspoons dried) marjoram, chopped

Gently stir-fry the shallots, garlic, fennel seeds, cilantro, fennel, and zucchini in the oil. Add the peas and the tomatoes, heat through, then add the bouillon and tomato paste. Bring to boil and add the salt, pepper and half the marjoram. Cover and simmer for 20 minutes. Add rest of the marjoram. Season and serve.

creamy cauliflower soup

1 cauliflower
2 tablespoons olive oil
2 shallots, chopped
1 small carrot, chopped
2 potatoes, chopped
5 cups diluted basic vegetable bouillon *(see page 104)*
1 cup soy milk
Sea salt and freshly ground black pepper to taste
1 bunch of parsley, finely chopped

Cut off the cauliflower flowerets and steam until tender. Chop up the rest of the cauliflower and stir-fry in the oil together with the other vegetables. Add the bouillon, bring to the boil and simmer for about 30 minutes. Blend, then add the soy milk together with the flowerets, seasoning and parsley. Heat through (but don't let it boil) and serve.

italian butterbean soup

14 ounces butterbeans, cooked
4 tablespoons olive oil
1 red onion, finely chopped
2 garlic cloves, finely chopped
4 stalks celery, chopped
1 pound 2 ounces tomatoes, peeled and chopped
5 cups diluted basic vegetable bouillon *(see page 104)*
1 tablespoon fresh thyme
1 teaspoon yeast extract
Sea salt and freshly ground black pepper to taste

Stir-fry the onion, garlic, and celery gently in the olive oil. Blend half the cooked beans with the tomatoes and half the bouillon, then add them together with the whole beans and the remaining bouillon. Stir well, then add the thyme, yeast extract, salt, and pepper. Bring to the boil and simmer for 20 minutes. Adjust the seasoning and serve.

pumpkin soup

3 tablespoons olive oil
1 red onion, chopped
1 garlic clove, chopped
2 pounds pumpkin, peeled, deseeded, chopped
3 tablespoons fresh (or 3 teaspoons dried) marjoram, plus some to garnish
5 cups diluted basic vegetable bouillon *(see page 104)*
2 cups coconut milk
Sea salt and freshly ground black pepper to taste

Heat the oil gently in a big saucepan. Add the onion, garlic, and pumpkin. Stir-fry for 5 minutes, then add the marjoram, bouillon, and coconut milk. Bring to the boil, cover and simmer for 15 minutes or until the vegetables are soft. Add salt and pepper. Blend and serve, garnished with marjoram.

shiitake mushroom soup

3 ounces dried shiitake mushrooms (or 9 ounces fresh/bottled)
2 tablespoons olive oil
2 scallions, finely chopped
1 garlic clove, finely chopped
1 carrot, finely chopped
1-inch cube fresh ginger root, finely chopped
1 tablespoon soy sauce
1 teaspoon maple syrup
7½ cups water with 1 teaspoon miso
Sea salt and freshly ground black pepper

If using dried mushrooms, soak them in plenty of water for 20 minutes. Discard the stems. Heat the oil gently in a big skillet and stir-fry the scallions, garlic, carrot, and ginger root for 2 minutes. Add the mushrooms and sauté for another 5 minutes. Add the soy sauce, maple syrup, and bouillon one after the other. Bring to the boil, cover and simmer gently for 30 minutes. Add the salt and pepper to taste.

spicy moroccan soup

2 ounces garbanzo beans
2 ounces pinto beans (or haricots)
3½ ounces green lentils, rinsed
3 tablespoons olive oil
1 garlic clove, finely chopped
1 onion, chopped
1 teaspoon ground black cumin (or ground cumin)
1 teaspoon ground cilantro (coriander)
1 teaspoon caraway seeds
½ teaspoon cayenne
1 tablespoon turmeric
2 carrots, chopped
2 potatoes, chopped
3 celery stalks, finely chopped
1-inch piece fresh ginger root, finely chopped
1 pound tomatoes, blended
5 cups diluted basic vegetable bouillon *(see page 104)*
Sea salt and freshly ground black pepper to taste
2 tablespoons lemon juice

Rinse and soak the garbanzos and pinto beans overnight. Rinse again and place in a saucepan with the lentils. Add lots of water and cook for 30 minutes. Meanwhile heat the oil gently in a soup pan. Stir-fry the garlic and onion. Add the spices, then carrots, potatoes, celery, and ginger. Stir-fry for 5 minutes. Add tomatoes and simmer. Drain the cooking water off the pulses and rinse them. Add the pulses to the pan together with the bouillon. Bring to boil and simmer for 45 minutes, adding more water if necessary. Season, add lemon juice. Serve.

tibetan dumpling soup

10 ounces wholewheat flour
10 ounces white flour
½ teaspoon salt
2 tablespoons olive oil
½ teaspoon fenugreek seeds
1 garlic clove, crushed
1 red onion, sliced
3 tomatoes, chopped
1-inch piece of ginger root, finely chopped
½ teaspoon nutmeg, grated
½ teaspoon turmeric
3 tablespoons soy sauce
1 bunch of radishes, sliced
3½ ounces green peas
7½ cups diluted basic vegetable bouillon *(see page 104)*
3 salad onions, sliced
Sea salt and freshly ground black pepper to taste

Combine the flours and salt. Add enough water to make a stiff dough. Roll on a floured surface to form a long, finger-thick snake. Cut into ½-inch pieces and sprinkle with flour to prevent them sticking together. Heat the oil in a soup pan and add the fenugreek seeds. Stir-fry until dark brown, then add the garlic and onion. Stir for 3 minutes, then add the tomatoes, spices, and soy sauce. Stir, cover, and simmer gently for 5 minutes, then add the radishes and peas. Cook for 2 more minutes. Add the bouillon, bring to the boil and add the dumplings. Boil for 6–8 minutes until the dumplings are done. Add the salad onions. Season and serve.

welsh leek and potato soup

4 leeks, sliced
2 ounces vegetable margarine
4 medium potatoes, chopped into small cubes
7½ cups basic vegetable bouillon *(see page 104)*
Sea salt and freshly ground black pepper
1 bunch of chives

Gently sauté the leeks in the margarine, add the potatoes, cook for a few more minutes before adding the bouillon. Heat through and simmer for 30 minutes. Garnish with chives and serve hot. It is also delicious blended.

APPETIZERS

asparagus with ravigote

(below right)

2 bunches of asparagus, peeled
1 tablespoon lemon juice
Ravigote *(see page 111)*

Cut off the woody ends of the asparagus. Cook in lightly salted boiling water for about 10 minutes. (One method is to tie the asparagus in a bundle with cotton string and boil with tips sticking out of water.) Serve with ravigote dressing.

hummus with crudités and warm pitta bread

10 ounces garbanzo beans, cooked and drained
2 garlic cloves, crushed
4 tablespoons lemon juice
1 teaspoon sea salt
2 tablespoons tahini
1 tablespoon fresh parsley, finely chopped
1 teaspoon paprika
1 tablespoon olive oil

For the crudités:
2 carrots and 8 long radishes, sliced into slim sticks
2 celery stalks, sliced into sticks
¼ cucumber, sliced into sticks
8 cherry tomatoes (kept whole)

Blend the garbanzos with the garlic, lemon juice, 4 tablespoons cold water, and sea salt. Add the tahini and blend again to a smooth paste. Adjust the seasoning and place in a serving bowl. Garnish with parsley and paprika and sprinkle with a little olive oil. Serve with crudités and warm pitta bread in wedges.

korean kimchi-style salad

1 small Chinese cabbage, finely chopped
1 teaspoon unrefined sea salt
2 garlic cloves, finely chopped
1-inch piece of fresh ginger root, finely chopped
1 fresh chilli pepper, finely chopped
2 tomatoes, finely chopped
1 green bell pepper, finely chopped
1 carrot, finely chopped
½ cucumber, finely chopped

Place the Chinese cabbage in a bowl. Add the salt and mix well. Add the rest of the ingredients and serve with fresh bread.

broiled bell peppers

3 bell peppers, quartered longways and deseeded
Rich garlic dressing *(see page 69)*

Broil the peppers, with the skin facing the heat, until the skin is charred. Leave to cool in a paper bag, then peel off the skin. Cut into long strips and place in a shallow dish. Sprinkle with rich garlic dressing and serve with French bread.

vegetable kebabs

(pictured page 109)

16 button mushrooms, kept whole
12 cherry tomatoes, kept whole
1 red bell pepper, in chunks
1 green bell pepper, in chunks
2 zucchini, in chunks
1 big sweet potato or yam, parboiled, in chunks
1 eggplant, in chunks
4 shallots, halved
4 bay leaves, halved
4 barbecue skewers

For the marinade (makes 1 pint):
12 ounces tomato ketchup *(see page 111)*
Juice of 1 lemon
¾ cup red wine vinegar
6 garlic cloves, crushed
2 tablespoons raw cane sugar
2 tablespoons olive oil
2 tablespoons mustard

Mix all the marinade ingredients together in a bowl. Add the prepared kebab ingredients. Mix gently, cover and leave to marinate for 2 hours. Thread the vegetables on to the skewers and brush with marinade. Place the kebabs on a hot barbecue and broil for 10 minutes, turning from time to time. Serve hot.

baba ganoush

1 big eggplant
2 garlic cloves, crushed
4 tablespoons tahini
4 tablespoons lemon juice
1 teaspoon ground black cumin, toasted
1 tablespoon fresh parsley, finely chopped
Sea salt to taste
1 teaspoon paprika

Prick the eggplant with a fork. Toast, turning from time to time, until the skin is black and charred. Cool under running water, then cut in half and scoop out the flesh. Chop the flesh finely, place in a bowl and mix in the rest of the ingredients, reserving a little parsley and the paprika to garnish. Adjust the seasoning, garnish, and serve with warm pitta bread, green salad leaves, tomato, and cucumber.

samosa parcels

4 scallions, finely chopped
1 tablespoon fresh ginger root, finely chopped
1 garlic clove, finely chopped
9 ounces marinated tofu, in small cubes
8½ ounces phyllo pastry
Sunflower oil
2 tablespoons soy sauce

Mix the scallions, ginger root, and garlic in a bowl. Gently stir-fry the tofu in a little oil. Turn off heat, add the soy sauce, stir, transfer to the bowl and mix well. Cut the phyllo pastry into long strips, about 3 inches wide. Brush each strip with oil. Take the first strip and put 1 teaspoon of filling on one end. Fold the end of the pastry over to form a triangle covering the filling. Keep folding the strip over itself to form a triangular parcel. Repeat with the other strips. Brush the parcels with oil, bake at 425°F for 10 minutes until golden. Serve hot.

toasted tempeh with herb salad

8 tempeh slices
Sunflower oil
Sea salt
1 small red lettuce
1 bunch of watercress
1 bunch of nasturtium leaves and flowers (optional)
1 carrot, finely sliced
1 bunch chives, finely chopped
Lime dressing *(see page 111)*

Brush the tempeh slices with oil and toast them on a dry pan till golden. Sprinkle with sea salt and remove from heat. For each individual serving, arrange some salad and two slices of tempeh on a plate, sprinkle with dressing and serve.

tofumasalata

7 ounces smoked tofu
4 tablespoons lemon juice
1 teaspoon grated lemon rind
8 tablespoons water
1 shallot, chopped
1 garlic clove, chopped
3 tablespoons breadcrumbs
4 tablespoons olive oil
1 teaspoon paprika
Sea salt and freshly ground black pepper to taste

Crumble the tofu, and blend with the lemon juice, lemon rind, water, shallot, garlic, breadcrumbs, olive oil, and paprika. Adjust the seasoning and chill before serving with warm pitta, olives, and slices of cucumber.

SNACKS
marinated olives

10 ounces olives
4 tablespoons olive oil
2 fresh or dried chilli peppers, chopped
½ lemon (unpeeled), quartered and sliced
2 garlic cloves, sliced
1 teaspoon cilantro (coriander) seeds, crushed
1 teaspoon dried thyme
1 teaspoon dried oregano

Gently press the olives with a rolling pin. Place in a bowl with the chilli peppers, lemon, garlic, cilantro, thyme, and oregano. Mix well, cover and allow to marinate overnight before serving.

toasted nuts and seeds

1 tablespoon cashew nuts
1 tablespoon melon seeds
1 tablespoon almonds
1 tablespoon walnuts
1 tablespoon hazelnuts
1 tablespoon sunflower seeds
1 tablespoon Brazil nuts
Soy sauce
½ teaspoon sea salt
Few drops of tabasco (optional)

Mix together the cashew nuts, melon seeds, almonds, walnuts, hazelnuts, sunflower seeds, and Brazil nuts and dry roast in a heavy skillet. Turn off the heat. Immediately add the soy sauce, sea salt, and tabasco. Stir well, remove from pan and serve.

tomato and cucumber canapés

1 cucumber, in thick slices
8 cherry tomatoes, halved
7 ounces walnuts, shelled
1 garlic clove
4 tablespoons water
5 tablespoons olive oil
Sea salt to taste
1 bunch of fresh parsley, finely chopped

Arrange the cucumber slices and the tomato halves on a large plate. Blend the walnuts, garlic, water, and olive oil to a smooth pâté. Season to taste. Place a small spoonful of the pâté on top of each slice of cucumber and tomato. Garnish with parsley and serve.

guacamole

4 small ripe avocados
2 teaspoons ground cilantro (coriander)
2 teaspoons ground cumin
¼ teaspoon cayenne pepper
4 tablespoons lemon juice
2 garlic cloves, finely chopped
½-inch cube fresh ginger root, finely chopped
2 ripe tomatoes, finely chopped
Sea salt and freshly ground black pepper to taste
1 small bunch fresh cilantro (coriander) leaves, chopped
2 carrots cut into sticks
1 packet tortilla chips

Blend the avocados with the ground cilantro, cumin, cayenne, lemon juice, garlic, and ginger until almost smooth. Transfer to a bowl, stir in the tomatoes, season, cover and chill before serving. Garnish with the fresh cilantro leaves and serve with tortilla chips and carrot sticks.

tofu balls

1 onion, grated
1 green chilli, deseeded and finely chopped
1 pound 2 ounces tofu, grated or crumbled
2 teaspoons ground cumin
1 garlic clove, crushed
1 organic lemon, juice and grated rind
Sea salt and freshly ground black pepper to taste
1 tablespoon olive oil
Grapeseed oil for shallow frying
Salad leaves (according to season)

Put the onion, chilli, tofu, cumin, garlic, lemon juice and rind, and olive oil in a bowl. Season to taste and mix well. Shape into small balls and shallow fry in the grapeseed oil till golden. Serve with a selection of salad leaves.

tzaziki

½ cucumber, finely diced
1¼ cups plain soy yogurt
1 teaspoon olive oil
2 garlic cloves, finely chopped
2 tablespoons fresh mint, finely chopped
Sea salt and freshly ground black pepper to taste

Place the cucumber in a bowl along with the yogurt, olive oil, garlic, and mint. Mix well. Cover and chill. Adjust seasoning. Serve with green salad leaves and warm pitta.

pan amb oli

4 slices of bread to toast
2 garlic cloves, halved
2 ripe tomatoes, halved
2 teaspoons olive oil
Sea salt and freshly ground black pepper

Toast the bread on both sides. Rub one side with the garlic, then squeeze on a half tomato and rub in the tomato pulp (discard the skin). Sprinkle with ½ teaspoon of oil. Repeat for remaining slices. Season and serve immediately.

SAUCES

lemon tahini dressing

(far left, bottom)

2 tablespoons lemon juice
1 tablespoon tahini
1 tablespoon maple syrup
1 tablespoon Dijon mustard
7 tablespoons olive oil
Sea salt and freshly ground black pepper

Mix together the lemon juice, tahini, maple syrup, Dijon mustard, and olive oil and blend or whisk to a thick, smooth consistency. Add seasoning to taste.

lime dressing

2 tablespoons lime juice
1 tablespoon Dijon mustard
1 teaspoon raw cane sugar
Sea salt and freshly ground black pepper
Olive oil

Combine all the ingredients, except the oil, in a small bowl and whisk together. Add the oil slowly, whisking continuously until you have a smooth dressing. (If you can't get the dressing to emulsify, try adding a little cold water.)

pesto sauce

(far left, top)

2 tablespoons pine nuts
1 bunch of fresh basil
2 garlic cloves, crushed
1 teaspoon coarse sea salt
4 tablespoons olive oil

Grind the nuts in a mortar or blender. Add the rest of the ingredients and mix to form a coarse paste. Add a little extra oil if necessary.

ravigote

1 garlic clove
1 teaspoon tarragon
2 tablespoons parsley, chopped
2 tablespoons chives, chopped
2 teaspoons capers
1 tablespoon Dijon mustard
1 tablespoon red wine vinegar
Pinch of freshly ground sea salt
¾ cup olive oil

Blend all the ingredients except the oil. Add the oil very carefully, a little at a time, until the mixture emulsifies, then slowly add the rest of the oil. Serve with cooked vegetables.

tomato ketchup

(far left, centre)

½ pound onion, finely chopped
1 pound red bell peppers, finely chopped
1 pound tomatoes, finely chopped
3 tablespoons olive oil
3½ ounces unrefined cane sugar
3 garlic cloves, finely chopped
1 fresh chilli pepper, deseeded, finely chopped
1 teaspoon mustard powder
2 teaspoons paprika
½ cup red wine vinegar
4 whole cloves, crushed
Sea salt and freshly ground black pepper to taste

Stir-fry the onion, red bell pepper, and tomatoes in the oil, then simmer for 45 minutes until they break down. Filter through a sieve. Add the sugar, cloves, chilli pepper, mustard powder, paprika, vinegar, and crushed cloves, and simmer very gently for 2 hours until you have a thick paste. Season. (This will keep in the refrigerator for 3–4 days. But if you want to keep it longer, pour the ketchup into clean bottles, put the tops on and place in boiling water for 20 minutes to sterilize the contents.)

main courses, side dishes, and salads

MAIN COURSES

amaranth and tofu puffs

1 ounce polyunsaturated vegetable margarine
8½ ounces marinated tofu, cubed small
8½ ounces amaranth leaves (or fresh spinach), chopped
Pinch of nutmeg
Sea salt and freshly ground black pepper to taste
1 packet of puff pastry

Melt the margarine, add the tofu and sauté for a few minutes. Add the amaranth (or spinach) and nutmeg and stir-fry until it goes soft and the water has evaporated. Season and set aside. Preheat oven to 400°F. Cut the pastry into squares. Dampen the edges. Place a portion of amaranth mixture on each square, fold one side over diagonally to form a triangle, seal well. Place on a greased baking tray and bake for about 15 minutes or until golden.

casserole de puy

3½ ounces lentilles de Puy (brown lentils)
1 bay leaf
3 tablespoons olive oil
½ teaspoon cayenne
1 teaspoon turmeric
1 teaspoon each of cilantro (coriander), cumin and mustard seeds
1 garlic clove, crushed
1 red onion, chopped
1 leek, sliced
8 ounces button mushrooms
1 potato
2 carrots
1 pound tomatoes, peeled and chopped
Sea salt and freshly ground black pepper to taste
Fresh cilantro cilantro (coriander)

Put the lentils and the bay leaf on to boil in twice their volume of water. Cover and simmer while you prepare the other ingredients. Heat the oil in a large flameproof casserole. Crush the seeds in a mortar and add them with the other spices, then add the onion and leek. Stir-fry for 2 minutes, then add the mushrooms and stir-fry for a few more minutes. Add the potato, carrots, and tomatoes, heat through and add the partially cooked lentils (with the cooking water). Season with salt and pepper, add a little more water to make sure the dish doesn't dry out, then cover and cook in the oven at 350°F for 45 minutes. Garnish with fresh cilantro. Serve with mashed potato.

paella

3 tablespoons olive oil
8½ ounces long-grain rice
1 teaspoon turmeric
2 garlic cloves, finely chopped
1 onion, chopped
1 carrot, chopped
8½ ounces artichoke hearts
1 celery stalk, finely sliced
1 red bell pepper, deseeded and sliced
4 tomatoes, skinned and chopped
¼ cup basic vegetable bouillon (see page 104)
3½ ounces green peas
1 tablespoon fresh parsley, finely chopped
1 tablespoon fresh marjoram (or 1 teaspoon dried)
2 tablespoons cashew nuts
1 organic lemon, in thick slices
Sea salt and freshly ground black pepper to taste

Heat the oil in a large deep skillet and stir-fry the rice until golden. Add turmeric, garlic, onion, and carrot, and stir-fry for a few minutes. Add the artichoke hearts, celery stalk, and red bell pepper and stir-fry again for 2 minutes. Add the tomatoes and bouillon. Bring to boil and simmer for 5 minutes. Add the peas, then simmer until the rice is cooked. Add the herbs, cashews, and lemon slices. Season to taste. Serve hot.

artichoke hearts, fava beans, and shiitake

2 tablespoons olive oil
2 teaspoons ground cumin
1 bay leaf
1 teaspoon turmeric
8½ ounces shiitake mushrooms, halved
1 pound fava beans (shelled weight)
1 pound artichoke hearts, cooked
½ cup water
2 tablespoons lemon juice
1 small bunch of parsley, finely chopped
Sea salt and freshly ground black pepper to taste

Heat the oil gently in a large pan. Add the spices, then the mushrooms. Sauté for a few minutes, then add the fava beans with the artichokes and the water. Heat through, simmer until the beans are tender, then add the lemon juice and the parsley. Season and serve.

asparagus asian-style

1 bunch of asparagus, ends cut off
2 tablespoons olive oil
1 teaspoon cumin powder
1 stalk lemongrass, finely sliced
1-inch piece fresh ginger root, finely chopped
3 medium carrots, julienned
1 bunch of scallions, sliced
1 bell pepper, deseeded, finely sliced
2 tablespoons tamarind paste, dissolved in 1¼ cups hot water
1 handful of bean sprouts
2 tablespoons soy sauce
1 tablespoon maple syrup
1–2 tablespoons lemon juice
Sea salt and freshly ground black pepper to taste

Cut the asparagus into 2-inch pieces and set aside. Heat the oil in a wok, add the cumin, lemongrass, and ginger and stir-fry a few seconds. Add the asparagus, then the carrots, scallions, and bell pepper. Stir-fry for another 5 minutes. Add the dissolved tamarind paste. Simmer until the asparagus are cooked. Then add the bean sprouts, soy sauce, maple syrup, and lemon juice. Heat through, season to taste and serve with rice or noodles.

butternut squash with bell pepper and tomato

(below)

1 butternut squash, deseeded and peeled
2 tablespoons olive oil
1 red onion, chopped
1 garlic clove, chopped
1 bell pepper, in strips
6 ripe tomatoes, skinned and sliced
2 tablespoons tomato paste
2 tablespoons fresh (or 2 teaspoons dried) basil, chopped
1 teaspoon paprika
2 tablespoons parsley, chopped
Sea salt and freshly ground black pepper to taste

Chop the squash into chunks. Heat the oil in a large pan, add the onion, garlic, and the squash, sauté for 2 minutes and then add the bell pepper. Heat through and then add the rest of the ingredients except the parsley. Cover and simmer for 20 minutes. Season, garnish with parsley and serve with rice or hasselbach potatoes *(see page 118)*.

sweet and sour vegetable parcels

4 thick slices of tempeh, chopped
2 scallions, finely sliced into strips
2 carrots, julienned
2 celery sticks, julienned
1-inch piece ginger root, cut into fine sticks
4-inch lemon grass stem
1 handful of bean sprouts
8 sheets of phyllo pastry
Grapeseed oil
1 tablespoon soy sauce
2 tablespoons lemon juice
1 tablespoon vinegar
1 tablespoon maple syrup
1 tablespoon tomato paste
1 garlic clove, crushed
1 teaspoon paprika
1 broccoli, cut into flowerets
3½ ounces baby corn cobs
1 red bell pepper, cut into strips

Stir-fry the tempeh. Add the vegetables one at a time in the order above, stir-frying in between. Add the lemongrass and bean sprouts. Stir-fry again and season to taste. Brush the pastry with the oil. Divide the filling between the 8 sheets. Fold the corners of each sheet into the center and pinch the parcels together. Brush with oil and bake at 400°F for 20 minutes until golden. For the sweet and sour vegetables, mix together soy sauce, lemon juice, vinegar, syrup, tomato paste, garlic, and paprika. Sauté the broccoli, baby corns, and red bell peppers for 5 minutes. Add the sauce, heat through, and serve with parcels.

french onion tart *(left)*

For the short-crust pastry:
8½ ounces wheat flour
½ teaspoon salt
4½ ounces cold vegetable margarine
¾ cup cold water

For the filling:
1 pound 9 ounces onions, finely sliced
¾ teaspoon salt and a pinch of black pepper
8½ ounces tofu, crumbled
1 cup soy milk
1 tablespoon flour

Mix the flour and salt, then add the margarine by chopping it into the flour with a knife and a spoon until it forms small lumps. Crumble the dough with your hands until it looks like Parmesan (taking care not to let the dough get warm), then add cold water and knead the dough lightly to a smooth lump. Refrigerate until needed. Sauté the onions very gently in the oil. Stir from time to time, taking care not to let them brown. After 10 minutes, add the salt and pepper. Stir, then cover and simmer very gently for 15 minutes. Remove the lid and let the liquid reduce for 5 minutes. Remove from heat. Blend the tofu, soy milk, and flour, and mix with the onions. Season to taste. Roll out the dough and place in a greased baking case. Add the filling and bake at 350°F for 25–30 minutes. Delicious hot or cold.

provençale-style kidney beans

2 tablespoons olive oil
1 red onion, sliced
2 garlic cloves, sliced
1 can red kidney beans
2 small zucchini, sliced
4 ripe tomatoes, skinned and chopped
½ cup basic vegetable bouillon (*see page 104*)
2 tablespoons fresh basil, chopped
3½ ounces small niçoise olives
Sea salt and freshly ground black pepper to taste

Heat the oil and sauté the onion and garlic gently for 2 minutes. Add the kidney beans, zucchini, and tomatoes and cook for 2 more minutes. Add the bouillon and the basil. Bring to the boil and simmer for 10 minutes. Add the olives. Heat through, season, garnish with basil, and serve with wild rice.

greek casserole

4 tablespoons olive oil
8½ ounces tofu, cut into cubes
1 red onion, in thick slices
1 green bell pepper, in thick slices
2 garlic cloves, chopped
1 tablespoon wholewheat flour
1 pound 2 ounces ripe tomatoes, chopped
1 tablespoon tomato paste
2 teaspoons marjoram
Sea salt and freshly ground black pepper to taste

Stir-fry the tofu cubes in half the oil until they begin to brown. Remove from pan. Add the rest of the oil, then the onion. Sauté for a few minutes then add the green bell pepper and garlic. Sauté for a few minutes, turn down the heat and mix in the flour. Let it blend in for a minute, then add the tomatoes, turn up heat and stir well. Add the tomato paste, marjoram, and salt and pepper. Stir while you bring the mixture to boil. Add the tofu pieces and mix well. Place in an ovenproof dish and bake, covered, at 350°F for about 30 minutes.

spinach bouillabaisse

3 tablespoons olive oil
2 white onions, sliced
2 potatoes, sliced
1 pound 2 ounces fresh spinach, chopped
2 garlic cloves, crushed
1½ cups diluted basic vegetable bouillon (*see page 104*)
Pinch of cayenne
1 tablespoon fresh dill, chopped (optional)
1 tablespoon fresh parsley, chopped
Sea salt and freshly ground black pepper to taste

Sauté the onion and potato in the oil. Add the spinach and stir until it goes soft, then add the garlic, bouillon, and cayenne. Simmer for 10 minutes, add dill and parsley, and season to taste. Heat through and serve with fresh bread.

okra in sweet and sour tamarind sauce

4 tablespoons olive oil
1 teaspoon black mustard seeds
1 teaspoon ground cumin
1 teaspoon ground cilantro (coriander)
Pinch of cayenne pepper
½ teaspoon turmeric
3 garlic cloves, finely chopped
1 pound fresh okra, trimmed
1¼ cups water
6½ ounces green beans, trimmed
2 tablespoons tamarind paste
2 tablespoons maple syrup
Sea salt and freshly ground black pepper to taste

Heat the oil gently in a skillet. Add mustard seeds, cumin, cilantro, cayenne, turmeric, and garlic. Stir-fry ½ minute, then add the okra. Stir-fry for 1 minute then add the water and the beans. Heat through and simmer for 10 minutes, stirring occasionally. Add the tamarind paste and the maple syrup. Simmer again for another 5 minutes. Season and serve with basmati rice.

shepherdess' pie

4 ounces lentilles de Puy (brown lentils)
3 tablespoons olive oil
1 bay leaf
1 teaspoon thyme
2 garlic cloves, finely chopped
2 shallots, chopped
2 carrots, finely chopped
10 ounces mushrooms, quartered
1 pound tomatoes, skinned and chopped
⅔ cup vegetable juice or bouillon (see page 104)
1 tablespoon soy sauce
2 tablespoons fresh basil, chopped
Sea salt and freshly ground black pepper to taste

For the topping:
3 large potatoes, chopped
2 sweet potatoes, chopped
2 ounces polyunsaturated vegetable margarine
Soy milk
Paprika

Put the lentils on to boil in three times their volume of water. Boil the potatoes and sweet potatoes in salted water until tender. Meanwhile heat the oil gently and add the bay leaf, thyme, garlic, shallots and carrots. Stir and add the mushrooms. Sauté for a few minutes (until the mushrooms give off their moisture) then add the tomatoes. Drain any remaining cooking water from the lentils and add them together with the bouillon and soy sauce. Simmer gently for 10 minutes. Add the basil and adjust seasoning. Remove from the heat and place in a large shallow ovenproof dish. Mash the potatoes with the margarine and soy milk. Add seasoning to taste and spread over the filling. Sprinkle with paprika and bake at 470°F for 10 minutes or until golden.

sweet potato curry

3 tablespoons olive oil
2 teaspoons black mustard seeds
1 teaspoon curry powder
1 red onion, sliced
2 green chillies, sliced
12 ounces sweet potatoes, peeled and cubed
8½ ounces corn kernels
1 spear broccoli, cut into flowerets
5 ounces fresh spinach, chopped
2 cups coconut milk
Sea salt and freshly ground black pepper to taste
2 tablespoons lime juice
1 bunch of fresh cilantro (coriander) leaves, chopped

Heat the oil and add the black mustard seeds and the curry powder and stir-fry until the seeds start to pop. Add the onion and chillies, and stir-fry for another 2 minutes. Add the sweet potato, sweetcorn, and broccoli. Stir-fry for 5 minutes then add the spinach and mix well. Add the coconut milk and simmer gently for 10 minutes until the vegetables are soft. Season with salt, pepper, and lime juice. Garnish with fresh cilantro and serve with rice.

mushrooms with sage and thyme stuffing

12–16 large flat open mushrooms
2 tablespoons olive oil
3 garlic cloves, crushed
2 teaspoons thyme
3 tablespoons soy sauce
8 tablespoons breadcrumbs
4 tablespoons fresh parsley, finely chopped

Remove the stalks from the mushroom caps and scrape out the lamellae (gills) with a teaspoon. Place the caps upside down on a greased ovenproof dish or baking tray. Finely chop the mushroom stalks and stir-fry them in the oil with the garlic. Add the thyme and the soy sauce and stir-fry until the mushroom stalks give off their moisture. Add the breadcrumbs and stir until the liquid is soaked up. Remove from heat and add the chopped parsley. Fill the mushroom caps with the mixture and bake for about 10 minutes at 400°F.

winter hot pot

3 tablespoons olive oil
1 onion, sliced
2 carrots, sliced
1 parsnip, sliced
1 celery stick, sliced
7 ounces cooked garbanzo beans
10 ounces shiitake mushrooms, kept whole
¾ cup basic vegetable bouillon (see page 104)
Sea salt and freshly ground black pepper to taste
2 big potatoes, thinly sliced

Heat the oil in a deep, ovenproof casserole. Add the onion, carrots, and parsnip. Sauté for 5 minutes. Add the celery, garbanzos, and mushrooms. Stir-fry for another 5 minutes and then add the bouillon. Heat through, season, and cover with potato slices. Place in a preheated oven and cook at 350°F for 45 minutes.

spicy tofu burgers

1 tablespoon olive oil
1 onion, grated
1 carrot, grated
2 teaspoons ground cilantro (coriander)
1 garlic clove, crushed
2 teaspoons tomato paste
8½ ounces tofu, crumbled
2 tablespoons breadcrumbs
2 tablespoons Brazil nuts, finely chopped
Sea salt and freshly ground black pepper to taste
Flour for coating
Grapeseed oil for frying

Heat the oil and gently stir-fry the onion and carrot until soft. Add the cilantro, garlic, and tomato paste and stir-fry for 2 more minutes. Place in a bowl and mix with the tofu, breadcrumbs, and nuts. Season and stir until the mixture sticks together well. Shape into burgers, dip in flour and fry till golden. Drain on paper and serve with steamed vegetables.

sweet chestnuts and kumquats

1 pound fresh (12 ounces dried) sweet chestnuts, shelled
3 tablespoons olive oil
1 garlic clove, sliced
1 bay leaf
2 celery sticks, sliced
2 leeks, sliced
3 tablespoons wholewheat flour
½ cup red wine
1¾ cups basic vegetable bouillon (*see page 104*)
Juice of 1 tangerine
3½ ounces kumquats
Sea salt and freshly ground black pepper to taste

If using dried chestnuts, you will need to soak them for 8 hours before cooking. If using fresh chestnuts, drop them in boiling water and peel them with a sharp knife. Heat the oil in a casserole, add the garlic and bay leaf, and stir for a few seconds. Add the chestnuts, celery, and leeks. Sprinkle with the flour, mix well, then slowly add the wine, the vegetable bouillon, and the tangerine juice. Heat through, then add the kumquats and salt and pepper. Cook covered in the oven at 350°F for about an hour. Serve with broccoli and wild rice.

SIDE DISHES

cucumber, tomato, and pepper relish

½ cucumber, chopped
8½ ounces tomatoes, chopped
1 red onion, chopped
2 green chilli peppers, finely sliced
2 tablespoons lime juice
Pinch of unrefined sugar
Pinch of salt
2 tablespoons fresh cilantro (coriander) leaves, chopped

Mix all the ingredients in a bowl and store in the refrigerator until needed.

red chilli relish

4 red chillies and 2 red bell peppers, stalk and seeds removed, chopped
4 ripe tomatoes, stalk removed, chopped
2 garlic cloves, peeled and chopped
3 tablespoons lime juice
Sea salt to taste

Blend all the ingredients, store in the refrigerator until needed.

khichuri—rice with lentils

7 ounces basmati rice, washed
3½ ounces red lentils, washed
1 bay leaf
2-inch cinnamon stick
1 teaspoon ground turmeric
5 cups water (approximately)
Sea salt to taste

Place the rice and the lentils in a saucepan with the spices. Add the water, bring to boil and simmer until rice is soft (about 30 minutes, depending on type).

lemon rice

10 ounces basmati rice, rinsed
2 lemon grass stalks, finely sliced
5 cups water (approximately)
Sea salt to taste
3 tablespoons lemon juice

Place the rice in a saucepan and add the water and the salt. Bring to the boil. Add the lemon grass and simmer for about 30 minutes until the rice is tender. Sprinkle with lemon juice and serve.

hasselbach potatoes

3 pounds potatoes, halved
Sunflower oil
Gomassio (sesame salt)
1 bunch of fresh dill, finely chopped

Place the halved potatoes on a chopping board, flat side down, and cut grooves in each (nearly all the way through to the bottom). Then parboil the potatoes in lightly salted water for 5 minutes, drain and cool under running water. Dry gently and place in a lightly greased large roasting tin. Brush well with oil. Bake in a preheated oven at 425°F for 25 minutes, or until crisp and golden. Sprinkle with gomassio and garnish with the fresh dill.

pan bread

8½ ounces wholewheat flour
2 teaspoons baking powder
½ teaspoon unrefined sea salt
1 teaspoon caraway seeds (optional)
1 cup water (approximately)

Sift the flour, baking powder, and salt together. Add the caraway seeds and then enough water to form a soft dough. Knead to a smooth consistency. Roll the dough into a sausage and divide it into 12 balls. Roll each ball on a floured surface into 5-inch rounds. Heat a dry heavy skillet and cook each bread (without oil) for 2 minutes on each side (or until brown spots appear).

spring greens and macadamia nuts

2 ounces macadamia nuts
2 tablespoons olive oil
2¼ pounds spring greens (or other greens), shredded
½ cup water or bouillon
1 tablespoon lemon juice
Sea salt and freshly ground black pepper

Toast the macadamia nuts in a dry skillet, then remove from heat. Heat the oil in a large pan or wok, add the spring greens and stir-fry for 5 minutes. Add the water, cover and simmer for another 5 minutes. Add the lemon juice and macadamia nuts, season and serve.

tomato salsa

1 pound ripe tomatoes, finely chopped
2 scallions, finely chopped
1 red chilli pepper, finely chopped
4 tablespoons lime juice
1 bunch of fresh basil, finely chopped
Sea salt and freshly ground black pepper to taste

Mix all the ingredients well in a bowl. Season and serve.

swiss chard and juniper berries

2 tablespoons olive oil
6 juniper berries, crushed
1 pound Swiss chard (or other greens), shredded
Sea salt and freshly ground black pepper
½ cup water

Heat the oil gently in a large pan. Add the juniper and stir. Add the greens. Stir-fry for 2 minutes. Add water, cover and simmer for 10 minutes. Season and serve.

SALADS

carrot 'n' beet salad

10 ounces carrots, grated
10 ounces beet, grated
1 tablespoon fresh ginger root, finely chopped
2 tablespoons sunflower oil
4 tablespoons lemon juice
3 ounces bean sprouts
3 tablespoons sunflower seeds, roasted
3 tablespoons pumpkin seeds, roasted

Mix the grated carrots and beet with the ginger. Add the oil and the lemon juice, and mix well. Add the bean sprouts and mix gently. Garnish with the seeds.

salad niçoise

½ cup olive oil
2 tablespoons white wine vinegar
1 tablespoon lemon juice
1 tablespoon Dijon mustard
1 tablespoon maple syrup
7 ounces new potatoes in their skins, boiled in lightly salted water
Sea salt and freshly ground black pepper to taste
4 ounces marinated tofu, in small cubes
Soy sauce
8½ ounces tomatoes, in boats
½ cucumber, chopped into sticks
½ iceberg lettuce
4 tablespoons small niçoise olives
8½ ounces green beans, topped, tailed, and steamed
2 tablespoons fresh parsley, finely chopped
2 tablespoons fresh basil, finely chopped

Combine the oil, vinegar, lemon juice, mustard, and maple syrup in a bowl, whisk or hand-blend, then season to taste. Cut the cooled potatoes in half and add them to the dressing. Mix well and set aside. Sauté the tofu in a little oil, turn off heat and add a few drops of soy sauce. Add to the potatoes. Leave to cool a little, then add the rest of the ingredients and serve with French bread.

bulgur wheat salad

8½ ounces bulgur wheat, cooked and allowed to cool
1 bunch of scallions, sliced
2 tomatoes, chopped
1 green bell pepper, deseeded and cut into strips
½ cucumber, chopped
1 garlic clove
2 tablespoons fresh mint, chopped
2 tablespoons fresh parsley, chopped
2 tablespoons fresh cilantro (coriander) leaves, chopped
4 tablespoons olive oil
3 tablespoons lemon juice
Sea salt and freshly ground black pepper to taste

Place the bulgur in a salad bowl and mix with other ingredients. Serve cold.

artichoke salad

8 artichoke hearts
4 big ripe tomatoes, cut into boats
1 red onion, sliced
3½ ounces green olives
1 pound flageolet beans (cooked weight)
Lemon tahini dressing *(see page 111)*

If using fresh artichokes, prepare them by breaking off the outer "petals." When you get to the softer inner ones, cut them off with a sharp knife as close to the heart as possible. Scrape out the "choke" with a teaspoon. (Leave the hearts in cold water while you prepare the others, to avoid discoloration.) Plunge the hearts into boiling water and cook for about 20 minutes (or until tender). Cool and place with the other ingredients in a salad bowl and serve with French bread and lemon tahini dressing.

provençal mesclun salad

1 butterhead lettuce, shredded
A small handful of the following green leaves and herbs:
Arugula, sorrel, radicchio, mustard cress, nasturtium leaves and flowers, parsley, mint, and/or basil
Rich garlic dressing *(see page 69)*

Place the shredded lettuce in a large salad bowl, add the green leaves and herbs, mix lightly and add the dressing just before serving.

arugula salad

4 handfuls of arugula, shredded
1 small red onion, finely chopped
4 small ripe tomatoes, cut into boats
Lime dressing *(see page 111)*
4 tablespoons walnuts, roughly chopped

Place the arugula in a salad bowl, add the onion and tomato, and the dressing. Garnish with the walnuts and serve with fresh crusty bread.

catalan salad

2 pounds potatoes, boiled in their skins and allowed to cool
1 broccoli, cut into flowerets, steamed and allowed to cool
1 avocado, sliced
1 scallion, chopped
1 red bell pepper, deseeded and sliced
1 yellow bell pepper, deseeded and sliced
3 tablespoons capers
4 tablespoons olives
3 tablespoons fresh parsley, finely chopped
1 tablespoon fresh thyme
Lime dressing *(see page 111)*

Cut the potatoes into thick slices. Place in a salad bowl and combine with the rest of the ingredients.

chinese salad *(pictured page 118)*

¼ Chinese cabbage, finely sliced
1 teaspoon fresh ginger root, finely chopped
1 teaspoon garlic, finely chopped
1 small red chilli pepper, deseeded and finely chopped
1 small bunch of watercress, chopped
3½ ounces mangetout peas, trimmed
2 scallions, finely sliced
8 ounces bean sprouts
1 portion lime dressing *(see page 111)*

Place the Chinese cabbage in a salad bowl and add all the other ingredients. Mix well, add the dressing and serve.

florence fennel salad

1 bulb Florence fennel, thinly sliced
1 avocado, thinly sliced
3½ ounces pecan nuts
3½ ounces green olives
1 cucumber, thinly sliced
Rich garlic dressing *(see page 69)*

Mix all the ingredients with the dressing. Garnish with fennel tops and serve.

green lentil salad

2 ounces green lentils (dry weight), cooked and allowed to cool
1 small cauliflower, in flowerets
2 carrots, cut into peelings
7 ounces green peas, shelled
1 young zucchini, thinly sliced
1 bunch of watercress, chopped
7 ounces yellow beans, steamed and cooled
Lemon tahini dressing *(see page 111)*

Mix all the ingredients with the dressing and serve.

orange mango salad

1 orange, peeled and chopped
2 mangos, peeled and chopped
2 carrots, cut into peelings
1 handful of radicchio, finely shredded
1 red chilli, deseeded and finely sliced
1 teaspoon ginger root, finely chopped
3 tablespoons lemon juice

Mix all the ingredients in a salad bowl and serve.

pasta salad

12 ounces three-colored pasta twists, cooked
1 zucchini, grated
2 tomatoes, in boats
1 bunch of asparagus, trimmed and cooked, in pieces
1 bunch of fresh basil, finely chopped
Lime dressing *(see page 111)*

Cool the pasta and place in a salad bowl. Add all the other ingredients, add the dressing and serve.

potato salad

2¼ pounds new potatoes, boiled in their skins
1½ cups plain soy yogurt
1 shallot, finely chopped
1 small red bell pepper, finely chopped
2 tablespoons capers
1–2 tablespoons lemon juice
Sea salt and freshly ground black pepper to taste
1 small bunch of chives, finely chopped

Allow the potatoes to cool and cut them into thick slices. Combine the rest of the ingredients to make the dressing. Place the potatoes in a salad bowl and add the dressing, mix gently, garnish with chives and serve.

sweetcorn (maize) and sun-dried tomato salad

4 sweetcorns (maize), cut into chunks and boiled for 3 minutes
2 ounces sun-dried tomatoes, cut into strips
1 handful of arugula
1 small lettuce, shredded
2 tablespoons fresh basil, chopped
4 tablespoons walnut oil
2 tablespoons balsamic vinegar
Sea salt and freshly ground black pepper to taste

Put the corn in a bowl on a bed of tomatoes, arugula, lettuce, and basil. Whisk together the oil and vinegar and toss with the salad. Season and serve.

salad with sorrel and tempeh

2 tablespoons olive oil
8 tempeh rashers
1 handful of young sorrel leaves, shredded
1 little gem lettuce, shredded
Rich garlic dressing *(see page 69)*

Fry the tempeh in the olive oil until crisp and golden. Sprinkle with salt then cut into bite-size pieces. Place the sorrel and lettuce leaves in a bowl and add the tempeh. Pour the dressing over and mix gently.

tropical sunshine salad

3 carrots, cut into peelings
1 avocado, sliced
1 mango, peeled and sliced
1 handful of nasturtium leaves and flowers
1 pomegranate, peeled and cut into segments
4 scallions, sliced
1 garlic clove, finely chopped
1-inch piece of ginger root, finely chopped
3 tablespoons safflower oil
3 tablespoons lime juice
Sea salt and freshly ground black pepper to taste

Combine all the ingredients in a salad bowl and mix well. Season and serve.

wild rice salad *(below)*

2 ounces wild rice (dry weight), cooked and cooled
1 bulb Florence fennel, steamed, cooled and sliced
1 bell pepper, broiled and skinned *(see broiled bell peppers—page 107)*
2 tomatoes, cut into boats
2 scallions, sliced
1 celery stalk, sliced
3½ ounces black olives, pitted
2 garlic cloves, crushed
Lemon tahini dressing *(see page 111)*
2 tablespoons fresh parsley, finely chopped, to garnish
2 tablespoons fresh basil, finely chopped, to garnish

Place the rice and fennel in a salad bowl, then add the rest of the ingredients. Add the lemon tahini dressing, garnish with the fresh herbs and serve.

desserts

raspberry gateau

8½ ounces wholewheat flour
1 tablespoon baking powder
2 ounces ground almonds
4 ounces raw cane sugar
½ cup sunflower oil
2 tablespoons malt extract
½ teaspoon vanilla (or almond) essence
1¼ cups warm water

For the topping:
1 cup plain soy yogurt
2 ounces blanched almonds, finely chopped and lightly toasted
12 ounces fresh raspberries
3 tablespoons maple syrup (optional)

Sift the flour and baking powder together. Add the ground almonds and sugar. Preheat the oven to 350°F. Grease a round cake tin with oil and sprinkle with flour. Combine the oil, malt, vanilla (or almond) essence, and warm water and quickly add the mixture to the flour. Mix as quickly as possible. Pour the mixture into the cake tin, smooth the top and bake for 20–30 minutes (until it doesn't stick to a skewer). Leave to cool a little, then remove from tin and place on a round serving plate and spread the yogurt evenly over it. Arrange the almonds and the raspberries over the yogurt and sprinkle with maple syrup.

baked apples

4 cooking apples, cored
10 dates, pitted and chopped
4 bananas, mashed
4 tablespoons macadamia nuts, chopped
3 tablespoons tahini
3 tablespoons lemon juice
½ cup maple syrup

Preheat oven to 350°F. Cut a line horizontally around the middle in the skin of each apple. Mix half the mashed banana with the chopped dates and stuff the mixture into the apple. Sprinkle the nuts on top. Bake for 20 minutes. Mix the tahini with the rest of the banana, lemon juice, and maple syrup. Add a little water and stir to a rich sauce. Pour over the baked apples.

passion-fruit sorbet *(far right, back)*

1½ cups passion-fruit pulp, blended
4 ounces raw cane sugar
½ cup water

Heat the water and the sugar gently in a small heavy-based casserole until the sugar dissolves. Stir gently from time to time to loosen the sugar from the base of the pan. Bring to the boil and simmer for 1 minute. Cool, then mix with the passion fruit. Stir well then freeze the mixture in a shallow non-metal container until solid (4–6 hours). Just before serving, break up the frozen mixture into chunks and blend until smooth. Serve immediately.

blackberry crumble *(below left)*

2¼ pounds blackberries (or bilberries, raspberries or blueberries)
3 tablespoons raw cane sugar
2 tablespoons white flour

For the topping:
3½ ounces wholemeal flour
3½ ounces rolled oats
4 tablespoons chopped nuts
5 ounces vegetable margarine
4 tablespoons honey

Preheat oven to 400°F. Mix the blackberries with the sugar and flour in a pie dish. For the topping, mix the flour, oats, and nuts in a bowl, then rub in the margarine and honey. Cover the berries with crumble mixture and lightly smooth the surface. Bake for 30 minutes, until golden. Serve warm or cold.

nectarine surprise

4 nectarines, thinly sliced
4 tablespoons maple syrup
1 teaspoon fresh ginger root, grated
1 tablespoon fresh mint, finely chopped

Place the sliced nectarines in a bowl. Heat ½ cup of water and add the maple syrup and the ginger. Cool and pour over the nectarines. Leave to marinate in the refrigerator for a couple of hours before serving, garnished with mint.

raspberry sorbet *(right, front)*

1½ cups raspberries, juiced
6 ounces raw cane sugar
½ cup water

Heat the water and the sugar gently in a small heavy-based casserole until the sugar dissolves. Stir gently from time to time to loosen the sugar from the base. Bring to boil and boil for 1 minute. Cool before mixing with the raspberry juice. Stir well, then freeze in a shallow non-metal container until solid (4–6 hours). Just before serving, break into chunks and blend until smooth. Serve immediately.

tropical fruit salad

1-inch cube ginger root, finely chopped
4 tablespoons maple syrup (optional)
1 lemon, grated rind and juice
½ cup pineapple juice
8 lychees, peeled and pitted
1 mango, peeled and cut into cubes
1 pineapple, peeled, cored and sliced
4 kiwis, peeled and sliced
1 papaya, peeled, deseeded and sliced

Put the ginger, syrup, and juices in a pan. Heat gently and simmer for 1 minute. Pour into a bowl. Cool. Add the fruit and serve.

pear tart

4 big ripe pears, peeled, halved longways, cored and deseeded
Marzipan (optional)

For the short-crust pastry:
8½ ounces wholewheat flour
½ teaspoon salt
2 ounces raw cane sugar
4½ ounces cold vegetable margarine

Mix the flour, salt and sugar, and chop in the margarine with a knife and a spoon until it forms small lumps. Crumble the mixture with your hands until it looks like Parmesan (taking care not to let the dough get warm). Add 5 tablespoons cold water and knead the dough lightly into a smooth lump. Refrigerate until needed. Preheat oven to 400°F. Divide the pastry in two, roll out one half and place in a greased flan case. Press a lump of marzipan into the core of each pear half, then place the pears, face down, in the flan shell. Cover with the other half of the pastry. Press lightly down between the pears and firmly around the edge. Bake for 20–30 minutes, until golden. Serve warm or cold.

juices

apricot and ginger

5 apricots, pitted
1 teaspoon fresh ginger root, chopped
½ cup apple juice
½ cup soy milk

Blend all the ingredients and serve with ice.

autumn fruit

2 apples, cored and quartered
2 pears, cored and quartered
½ grapefruit, peeled

Juice the ingredients and serve with ice.

beet and apple

8½ ounces fresh beet, quartered
3 apples, cored and quartered

Juice the beet and the apple and mix well. Pour into a tall glass and garnish with a slice of lime.

blackberry cream *(far right, front)*

3½ ounces blackberries
1 ripe banana
1 pear, cored and quartered
½ cup plain soy yogurt
1 tablespoon sunflower seeds

Blend all the ingredients and serve chilled.

caribbean smoothie

¼ pineapple, peeled, cored and chopped
½ mango, peeled and chopped
1 banana, peeled

Blend and serve chilled.

carrot and lemon with garlic

8½ ounces carrots
1 garlic clove, peeled
½ lemon, squeezed

Press the garlic through the juicer together with the carrot. Mix with the squeezed lemon and serve.

cool cucumber

1 cucumber
1 tomato
1 garlic clove, peeled
1 green bell pepper, quartered and deseeded
2 sprigs of fresh dill

Juice the ingredients, but keep a little dill as a garnish. Serve chilled.

cranberry spritzer

10 ounces cranberries (or ½ cup cranberry juice)
½ cup fizzy water
1 lemon slice

Juice the cranberries and mix with the fizzy water. Garnish with lemon.

creamy mango *(right, back)*

1 mango, pitted, peeled and cubed
1 banana, peeled
1 wedge of fresh coconut
1 orange, squeezed

Blend the mango, banana and coconut. Add the orange juice, mix well and serve.

green party

2 celery stalks with leaves
¼ bulb Florence fennel
1 handful of arugula leaves (or other green leaves)
½ cucumber
1 tomato
Few sprigs of fresh basil
Slice of lime

Juice the celery, fennel, green leaves, cucumber, tomato, and basil. Garnish with lime and serve cool.

guava and apple

1 guava, peeled
¾ cup apple juice
1 slice of orange

Blend the guava with the apple juice. Serve in
a tall glass garnished with a slice of orange.

heart warmer

3½ ounces carrots
3½ ounces beet
2 celery sticks with leaves
2 garlic cloves, peeled
1-inch piece of ginger root, peeled
½ lemon, squeezed

Juice the carrot, beet, celery, garlic, and ginger.
Add the lemon juice, mix well, and serve.

height of passion

3 passion-fruits, peeled
½ mango, peeled
¼ pineapple, peeled

Juice the fruits and serve with ice.

mango and lime

1 mango, peeled and pitted
½ cup almond milk
1 lime, squeezed
Pinch of cinnamon

Blend, garnish with a sprinkle of cinnamon, and serve chilled.

melon and orange

7 ounces cantaloupe melon, deseeded and peeled
1 orange, squeezed

Blend the melon with the orange and serve with ice.

natural beauty *(far right)*

2 apples
½ cantaloupe melon

Juice and serve.

nirvana

1 ripe pear
6 strawberries
4 apricots
1 peach
1 slice of tangerine

Juice the fruits and serve garnished with a slice of tangerine.

papaya power

1 papaya, peeled, and pitted
1 lemon, squeezed

Blend the papaya with the lemon juice and serve with ice.

piña colada

½ pineapple, peeled, cored and chopped
4 tablespoons coconut milk
1 teaspoon lime juice
2 teaspoons maple syrup

Blend all the ingredients and serve with ice.

passion and lime

2 passion-fruits
1 tablespoon maple syrup
1 orange, squeezed
½ lime, squeezed
2 tablespoons plain soy yogurt
Pinch of vanilla powder

Blend passion-fruits, maple syrup, and orange and lime juice with yogurt and vanilla. Pour into a glass and add fizzy water to taste. Serve with ice.

tomato cocktail

7 ounces tomatoes, quartered
1 carrot
1 small beet, quartered
3 lettuce leaves
3 spinach leaves
6 sprigs of watercress
4 sprigs of parsley
1 celery stalk with leaves
Few drops of tabasco (optional)
Pinch of celery salt

Juice the vegetables and greens. Pour into a glass and mix well, add a few drops of tabasco and a pinch of celery salt, stir, and serve garnished with lemon.

pink pineapple *(far left)*

¼ pineapple, peeled, cored and chopped
1 orange, squeezed
5 ounces strawberries

Blend all the ingredients and serve.

grape and raisin smoothie

1 bunch of seedless grapes
1 carrot
2 tablespoons raisins, soaked in water overnight

Juice the ingredients and serve.

soft tutti fruity

6 strawberries
5 apricots
2 peaches
4 tablespoons apple juice
Maple syrup to taste (optional)

Blend the fruits with the apple juice and serve.

sunrise

1 apple, cored and quartered
2 carrots
1 tomato, quartered
1 orange, squeezed
1 slice of orange
Fresh mint

Juice the apple, carrots, and tomato and mix with the orange juice. Serve in a tumbler garnished with a slice of orange and a sprig of fresh mint.

vegetable cocktail

1 small beet, quartered
1 handful of arugula (or other green leaves)
1 red bell pepper, deseeded and quartered
2 tomatoes, quartered
3 celery stalks, with tops
5 carrots
1 wedge of cabbage (or spring greens)
1 garlic clove, peeled

Juice the ingredients and serve.

herbal drinks and syrups

calming tea

1 part lavender flowers
1 part chamomile
1 part lemon balm
1 part St. John's wort

Mix the herbs well. Use 1 teaspoon herb mixture per cup of boiling water. Place the herbs in a warmed teapot and pour boiling water over them. Cover and leave to infuse for 10 minutes.

chamomile tonic

2 ounces chamomile flowers
2 tablespoons lemon juice
3 tablespoons honey
3¾ cups organic white wine

Mix all the ingredients in a bowl. Cover and leave in a cool, dark place for 10 days. Strain through a cheesecloth and store in sterile bottles.

cold buster

½ teaspoon wild marjoram
½ teaspoon yarrow
½ teaspoon elderflowers
Small pinch of cayenne
1 cup boiling water
2 tablespoons lemon juice
Honey to taste

Place the herbs in a mug in a tea filter or strainer. Add boiling water. Cover and leave to infuse for 10 minutes. Remove the herbs, add the lemon juice and honey. Drink hot.

cough mixture

½ teaspoon licorice root
½ teaspoon thyme
½ teaspoon wild marjoram
½ teaspoon borage
1 teaspoon sweet violet
1 cup boiling water
1 teaspoon honey
Squeeze of lemon juice

Place the herbs in a warmed teapot. Add the boiling water, cover and leave to infuse for 10 minutes. Pour into a mug, add the honey and the lemon juice.

circulation booster

3 parts hawthorn flowers or berries
2 parts yarrow
1 part black mustard seeds

Mix the herbs. Use 1 teaspoon herb mixture per cup of boiling water. Place the herbs in a warmed teapot and pour boiling water over them. Cover and leave to infuse for 10 minutes.

cystitis relief

1 part yarrow
1 part echinacea
1 part cleavers
1 part celery seeds
1 part sweet violets

Mix the herbs well. Use 1 teaspoon herb mixture per cup of boiling water. Place the herbs in a warmed teapot and pour boiling water over them. Cover and leave to infuse for 10 minutes.

elderberry cordial

2¼ pounds ripe elderberries, rinsed, with stalks removed
2½ cups spring water
2 tablespoons lemon juice
1 teaspoon citric acid (optional)
12 ounces unrefined cane sugar

Place the berries in a saucepan with the water, lemon juice, and citric acid. Bring to boil and simmer gently until the berries burst. Strain through a cheesecloth, add the sugar and bring back to the boil. Simmer again for 5 minutes. Skim and pour into sterilized warm glass bottles. Seal and store in a cool, dark place. Drink diluted with hot water.

elderflower spritzer

1 head of fresh elderflowers
1 slice of lemon
½ cup boiling water
1 teaspoon honey
Ice cubes
½ cup fizzy water

Place the elderflowers and the lemon slice in a small bowl. Add the boiling water and the honey. Cover and leave to cool. Strain and pour into a tall glass with ice, add the fizzy water, and serve immediately.

eucalyptus mix

3 parts eucalyptus leaves
2 parts chamomile
2 parts thyme

Mix the herbs well. Use 1 teaspoon herb mixture per cup of boiling water. Place the herbs in a warmed teapot and pour boiling water over them. Cover and leave to infuse for 10 minutes.

garlic oxymel *(below)*

1 cup red wine vinegar
3 tablespoons fresh garlic, chopped
2 teaspoons black cumin seeds
9 ounces honey

Place the vinegar, garlic, and cumin in a small saucepan. Bring to the boil, cover, and simmer for 5 minutes. Strain and add the honey. Bring to the boil and simmer again, very gently, for another 5 minutes. Remove from heat and store in a clean jar. Take 1 tablespoon at a time.

green tea with mint

1 teaspoon green tea
1 tablespoon fresh mint, chopped
1 cup boiling water

Place the green tea and the mint in a warmed teapot. Add the boiling water, cover and leave to infuse for 5 minutes. Serve hot or chilled.

hay fever relief

1 teaspoon fresh horseradish, grated
1 teaspoon honey
1 glass of water

For the tisane:
2 parts elderflowers
1 part echinacea
1 part eyebright
1 part chamomile
1 part licorice
1 part peppermint

Mix the grated horseradish with the honey and take with a glass of water. Make the tisane by mixing the herbs and adding 1 teaspoon of herbs per cup of boiling water to a warmed teapot. Add boiling water, cover, and leave to infuse for 10 minutes.

heart chai

1 teaspoon green tea
1 teaspoon black cumin seeds
½-inch piece cinnamon stick
Small pinch of cayenne
1 teaspoon lemon balm
1½ cup soy (or rice) milk
1 teaspoon honey (optional)

Place all the ingredients, except the honey, in a small saucepan, bring to the boil and simmer gently for 2 minutes. Strain into a large cup, add honey (if liked), and serve.

immuni-tea

2 parts nettles
1 part licorice
1 part echinacea
1 part cleavers
1 part thyme
1 part borage

Mix the herbs well. Use 1 teaspoon of herb mixture per cup of boiling water. Place the herbs in a warmed teapot, add the boiling water, cover, and leave to infuse for 10 minutes.

licorice mix

½-inch piece licorice root, chopped
½-inch piece cinnamon stick
½ teaspoon fennel seeds
½ teaspoon fresh ginger, chopped
1 cup water

Place all the ingredients in a small saucepan and bring to boil. Simmer gently for 5 minutes. Strain and serve.

lung-cleansing tea mix

1 part licorice root
1 part thyme
1 part eucalyptus leaves
1 part peppermint
1 part sweet violets
1 part elderflowers

Mix all the herbs well. Use 1 teaspoon per cup of boiling water. Place the herbs in a warmed teapot. Add the boiling water. Cover and leave to infuse for 10 minutes.

pick-me-up

1 part oats, whole grains, crushed
1 part lavender
1 part rosemary
1 part lemon balm
2 parts rosehips
1 part jasmine tea

Mix all the herbs together. Use 1 teaspoon per cup of boiling water. Place the herbs in a warmed teapot. Add the boiling water. Cover and leave to infuse for 10 minutes.

rosehip syrup

4 ounces rosehips
2½ cups water
4 ounces raw cane sugar

Place the rosehips and water in a saucepan. Bring to the boil, remove from heat and leave to cool. Strain through several layers of cheesecloth to make sure seeds and fine hairs are discarded with the fruit. Bring the liquid back to the boil, add the sugar and simmer gently until the volume is reduced by a third. Stir gently from time to time. Pour into sterile bottles and store in a cool dry place.

sage mix for sore throats

1 teaspoon sage
½ teaspoon cleavers
½ teaspoon fresh ginger, finely chopped
1½ cups boiling water

Place the sage, cleavers and ginger in a warmed teapot, add the water, and leave to infuse for 5 minutes.

si c

1 guava, peeled
3½ ounces black currants
3½ ounces strawberries
½ papaya, peeled and deseeded
1 banana

Blend the ingredients and serve with ice.

sleepy time

2 parts passion flower leaves
1 part lavender
1 part chamomile
1 part catnip

Mix all the herbs well. Use 1 teaspoon per cup of boiling water. Place the herbs in a warmed teapot. Add boiling water. Cover and leave to infuse for 10 minutes.

spicy chai

½-inch piece cinnamon stick
½ teaspoon black mustard seeds
½ teaspoon fennel seeds
½ teaspoon licorice root
¼ teaspoon caraway seeds
1½ cup rice milk
1 teaspoon honey (optional)

Place all the ingredients in a small saucepan and bring to the boil. Simmer for a few minutes. Pour into a mug and serve with honey.

stress relief

1 part borage
1 part lavender
1 part lemon balm
1 part basil
1 part peppermint

Mix all the herbs well. Use 1 teaspoon per cup of boiling water. Place the herbs in a warmed teapot. Add boiling water. Cover and leave to infuse for 10 minutes.

tea for aches and pains

2 parts St. John's wort
2 parts meadowsweet
1 part rosemary

Mix all the herbs well. Use 1 teaspoon per cup of boiling water. Place the herbs in a warmed teapot. Add boiling water. Cover and leave to infuse for 10 minutes.

tea for ear infections

1 part St. John's wort
1 part echinacea
1 part rosehips
1 part elderflowers
1 part licorice root
1 part peppermint
1 part cleavers

Mix all the herbs well. Use 1 teaspoon per cup of boiling water. Place the herbs in a warmed teapot. Add boiling water. Cover and leave to infuse for 10 minutes.

tea for fever

½ teaspoon catnip
½ teaspoon borage
½ teaspoon chamomile
Small pinch of cayenne
1 cup boiling water

Place the herbs in a warmed teapot. Add the boiling water. Cover and leave to infuse for 5 minutes.

tea for fungal infections

2 parts echinacea
1 part lemon balm
1 part calendula (marigold)
1 part cleavers

Mix the herbs well. Use 1 teaspoon herb mixture per cup of boiling water. Place the herbs in a warmed teapot and pour the boiling water over them. Cover and leave to infuse for 10 minutes.

thyme syrup

3 tablespoons dried thyme
2½ cups water
12 ounces unrefined cane sugar

Bring the water to the boil in a small saucepan. Add the thyme and remove from heat. Cover and leave to infuse for 20 minutes. Strain and add the sugar. Heat gently until sugar dissolves. Pour into sterile bottles and store in the refrigerator.

tea for glands

1 part borage
1 part cleavers
1 part echinacea
1 part calendula (marigold)

Mix all the herbs well. Use 1 teaspoon per cup of boiling water. Place the herbs in a warmed teapot. Add boiling water. Cover and leave to infuse for 10 minutes.

tea for headache

1 part feverfew
1 part rosemary
1 part marjoram
1 part peppermint

Mix all the herbs well. Use 1 teaspoon per cup of boiling water. Place the herbs in a warmed teapot. Add boiling water. Cover and leave to infuse for 10 minutes.

tea for joints

1 part elderflowers
1 part St. John's wort
1 part celery seeds
1 part nettles
1 part black mustard seeds

Mix all the herbs well. Use 1 teaspoon per cup of boiling water. Place the herbs in a warmed teapot. Add boiling water. Cover and leave to infuse for 10 minutes.

tea for the skin

1 part nettles
1 part echinacea
1 part cleavers
½ part calendula (marigold)
1 part sweet violets

Mix all the herbs well. Use 1 teaspoon per cup of boiling water. Place the herbs in a warmed teapot. Add boiling water. Cover and leave to infuse for 10 minutes.

winter tonic

7 ounces ripe blackberries
2 tablespoons maple syrup
1 banana
½ cup almond milk

Blend and serve.

diet plans

detox and elimination diet

If you suffer from any serious medical disorders, including cancer, diabetes mellitus, depression, eating disorders, severe asthma, or epilepsy, it is not advisable to undertake an elimination diet without medical supervision. The idea of this diet is to eat only things to which you are unlikely to be allergic—which may take a lot of willpower and support! Follow it for two weeks to give your system time to eliminate any offending food allergens.

If you suspect you have a food allergy, but you are unsure to what you are allergic, one way to find out for sure is to keep a diet diary. Take seven pieces of A4 paper and mark each one with a different day of the week. Carry the relevant piece of paper around with you everywhere each day for the following week, and record EVERYTHING you eat and drink and the time you had it. (It is easy to forget what you've eaten if you don't write it down immediately.)

At the end of each day, write down how (and where) you've been that day, whether you've had any allergy symptoms (such as migraine or stomach ache) and, if you are suffering from arthritis, whether your arthritis was better or worse (on a scale of 1 to 10) that day. Food allergy symptoms can start up to 24 hours after the allergen was consumed, so keeping a diet diary enables you to look back and identify possible offenders more easily.

If after a week it is clear that you have "good" days and "bad" days according to what you eat (and provided you feel well when you wake up the next morning after a good day), you can start to plan your own elimination diet by keeping your diet diary up to date and eliminating the foods you have found are not good for you.

If your symptoms are not that clear cut, try the following elimination diet plan to discover which things to leave out of your diet (you can always reintroduce them after a while, to see if you still react to them). Choose a time when you haven't got too many commitments—choosing different foods from those you are used to is inevitably time consuming.

When following this diet plan, you may experience symptoms of withdrawal and detoxification (such as nausea, headache, the feeling that your teeth and tongue have a furry coat, and even diarrhea) but these symptoms should diminish after a couple of days, leaving you feeling fresher and more alert. Eat and drink (water or mild herbal tea) every 2–3 hours and have plenty of the foods on the "allowed" list. Keep a record of everything you consume and note any reaction you experience. Avoid using toothpaste during the diet—use salt or baking powder instead.

DAY ONE

Cut out all stimulants (tea, coffee, chocolate, cigarettes, alcohol), processed "convenience" foods, and foods containing additives.

DAY TWO

Cut out all dairy products, wheat, buckwheat, and sugar (including honey and syrups), and any foods containing these.

DAY THREE

Cut out all meat, fish, and shellfish.

DAY FOUR

Cut out all corn, nuts, and pulses, and foods containing these.

DAY FIVE

Cut out all foods belonging to the nightshade family (solinaceae): potato, eggplant, bell peppers, chillies, cayenne, paprika, and tomatoes. Eat only steamed or raw vegetables, rice, and fruit.

DAY SIX

Cut out all citrus fruits (lemon, orange, grapefruit, lime, tangerine, kumquat, mandarin, clementine). Eat only vegetables and those fruits not belonging to the citrus and nightshade families.

DAY SEVEN

Drink only water, fruit and/or vegetable juices. Make your own mixtures according to taste.

DAY EIGHT

Eat vegetables and fruits, except citrus fruits and members of the nightshade family.

DAY NINE

Eat vegetables, fruits, and rice. Drink water and juices. Reintroduce foods from the nightshade family. Observe any reaction.

DAY TEN

Eat vegetables, fruits, and rice. Drink water and juices as on day seven. Reintroduce citrus fruits. Observe any reaction.

DAY ELEVEN

Eat vegetables, fruits, and rice. Drink water and juices as on day seven. Reintroduce corn, nuts and pulses. Observe any reaction.

DAY TWELVE

Eat vegetables, fruits, and rice. Drink water and juices as on day seven. Reintroduce wheat, sugar, and fish. Observe any reaction.

DAY THIRTEEN

Eat vegetables, fruits, and rice. Drink water and juices as on day seven. Reintroduce dairy products. Observe any reaction.

DAY FOURTEEN

Eat vegetables, fruits, and rice. Drink water and juices as on day seven. Reintroduce shellfish. Observe any reaction.

DAY FIFTEEN

Start eating "normally" again, but note your reactions carefully when you reintroduce meat, stimulants, and food additives. Review your diet diary and take note of the food groups to which you reacted negatively. Base your future diet on what you have discovered.

traditional grape fast

A grape fast is cleansing and detoxifying. The best time to do it is at the end of the summer when grapes are fresh, cheap, and plentiful. Choose organic grapes, and eat as many as you like on the "grape" days. You should also drink plenty of clean water and have unsweetened organic grape juice, little and often, throughout. Take plenty of time to rest, too. Avoid smoking during the fast.

DAYS ONE, TWO, AND THREE

Eat only grapes and drink only water and grape juice.

DAY FOUR

Eat nothing but drink plenty of water and grape juice.

DAYS FIVE, SIX, AND SEVEN

Eat only grapes and drink only water and grape juice.

gentle healing diet

If you are suffering from a chronic illness, or have been through a period of physical, mental, emotional, or spiritual stress, a gentle healing diet is a necessity to provide resources for healing. It is made up of foods that are highly nutritious, easily digested, and easily absorbed and used by the body. The diet contains the right amount of protein for growth and repair, and plenty of complex carbohydrates for sustained energy. It is low in fat but contains all the necessary essential fatty acids, and it is high in vitamins, minerals and other healing phytochemicals.

Eat as many of the following foods as you like, and in any combination that suits you.

COMPLEX CARBOHYDRATES

Grains, roots, and tubers—rice, pasta, couscous, bulgur, parsnips, celeriac (celery root), carrots, potatoes, sweet potatoes, beet.

VEGETABLE PROTEIN

Beans, peas, grains, and green leaves. (Meat is not suitable for this gentle healing diet because it is a very concentrated food containing no fiber, and it may contain residues of hormones, antibiotics, nitrates, and other additives or harmful substances.)

VITAMINS, MINERALS, AND PHYTOCHEMICALS

Organically grown vegetables, either raw or cooked, boiled, baked, or steamed depending on your taste, your state of health, and your digestion. Start with cooked vegetables if you find raw foods hard to digest and add some raw ones little by little. Organic vegetables contain more nutrients and less water than those produced by intensive farming methods, and they are not contaminated by sprays and fertilizers, which the body needs energy to deal with.

Fruit is also a very healthy food, and you should eat one or two pieces each day. But in this diet the emphasis is on building up resources by eating food that provides steady energy without too many short bursts upsetting blood-sugar levels. Most fruits contain simple sugars (disaccharides) that are digested and absorbed into the blood stream more quickly than the complex carbohydrates (polysaccharides) found in grains and many vegetables. Eat fruits that are in season, and particularly fruits that improve digestion, such as papaya, pineapple, banana, and grapefruit. Lemons contain a lot of vitamin C and not too much sugar.

UNSATURATED FAT

Nuts, seeds, and olive oil all contain unsaturated fatty acids that are beneficial to health.

DRINKS

The aim is to build up resources by eating nutritious foods and keeping the digestive load to a minimum. Drinks should follow the same guidelines and be limited to water, vegetable juices (without sugar), and herb teas (avoid the artificially flavored ones).

SUGGESTED MENU
(CHOOSE ONE FROM EACH CATEGORY)

BREAKFAST

SALAD AND SOUP LUNCH

DINNER
Starters

Main course

SNACKS

spicy brazil nut pâté (page 57)

marinated olives (page 108)

pan amb oli (page 111)

toasted nuts and seeds (page 108)

tomato and cucumber canapés (page 110)

guacamole (page 110)

tzaziki (page 111)

DRINKS

Pure water, herbal tea, freshly made vegetable juices, dandelion or chicory coffee substitutes.

FOODS TO AVOID

● All sugars and foods containing added sugar

● All refined or processed foods and junk foods

● Fruit juices

● Stimulants (such as tea, coffee, alcohol, chocolate, fizzy drinks)

● Non-prescription drugs and supplements

● All foods containing saturated fats

● Additives

● Dairy products

● Meats

● Fish

If you suffer from an arthritic condition, this healing diet may bring you relief from symptoms and pain. If it does not, you should consider modifying your diet to exclude the following: wheat, potatoes, tomatoes, peppers, eggplants, acidic fruits and vinegar.

glossary

Words in **bold** type also appear in this glossary.

ACETYLCHOLINE a chemical messenger needed for normal functioning of the central and autonomic nervous systems.

ANTHOCYANINS dark-blue **antioxidants** that may reduce the "stickiness" of blood platelets and help prevent blood clots.

ANTIBIOTIC a treatment for infectious disease that works by killing, or inhibiting the growth of, infecting organisms.

ANTI-CATARRHAL a substance capable of reducing secretions from mucous membranes.

ANTICOAGULANT reduces the tendency of the blood to clot.

ANTIOXIDANT a substance that inhibits and controls the harmful action of **free radicals**. Vitamins C and E, zinc, and the trace element selenium are important antioxidants.

ANTISCORBUTIC prevents scurvy—a beneficial property of any food containing vitamin C (ascorbic acid).

ASTRINGENT causes binding and drying, for example to treat bleeding and diarrhea.

BENZOIC ACID an antiseptic primarily used to treat urinary-tract infections, and as a preservative in cordials and pickles.

BETA-SITOSTEROL a plant sterol that lowers blood cholesterol levels and is also believed to reduce tumor growth, particularly in the colon.

BIO-ACTIVE COMPOUNDS chemical substances, such as **antioxidants**, that are found in foods and known, or believed to have, beneficial effects on human health.

BIOFLAVONOIDS also known as flavonoids, a group of **bio-active compounds**, including **quercetin**, **kaempferol**, **rutin**, and hesperidin with **antioxidant**, **diuretic** and other wide-ranging properties. They reduce blood-cholesterol levels, and may protect against heart disease and some cancers.

BITTER PRINCIPLES a group of plant chemicals with a distinctive bitter taste. They stimulate secretion of digestive juices, activate the liver, and may act as natural **antibiotics**, antifungals, and anti-cancer agents.

BROMELAIN a protein-digesting enzyme found in pineapple. It mimics the action of pancreatic enzymes, and may reduce inflammation and swellings.

CAMPHOR a component of some volatile oils with warming, numbing, pain-relieving, and insecticidal properties.

CARMINATIVE relieves intestinal gas (flatulence).

CAROTENE a **carotenoid** in orange-colored plant foods.

CAROTENOIDS pigments with strong **antioxidant** properties found in brightly-colored plant foods. They are converted into vitamin A in the body.

CHLOROPHYLL a green pigment responsible for photosynthesis in plants that stops the growth of bacteria and soothes inflammation.

CITRIC ACID a plant acid that gives the distinctive sharp taste to lemons, limes, unripe oranges, currants, and raspberries. It has a cooling, thirst-quenching effect.

COUMARINS phytochemicals with natural anti-blood-clotting properties. May protect against stomach and breast cancer.

CRUCIFEROUS a member of the Cruciferae family of plants that includes cabbages, kale, mustard greens, turnips, and rutabaga. Cruciferous plants are rich in **glucosinolates**.

CURCUMINOIDS yellow pigments found in turmeric with anti-inflammatory properties. They enhance the action of adrenal hormones, and are beneficial to the liver.

CYANOGLYCOSIDES **bio-active compounds** found in some plants that may have medicinal properties.

DECOCTION a medicinal preparation made by boiling plant material (such as roots, wood, bark, nuts, or seeds) in water, usually for 10 to 15 minutes.

DEPURATIVE encourages the body to eliminate impurities.

DIAPHORETIC encourages sweating.

DIURETIC increases the flow of urine.

ESSENTIAL OILS also known as volatile oils, these are strong-smelling oils that give plants their characteristic odor, and have many pharmacological actions.

EXPECTORANT provokes the expulsion of mucus and impurities from the lungs.

FEBRIFUGE a remedy that cools fever.

FLAVONOID see **bioflavonoid**.

FOLATE, or folic acid, a type of B-vitamin so called because it is found in foliage.

FOLIC ACID see **folate**.

FORMIC ACID an irritant acid found in nettles.

FREE RADICALS by-products of metabolism that can cause damage to cell membranes by oxidation of fatty acids. Free radicals are neutralized by **antioxidants**.

GLUCOKININ a chemical found in various plants including blueberry and garlic that lowers blood-sugar levels.

GLUCOQUINONE a chemical found in nettle that may help lower blood-sugar levels.

GLUCOSINOLATES a group of more than 20 chemicals (including indoles and isothyocyanates) found in edible plants such as cabbage, cauliflower, and broccoli. They increase the activity of enzymes that help the body eliminate potential carcinogens, and thus help to protect against cancer. However, glucosinolates may inhibit iodine uptake by the thyroid gland if eaten in large quantities.

GLUTATHIONE a **free-radical** "scavenger" dependent on selenium for its **antioxidant** activity.

GLUTEN a protein contained in cereals such as wheat, barley, rye, and oats. Components of gluten called gliandins can provoke the immune reaction that causes celiac disease.

GLYCOSIDES compounds made up of a combination of sugars and non-sugars, found widely in nature, many of which have powerful medicinal actions (such as digitalis in foxglove).

HISTAMINE derived from the amino acid histidine and found in the tissues of animals and plants, it has various powerful effects on the body (including dilating small blood vessels, constricting the bronchial tubes, and stimulating the production of gastric juice), and is responsible for urticaria ("hives").

HYDROGENATED FATS found in many processed foods, these are made by adding hydrogen to polyunsaturated fats in a process known as hydrogenation. Hydrogenated and partially hydrogenated fats are more solid at room temperature than **polyunsaturated fats** (or oils), but the chemical and physical techniques used to produce them cause unwelcome changes, such as the production of unhealthy "trans" fats.

IMMUNO-STIMULANT boosts the body's natural defenses.

INFUSION a remedy made by steeping plant material (usually flowers and leaves) in hot water.

ISOFLAVONES a group of **bio-active compounds** found in cereals and pulses (including soy) that are structurally similar to human estrogen. Isoflavones may protect against breast cancer, but there is continuing debate about the effect of phytestrogens on infants fed on soy-based formula foods.

KAEMPFEROL a **bioflavonoid** found in many plant foods.

LACTOBACILLI a bacterial species that forms part of the body's healthy microbial ecology. Also found in live yogurt.

LECITHIN a complex phospholipid fat found in many body tissues, particularly the brain and nerves. It is also found in various foods. Plant lecithin may help the body to deal with excess cholesterol, and help prevent abnormal blood clotting.

LENTINAN a polysaccharide found in shiitake mushrooms that enhances the immune response by stimulating T-helper cell activity. It is now being investigated as a possible treatment for A.I.D.S. (in conjunction with other drugs) and cancer.

LEUKOTRIENE one of the eicosanoid family of chemicals, derived from arachidonic acid. It causes contraction of smooth muscle and is involved in the inflammatory response to injury.

LINOLEIC ACID one of the "essential" fatty acids (so called because they cannot be made in the body and thus have to be consumed in the diet). It is found in vegetables, nuts, grains, fruits, plant oils, eggs, and fowl, and is one of the omega-6 family of **polyunsaturated fats**. It can be converted in the body to gamma-linolenic acid and arachidonic acid, both of which have powerful effects on immune function, the inflammatory response, and cell metabolism.

LINOLENIC ACID an essential fatty acid necessary for normal health. One of the omega-3 family of **polyunsaturated fats**, it is found in abundance in flax, mustard, and pumpkin seeds, soy and walnut oils, green leafy vegetables, meat, and meat products. It is converted in the body to eicosapentaenoic acid (E.P.A.—also found in fish oil) and docosahexaenoic acid (D.H.A.—also found in fish oil and some algae), both of which have beneficial effects on blood-fat levels and inhibit blood clotting.

LUTEIN an **antioxidant carotenoid** in many plant foods.

LYCOPENE an **antioxidant carotenoid** found in tomatoes. It is released from tomatoes when they are cooked, and its absorption into the body is improved by the presence of small amounts of oil or fat in the meal.

MONOUNSATURATED FAT a type of fatty acid that contains one chemical double-bond in its carbon chain. Olive oil is particularly rich in monounsaturated fat, which is found also in many animal, fish, and vegetable fats.

MUCILAGE a complex carbohydrate found in many plants. It has a slimy texture when dissolved in water. Herbal remedies containing mucilage soothe inflamed mucous membranes.

OLEIC ACID one of omega-9 family of unsaturated fats.

OMEGA-3 a group of unsaturated fatty acids containing **linolenic acid**, E.P.A. and D.H.A.

OMEGA-6 a group of unsaturated fatty acids containing **linoleic acid** and arachidonic acid.

OXALATE also known as oxalic acid, a chemical found in various foodstuffs, including tea, rhubarb, and spinach, which, when present in the body in large amounts, encourages the formation of urinary stones. People suffering from urinary stones (or any form of gastro-intestinal malabsorption) should avoid foods containing oxalates.

PAPAIN a substance obtained from the juice of the papaya that mimics the action of digestive juices, thus aiding digestion.

PECTIN a soluble non-starch polysaccharide (N.S.P.) found in fruits and plants and used as a gelling agent in jams and preserves. Soluble N.S.P. in the diet helps protect against diseases associated with high blood cholesterol, such as coronary heart disease and gallstones.

PHENOLIC ACIDS substances found in freshly picked vegetables and fruits, wines, and teas that encourage detoxification and inhibit the formation of cancer cells.

PHYTOCHEMICALS bio-active compounds found in foods of plant origin with health-enhancing effects. They include allium compounds, carotenoids, coumarins, and bioflavonoids.

PHYTOHORMONES plant-derived chemicals, such as phytoestrogens, that mimic the action of human hormones.

POLYSACCHARIDES large carbohydrate molecules made up of chains of simple sugar molecules linked together. Starch is a type of polysaccharide.

POLYUNSATURATED FAT a type of fatty acid containing two or more double bonds in its carbon chain. It is found mainly in plant oils, and is an essential part of a healthy diet.

PORPHYRINS pigments found in the blood and tissues of animals, and also in plants and micro-organisms.

POULTICE a hot pack applied to the skin, prepared by mixing herbs (such as oats, flaxseed, or comfrey) with hot water and wrapping the mixture in a piece of linen or muslin.

PROTEASE INHIBITORS proteins found in plants, such as cereals and pulses, that may help protect against cancer.

QUERCETIN a **bioflavonoid** found in foods such as onions, tomatoes, apples, berries, and tea. An **antioxidant**, it is thought to act as an antihistamine, to treat allergies, and prevent heart disease and cancer, but there is, at present, little evidence to support these claims.

QUINIC ACID a sugar compound found in fruits, such as apples, peaches, pears, plums, and some vegetables, that has antiviral and neuroprotective properties.

RUTIN a **bioflavonoid** with a reputation for toning and healing peripheral blood vessels.

SACCHARIDE another name for carbohydrate. Complex carbohydrates, fruit sugar, and glucose are also known as polysaccharides, disaccharides, and monosaccharides respectively.

SALICYLATE also known as salicylic acid, a chemical of plant origin that forms the basis for the drug aspirin. Plants containing salicylate have antiseptic, painkilling and anti-inflammatory effects.

SAPONINS bio-active compounds, traditionally used for their **expectorant**, **diuretic** and anti-inflammatory effects. They are found in many foods and herbs, including soy beans, licorice, violet, yarrow, oats, asparagus, and other vegetables.

SATURATED FAT a type of fatty acid containing the maximum number of hydrogen atoms. It is usually solid at room temperature. Animal fats (including butter, lard, and suet) contain a high proportion of saturated fat, as do solid vegetable fats like coconut oil. Saturated fat can be made in the body and so is not needed in the diet.

SULFUR a mineral found in some plant foods and medicinal plants that has a cleansing, anti-rheumatic effect.

TANNIN a plant constituent that causes tissue to contract by precipitating proteins. Traditionally used to make leather by tanning animal hides, and used therapeutically to reduce secretions and discharges. It has an **astringent** action.

TARTARIC ACID a fruit acid found in grapes.

THYMOL a volatile oil with strong antiseptic properties.

TRYPTOPHAN an amino acid that can be converted into vitamin B3 in the body.

VALERIANIC ACID a volatile oil with sedative properties.

VASODILATOR a substance that causes blood vessels to widen (dilate), thereby enhancing blood flow.

VOLATILE OIL see **essential oils**.

top ten foods

The following lists give the top ten sources of vitamins, minerals, and trace elements. In each case foods are listed according to amount per portion, beginning with the highest.

WATER-SOLUBLE VITAMINS

VITAMIN B1 (thiamin): peas, brown rice, yeast extract, potatoes, muesli, sunflower seeds, pinto beans, cabbage, tahini paste, leeks

VITAMIN B2 (riboflavin): yeast extract, tempeh, muesli, avocado, seaweed, oyster mushrooms, corn, mushrooms, peas, mustard leaves

VITAMIN B3 (niacin)—including proportion converted from tryptophan: yeast extract, tempeh, muesli, fava beans, peas, peanut butter, brown rice, soy beans, potato, wheat bran

VITAMIN B5 (pantothenic acid): fava beans, avocado, mushrooms, tempeh, Brussels sprouts, purple broccoli, endive, corn, sweet potato, potato

VITAMIN B6 (pyridoxine): tempeh, muesli, potato, avocado, bell pepper, banana, Brussels sprouts, leek, lentils, curly kale

VITAMIN B12 (cobalamin); (f) = fortified: yeast extracts (f), vegetable stock (f), vegetable margarines (f), soy milk (f), breakfast cereals (f), tempeh, seaweed, sourdough bread, shiitake mushrooms, soy sauce

FOLATE: black-eye peas, Swiss chard, Savoy cabbage, spinach, fava beans, pinto beans, endive, Brussels sprouts, curly kale, okra

BIOTIN: tempeh, soy beans, hazelnuts, peanuts, almonds, muesli, black-eye peas, mushrooms, avocado, mangetout

VITAMIN C: guava, red bell pepper, spring greens, blackcurrants, green bell pepper, Brussels sprouts, curly kale, papaya, strawberries, purple broccoli

FAT-SOLUBLE VITAMINS

VITAMIN A: sweet potato, carrot, red bell pepper, butternut squash, Swiss chard, spinach, curly kale, spring greens, mango, cantaloupe melon

VITAMIN D: Although a number of foods are fortified with vitamin D, only a few foods contain vitamin D naturally. The best way to ensure adequate vitamin D is to spend some time each day in the open air, as we all produce vitamin D internally by the action of sunlight on our skin

VITAMIN E: wheatgerm oil, sun-dried tomato, sweet potato, sunflower oil, safflower oil, sunflower seeds, avocado, hazelnuts, almonds, butternut squash

VITAMIN K: broccoli, spinach, parsley, cabbage, curly kale, spring greens, cauliflower, peas, soy-based margarines, vegetable oil

MINERALS

CALCIUM: tofu, okra, spring greens, spinach, curly kale, tempeh, sesame seeds, purple broccoli, scallions, dried figs

MAGNESIUM: Brazil nuts, okra, melon seeds, Swiss chard, brown rice, tempeh, sunflower seeds, sesame seeds, beans, spinach

PHOSPHORUS: brown rice, tempeh, tahini, muesli, peas, beans and lentils, nuts and seeds, corn, tofu, sweet potato

POTASSIUM: avocado, potato, sweet potato, dried apricots, squash, beans, banana, spinach, zucchini, Brussels sprouts

TRACE ELEMENTS

IRON: tempeh, lentils, potato, muesli, spring greens, endive, peas, tahini paste, cumin seeds, dried peaches

ZINC: aduki beans, tofu, tempeh, lentils, muesli, pasta, wheat bran, garbanzos, tahini paste, brown rice

MANGANESE: oyster mushrooms, brown rice, muesli, tempeh, pine nuts, tofu, blackberries, macadamia nuts, hazelnuts, aduki beans

COPPER: tempeh, brown rice, aduki beans, pigeon peas, mushrooms, melon seeds, sunflower seeds, cashew nuts, tahini, soy beans

IODINE: the most reliable sources come from the sea—fish and seaweeds, sea salt and iodized salt. The amount in plants varies depending on iodine levels in the soil

SELENIUM: Brazil nuts, lentils, wholemeal bread, pasta, sunflower seeds, pinto beans, red kidney beans, cashew nuts, mushrooms, soy beans

index

bibliography

R. Ballentine, *Diet & Nutrition* (Himalayan International Institute, U.S.A., 1982)

H. G. Bieler, *Food is Your Best Medicine* (Spearman, U.K., 1968)

K. Bock and N. Sabin, *The Road to Immunity* (Pocket Books, U.S.A., 1997)

A. Braine, *Des Plantes pour Tous les Jours* (Presse Pocket, France, 1993)

C. and C. Caldicott, *World Food Café* (Frances Lincoln, U.K., 1999)

W. Chan, J. Brown and D. H. Buss, *Miscellaneous Foods*, supplement to *McCance & Widdowson's The Composition of Foods* (Royal Society of Chemistry & Ministry of Agriculture, Fisheries and Food, U.K., 1994)

R. Creasy, *The Edible French Garden* (Periplus, U.S.A., 1999)

M. Delmas, *Les Mille Recettes aux Mille Vertus* (Magnard/Le François, France, 1990)

R. Elliot, *The Bean Book* (Fontana, U.K., 1979)

K. Fern, *Plants for a Future* (Permanent Publications, U.K., 1997)

J. S. Garrow, W. P. T. James and A. Ralph, *Human Nutrition & Dietetics*, 10th edition (Churchill Livingstone, U.K., 2000)

M. Grieve, *A Modern Herbal* (Tiger Books, U.K., 1992)

S. Harrod Buhner, *Herbal Antibiotics* (Newleaf, Ireland, 2000)

K. Hartvig and N. Rowley, *10 Days To Better Health* (Piatkus, U.K., 1998)

K. Hartvig and N. Rowley, *You Are What You Eat* (Piatkus, U.K., 1996)

R. K. Henderson, *The Neighborhood Forager* (Chelsea Green, U.S.A. and U.K., 2000)

A. Hirsch, *Drink to Your Health* (Marlow, U.S.A., 2000)

D. Hoffmann *The Complete Illustrated Holistic Herbal* (Element, U.K., 1996)

B. Holland, I. D. Unwin and D. H. Buss, *Cereals & Cereal Products*, supplement to *McCance & Widdowson's The Composition of Foods* (Royal Society of Chemistry & Ministry of Agriculture, Fisheries and Food., U.K., 1992)

B. Holland, I. D. Unwin and D. H. Buss, *Fruits & Nuts*, supplement to *McCance & Widdowson's The Composition of Foods* (Royal Society of Chemistry & Ministry of Agriculture, Fisheries and Food, U.K., 1992)

B. Holland, et al, *Vegetables, Herbs & Spices*, supplement to *McCance & Widdowson's The Composition of Foods* (Royal Society of Chemistry & Ministry of Agriculture, Fisheries and Food, U.K., 1991)

M. Jaffrey, *Eastern Vegetarian Cooking* (Arrow, U.K., 1990)

S. Mills, *The Dictionary of Modern Herbalism* (Thorsons, U.K., and U.S.A., 1985)

M. T. Murray and J. E. Pizzorno, *An Encyclopaedia of Natural Medicine* (Macdonald Optima, U.K., 1990)

C. R. Paterson, *Essentials of Human Biochemistry* (Pitman, U.K., 1983)

A. A. Paul and D. A. T. Southgate, *McCance & Widdowson's The Composition of Foods* (Royal Society of Chemistry & Ministry of Agriculture, Fisheries and Food, U.K., 1978)

A. A. Paul, D. A. T. Southgate and J. Russel, *Amino Acids & Fatty Acids*, supplement to *McCance & Widdowson's The Composition of Foods* (Royal Society of Chemistry & Ministry of Agriculture, Fisheries and Food, UK, 1991)

G. Reeves and E. Todd, *Immunology* (Blackwell Science, UK, 2000)

M. Romeyn, *Nutrition & H.I.V.* (Jossey-Bass, U.S.A., 1998)

E. Rothera, *Perhaps It's An Allergy* (Foulsham, U.K., 1988)

N. Rowley, *Basic Clinical Science* (Hodder & Stoughton, U.K., 1994)

N. Rowley and K. Hartvig *Energy Foods* (Duncan Baird Publishers, U.K., 2000)

N. Rowley and K. Hartvig, *Energy Juices* (Duncan Baird Publishers, U.K., 2000)

J. Santa Maria, *Chinese Vegetarian Cookery* (C.R.C.S., U.S.A., 1983)

K. Thesen, *Country Remedies* (Pierrot, U.K., 1979)

J. G. Vaughan and C. A. Geissler, *The New Oxford Book of Food Plants* (Oxford University Press, U.K., 1997)

R. F. Weiss, *Herbal Medicine* (A.B. Arcanum, UK, 1988)

World Cancer Research Fund in association with the American Institute for Cancer Research, *Food, Nutrition & the Prevention of Cancer: A Global Perspective* (American Institute for Cancer Research, U.S.A., 1997)

R. C. Wren, *Potter's New Cyclopaedia of Botanical Drugs & Preparations* (Daniel, U.K., 1988)

acknowledgments

Kirsten Hartvig would like to thank:
Judy Barratt, Pamela Blake-Wilson, Geoffrey Cannon, Richard Emerson, Peter Firebrace, Tara Firebrace, Allan Hartvig, Anders Hartvig, Simon Hickmott, Pip Martin, Jennifer Maughan, Ian Melrose, Anna Mews, Kathy Mitchison, Sue Mitchison, Françoise Nassivet, Manisha Patel, Liz Pearson, Dr Peter Pearson, Dr Nic Rowley, François Salies, Dr Joyce Thomas and Jaqueline Young for their help and inspiration in writing this book.

Duncan Baird Publishers would like to thank:
Vicky Carlisle (proofreader)
Emma Bentham-Wood (photographer's assistant)
Juss Herd (assistant food stylist)
Ingrid Lock (indexer)